Palgrave Studies in the Theory and History of Psychology

Series Editor
Thomas Teo
Department of Psychology
York University
Toronto, ON, Canada

Palgrave Studies in the Theory and History of Psychology publishes scholarly books that use historical and theoretical methods to critically examine the historical development and contemporary status of psychological concepts, methods, research, theories, and interventions. Books in this series are characterised by one, or a combination of, the following: (a) an emphasis on the concrete particulars of psychologists' scientific and professional practices, together with a critical examination of the assumptions that attend their use; (b) expanding the horizon of the discipline to include more interdisciplinary and transdisciplinary work performed by researchers and practitioners inside and outside of the discipline, increasing the knowledge created by the psychological humanities; (c) "doing justice" to the persons, communities, marginalized and oppressed people, or to academic ideas such as science or objectivity, or to critical concepts such social justice, resistance, agency, power, and democratic research. These examinations are anchored in clear, accessible descriptions of what psychologists do and believe about their activities. All the books in the series share the aim of advancing the scientific and professional practices of psychology and psychologists, even as they offer probing and detailed questioning and critical reconstructions of these practices. The series welcomes proposals for edited and authored works, in the form of full-length monographs or Palgrave Pivots; contact beth.farrow@palgrave.com for further information.

Serimes Editor:
Thomas Teo is Professor of Psychology at York University, Canada.

Series Editorial Board:
Alex Gillespie,
London School of Economics and Political Science, UK;
Suzanne R. Kirschner, College of the Holy Cross, USA;
Annette Mülberger, Universitat Autonoma de Barcelona, Spain;
Lisa M. Osbeck, University of West Georgia, USA;
Peter Raggatt, James Cook University, Australia;
Alexandra Rutherford ,York University, Canada.

More information about this series at
http://www.palgrave.com/gp/series/14576

Natasha Distiller

Complicities

A theory for subjectivity in the psychological humanities

Natasha Distiller
Gender and Women Studies
University of California, Berkeley
Berkeley, CA, USA

This book is an open access publication. This title is freely available in an open access edition with generous support from the Library of the University of California, Berkeley.

ISBN 978-3-030-79674-7   ISBN 978-3-030-79675-4 (eBook)
https://doi.org/10.1007/978-3-030-79675-4

© The Editor(s) (if applicable) and The Author(s) 2022, corrected publication 2022. This book is an open access publication.

Open Access This book is licensed under the terms of the Creative Commons Attribution 4.0 International License (http://creativecommons.org/licenses/by/4.0/), which permits use, sharing, adaptation, distribution and reproduction in any medium or format, as long as you give appropriate credit to the original author(s) and the source, provide a link to the Creative Commons licence and indicate if changes were made.

The images or other third party material in this book are included in the book's Creative Commons licence, unless indicated otherwise in a credit line to the material. If material is not included in the book's Creative Commons licence and your intended use is not permitted by statutory regulation or exceeds the permitted use, you will need to obtain permission directly from the copyright holder.

The use of general descriptive names, registered names, trademarks, service marks, etc. in this publication does not imply, even in the absence of a specific statement, that such names are exempt from the relevant protective laws and regulations and therefore free for general use.

The publisher, the authors and the editors are safe to assume that the advice and information in this book are believed to be true and accurate at the date of publication. Neither the publisher nor the authors or the editors give a warranty, expressed or implied, with respect to the material contained herein or for any errors or omissions that may have been made. The publisher remains neutral with regard to jurisdictional claims in published maps and institutional affiliations.

This Palgrave Macmillan imprint is published by the registered company Springer Nature Switzerland AG.
The registered company address is: Gewerbestrasse 11, 6330 Cham, Switzerland

The original version of the book was revised: The acknowledgement of the funding from the Library of the University of California, Berkeley, for this book is now included in the front matter. A correction to this book can be found at https://doi.org/10.1007/978-3-030-79675-4_8

*"Seeking innocence is a distraction of the highest order to critical thought"
(Imani Perry,* Vexy Thing *2018, p. 102).*

Preface

This book has been challenging to write. It is interdisciplinary to its core, a product of my own journey through knowledge collections that span literary studies, a range of critical, cultural and political theories, and psychology and psychotherapy. My hope is that it synthesizes its informing discourses clearly for those who are new to some of them, and interestingly for those who are not.

The title of this book was originally, and probably rather grandiosely, *Complicities: A Model for Subjectivity in the Twenty-First Century*. About halfway through writing it, I realized I was not, in fact, offering the reader a model for anything. "Model" suggests something that can be followed, a series of principles and actions that can be laid out and pursued as with an instruction manual. I changed the title to "theory," which more accurately captures what I am doing here: offering a way to think about human subjectivity that can be useful to critical psychologists and practicing psychotherapists if they are convinced that the humanities-style approach I detail is worthwhile. My colleague in the Beatrice Bain Research Group of the Gender and Women's Studies Department at the University of California Berkeley, Robin Clark, assessing the first part of the manuscript, declared it a manifesto, and that is perhaps the most accurate descriptor of all. This book is a summary of everything I have learned as I traversed disciplines. It aims to capture what I have learned accordingly, and how I think about what it means to be human—a concern both of literature, my first home, and psychotherapy, my second. So ultimately, this book may be offering a philosophy, a way of thinking that encodes a set of beliefs about the world and how it could be.

This may well be informative to critical psychologists and others concerned with social justice, feminism, decolonialism and other theories of human being. But how does it apply to therapeutic practice? In the final chapter, I offer some suggestions. I apply my theory to the modalities I use with clients, and hope to open up possibilities for doing, as well as thinking about, psychotherapy.

There are no case studies. I know providing some might well help to ground the more theoretical moments, especially in the first chapter. This is why there are no case studies: I have come to believe that it is a form of making use of clients in a way that does not feel congruent with my therapeutic philosophy. I consider each therapeutic relationship an invitation to a unique journey with someone. When the relationship goes well, the connection is special. I might even use the word sacred, although that will be the most spiritual this theoretical book will get. It does not feel right to me to share this journey for the purposes of my own gain. I learned this from a client whose journey I hold very close to my heart. I want to honor that lesson, and all my clients' sacred sharings. Instead, where appropriate, I will talk about my own journey. I hope this functions to ground some of the ideas.

This book, then, is unashamedly theoretical, although it does also aim to be accessible. For readers not used to the tone and jargon of critical theory, I hope the parts that require more from you are made up for by the illustrations and applications that come up from the third chapter and are the focus of the last chapter.

I would like to take a moment to address the choice of the notion of complicity to capture what I am trying to say. Complicity has a negative connotation. It suggests that one is guilty of collaborating with a wrong. In a sense, that is the point: As I will argue in detail, the term is meant to invoke the idea that we subjects of Western modernity are none of us unimplicated in the systems of oppression whose historical trajectories I account for in this book. It suggests that to be human is to be made by, participants in, resistors to, and beneficiaries of, the systems and institutions that we cannot help but inherit. Some suffer more, but no one of us is better than the other, a theoretical statement that will be fully explored in the course of the book. But another argument of this book is that binary thinking has to go if we want to improve things. Therefore, the binary innocent/guilty is not a helpful way to approach the idea of complicity. It keeps us in the realm of good/bad, self/other, right/wrong. If *Complicities* argues anything, it argues that we have to think about ourselves and each other in more complicated terms. This is how we finally exceed the terms that Western Enlightenment and then colonial processes, as consolidated in the psy disciplines as one of the technologies of modern subjectivity, have given us.

One last set of explanations about style choices: I have used the uppercased adjective Black to denote people of African descent. I do this to acknowledge that the specific history of oppression African people have suffered, because of the historical forces I detail in this book, has created specific material and identity outcomes for Black people. I have not used the uppercase for other descriptors of racialized groups indicated with reference to color. White supremacist groups sometimes capitalize white, a usage I have no intention of sharing. I wish to avoid the implication that white people share a history which outcome has been the need for a shared identity of solidarity. I do think, as I detail in this book, that until a majority of white people accept that whiteness is also a racialized construction, we cannot get very far in the project of racial justice. "Brown" is too general a term, used for many groups of people, to indicate specific, shared histories or identities.

I use the pronoun "he" to describe the subject of Western epistemology and personhood. When I use "he" to talk about the subject of the West, it is deliberate. As I argue in the book, the human subject of Western thought is, in the first place, male. So my "hes" are not thoughtless sexist throwbacks, and they do not occur everywhere. I hope the reader will bear with me on this, and allow the assertion implicit in the gendering of the Western liberal subject. I hope the book's argument of this position convinces you.

The first two chapters provide, broadly, the larger theoretical outlines for the argument. They address the necessity for an interdisciplinary mode, a psychological humanities; account for the emergence of psychology and its associated disciplines as part of a specific Western episteme; and locate the liberalism and whiteness of dominant subjects of Western culture against which human being has been forced to articulate itself in the places made, or affected, by Western systems of thought, economy, politics and meaning, including the psy disciplines. The third chapter focuses on race, the fourth on gender, sex and sexuality, the fifth on American public youth culture in the age of social media and the last chapter on how this all might affect psychotherapy practice. I hope this book's ambitious heart speaks to yours.

Berkeley, CA   Natasha Distiller

Acknowledgments

This book was made possible by the support and encouragement of Glen Retief and John Holmes. Two smarter, kinder midwives could not be hoped for.

I am grateful to my colleagues who agreed to read and comment on portions of the manuscript: David Azul, Robin Clark and Sara Thornton. My thanks also to the Palgrave reviewers, whose feedback helped improve the manuscript. This project was supported in part by the Beatrice Bain Research Group, University of California, Berkeley, and I thank the Department of Gender and Women Studies there, with whom I was a Beatrice Bain Research Scholar for the final part of this book's writing. Laura Nelson was a compassionate and generous chair and a great help to me. Sandra Young, Deborah Posel and Mel Y. Chen continue to offer me their professional support, and I am grateful for their time. A very big thank you to Hannah Hanson, who under the auspices of UC Berkeley's URAP program was a marvelous research assistant. Without her help, this project would have taken longer to complete. Erin Harrell offered support that was both personal and professional, and that made a difference.

My thanks to Stephanie Allais for taking care of my soul, and to Finn Gratton for being such a good friend. Lisa Retief took care of a lot of logistics to enable me to work, and continues to do so. My clients have allowed me to accompany them, and each journey has been a privilege to participate in.

This book, as with all things I do, is for Jesse and Lee, my most precious complicit relationships.

Praise for *Complicities*

"This is the kind of writing—I hope—members of allied health and medical disciplines have been waiting for, irrespective of whether they focus explicitly on providing support for the psychological aspects of human being or whether they work in fields that intersect with mental health practice.

Complicities offers a gentle, generous, highly knowledgeable, and accessible introduction to and application of transdisciplinarity at its best. Using arguments, ideas and theories from the critical humanities and cutting-edge approaches to neurobiology and psychotherapy, Natasha Distiller invites the reader into a world in which diversity and complexity are openly at play and the taken-for-granted is given a chance to dissolve. Guided by the author's carefully selected and convincingly elaborated gestures towards diverse knowledges, binary distinctions between e.g., self and other, mind and body, individual and context, power and oppression, clinician and client, clinical and everyday encounters, therapy and advocacy, are slowly replaced with a third space in which human being has always already been understood and practiced as intersubjectivity, relationality, mutuality, and being-with. This third space, which corresponds to the complicit mindset and the notion and practice of complicity as the only way in which we can live a human life, offers an alternative to the injustices and suffering that result from a rigid adherence to binary disciplinary, colonial, scientific, and capitalist regimes.

Complicities can be read as a guide to be (human and a professional) which allows us to drop the relentless but familiar fight for the upper hand position in all our relations (e.g., as expert, objective observer, a person who owns what is morally good and true) in favour of nurturing a non-judgmental stance towards human lives being with each other in the world. If we learn to acknowledge and accept our imperfection, vulnerability, and complicity as human beings, we can, so the book suggests, truly connect with each other and develop and maintain healing relationships.

Reading the book once is not enough. It leaves the reader with the desire to start all over again, for another go at engaging with the diverse dimensions and implications of the notion and practice of complicity."

—David Azul, *La Trobe University, Bendigo, Australia*

Contents

1 **Introduction: The Personal Is Still Political** 1
   Binary Thinking 7
   Complicities 12
   The Science of Psychology and the Psychological Humanities 15
   Self/Other 23
   The Subject of Psychology 27
   Conclusion 33
   Works Cited 35

2 **Well-Intentioned White People and Other Problems with Liberalism** 43
   Liberalism 44
   A Note on the Idea of the Universally Human 50
   The Liberal Subject of Psychology 56
   From Liberalism to Neoliberalism 59
   Complicit Intersubjectivity 62
   Works Cited 68

3 **Wakanda Forever** 73
   Race 75
   Racism 82
   Race and Racism in and Through Psychology 84

	Complicities: *Black Panther*	88
	Works Cited	99
4	**Thought Bodies: Gender, Sex, Sexualities**	107
	Binary Gender	110
	Transgender Complicities	115
	Heterosexual Consent	127
	Transnational Lessons	141
	Works Cited	152
5	**Love and Money**	163
	Neoliberalism and Identity	165
	The More Things Change	169
	Finding Oneself in the Public Eye	174
	Truth, Lies and Mediascape: Trump's Bullshit	178
	Being Millennial	180
	Love and Money	189
	Works Cited	204
6	**The Complicit Therapist**	211
	Stance	213
	Trauma-Informed, Body-Based Theories	216
	Internal Family Systems	223
	Beyond the Self/Other Binary: Thirdness	227
	A Social Justice Practice	232
	The Complicit Therapist: How Therapy Heals	239
	Works Cited	240
7	**Conclusion**	245
	Works Cited	250
	Correction to: Complicities	C1
	Index	253

1

Introduction: The Personal Is Still Political

The second wave of feminist activism in the United States gave us the adage, "the personal is political." It allowed women to insist that the difficulties they were having were not caused by their personal qualities or individual choices, but were the product of a system that positioned them as women, and structured their lives and the horizon of possibilities for their material and emotional experiences accordingly (see Shaw & Lee, 2015). The core lesson was (and is) that a person's individual experience is not theirs alone. Their sense of self is formed within, in relation to, and by, external forces. Feminism began with the understanding that gender is one apparently personal quality that is in fact formed by social factors, and, under patriarchy, in relations of power and oppression.

Naomi Alderman's feminist dystopian fiction, *The Power* (2016), explores the consequences of changing gender dynamics within a system of power. The book shows what happens when women are given superior physical power over men, and seize the reins of control accordingly. What begins as a satisfying ability to finally stand up to sexualized brutality becomes a reinscription of more of the same: patriarchal values, where might conveys right, remain in place, even as gender positions are inverted. Merely changing structural positions does not alter the nature of the structure.

The voice of someone who is most likely god says, at the book's conclusion (Alderman, 2016, p. 360),

> I'm giving you the crib sheet right now. Maybe you'll understand it and maybe you won't… Who's bad and who's good? Who persuaded the other one to eat the apple? Who has the power and who's powerless? All of these questions are the wrong questions.
>
> It's more complicated than that, sugar. However complicated you think it is, everything is always more complicated than that… You can't put anyone in a box. Listen, even a *stone* isn't the same as any other stone, so I don't know where you all think you get off labelling *humans* with simple words and thinking you know everything you need. But most people can't live that way, even some of the time. They say: only exceptional people can cross the borders. The truth is: anyone can cross, everyone has it in them.

Alderman slyly skewers sexism—the kind we have in our present world, where women are treated differently because of the social meanings made of their sexual difference—and also insists that human beings all have the ability to abuse, when the terms of valued personhood are based on who is stronger. The supernatural voice who sums it up in the extract above makes the point that *Complicities* aims to illustrate and unpack: There is a self/other binary at work in the power dynamics of Western social, interpersonal and intrapersonal dynamics. This binary has a specific material history. It is not inevitable. And it creates realities both psychological and material. In deconstructing binary thinking, and the version of the human that results, and by focusing on the messiness and complexity of human interactions in practice, a new model for human being emerges. This is a way out of the us and them positions that in the end serve to keep the structure in place.

The main argument of this book is that to be human means to be complicit in the systems we inherit, and are structured by. These systems, in a world which relies on binary thinking, are always systems of power. They comprise both symbolic structures like language, apparently natural units like the family, and larger social formations like communities and countries. They also include group and individual experiences which are given narrative shape and thus specific meanings, like history, and like identity. To be complicit means that human being is not an individualized enterprise. Each subject is made through genealogies, histories, inheritances which are by definition communal, and through their linkages and reactions to, and reliances on, other subjects.

To accept this argument is to see a way out of the current dominant binary thinking that continues to structure most ideas of human subjectivity at work in psychotherapy. The modern idea of the self as it is espoused through the psy disciplines (psychology, psychotherapy, psychiatry and psychoanalysis), a Western technology of knowing, is based on a self/other structure. Such a formulation also maps onto an oppressor/oppressed model for subjectivity, which currently informs much of the liberation work of identity politics. For a social justice-oriented psychotherapy practice, this can be limiting. *Complicities* will flesh out these assertions, concentrating in various chapters on aspects of modern identities important to liberation politics and practices. It will also connect modern identification practices to the liberalism that has helped shape the Western subject of psychotherapy, via the discipline of psychology and the work it has done to help construct the modern world. In the final chapter, some practices for social justice-oriented psychotherapy will be considered.

This work takes place under the rubric of the psychological humanities, which recognizes the conceptual limits of traditional psychological approaches to human being. This initial chapter is the most theoretical. Because, as an exploration of the potential of the psychological humanities as an interdiscipline, explored below, I draw on concepts that will be differently familiar to readers depending on their knowledge base, I considered it important to map out the frames of reference that inform my thinking. Some readers find theoretical language alienating, one of the relevant critiques against forms of high theoretical writing that nevertheless claims to be engaged with social justice issues and wants to be relevant to the world. I have done my best to make these ideas both interesting and accessible. If at times they are hard going, I beg your indulgence and assure you they are applied in later chapters.

My starting point, in feminism, locates my work within the group of psychological theories of human being that are concerned with acknowledging and addressing issues of social justice. Feminist therapy followed early feminist insight, born out of consciousness raising groups where women's experiences were validated. It was a practice that began by refusing the normative gender assumptions of the patriarchal authority that had structured the discipline (Rothblum & Cole, 2018; Williams, 1995). It grew to actively value the wisdom and experiences of all othered voices (Brown, 2018). Other psychologies concerned with political and psychic liberation also insist that knowledge is never neutral, that the standpoint of the observer-commentator shapes what they can understand and that institutions create systems of privilege and oppression that define and affect people along axes of gender, race, class, ablebodiedness, ethnicity, neurodiversity, location, nation and other markers of hierarchy and access. Transnational, postcolonial, indigenous and decolonial perspectives extend the definition of systems and the understanding of how they work to a global scale. Cultural and hermeneutic awareness has long been a part of the discipline and practice of psychology and psychotherapy, as will be discussed in more detail below. The acknowledgment that we are not, in fact, independent liberal subjects, free to choose (our identities, our experiences, our relation to ourselves and our access to resources if we just work hard enough), is not at all new.

And yet, in popular culture and in mainstream American political discourse, the modern subject is still the subject of liberalism, free indeed to choose his fate, at best, or fettered by injustice so that he cannot achieve this rhetorically god-given right. In the twenty-first century, he is neoliberalized into being responsible for ensuring his selfhood is profitable, as I will explain in Chaps. 2 and 5. He is, in the first place, gendered, classed and raced, although he believes these things do not matter to his ability to succeed. The discourses and technologies of psychology, psychoanalysis, psychiatry and psychotherapy have been central to the creation, authorization, dissemination and popularization of this liberal human subject. What we have today, as a result, is a popular idea of what it means to be a person that is saturated with historical meanings and specific economic processes, presented as natural, and dependent on binary thinking. This is true, despite decades of theoretical work in the academy which seeks to deconstruct, interrogate, problematize and locate the relations of power that comprise our institutions and the meanings we make of the world, ourselves and each other.

The unified self in search of its correct path, free to make the right or healthy choices to achieve knowledge of itself and thus be a better version of itself, is the model of the self that is still necessary in most versions of the psychotherapy session. Throughout this book, I use the term "psychotherapy" to refer to the practice of counseling undertaken by therapists who may or may not be psychologists: They might be licensed professional counselors, marriage and family therapists, or analysts. Such practitioners did not necessarily pass through academic psychology to achieve their licensure. They also did not necessarily encounter in much detail any of the more humanities-inflected ideas about human being of the last half century. In what follows, I am bringing together for a very broad church ideas about the theory and practice of psychology and psychotherapy, informed by feminist, queer, critical race, postcolonial and decolonial, and cultural studies insights developed most extensively in the academic humanities.

Who am I talking about, and for? On the one hand, a disembodied idea called the human subject. The statement that to be human means to be implicated in psychic and material structures is a statement intended to be universal. On the other hand, the subject under discussion here is the subject of psychology, which is to say, the subject of Western modernity. This subject is not, in theory or practice, universal, although the scientific subject of psychology can sometimes forget that it is not a collection of neurons and response times, of evolutionary logic and developmental absolutes. The human being I am invoking is a diverse collective, intended to acknowledge our very real experiential differences, the ways our systems of power and our institutions name and position people very differently based on the meanings made of their histories, communities and embodiments. And in so doing, shape (but not determine) their senses of selves. Through our differences, through our very different investments, profits and losses in the meanings made of our differences, "we" are connected. This is an audacious claim for a middle-class white person to make, and from that standpoint, it is an assertion of privilege. But my voice is also informed by being assigned female at birth and socialized female, by being queer, by being from the global South, by being an immigrant. I am a both-and, which is what I am suggesting the theoretical "we" I invoke should be seen as as well: both universalizing and specific, looking for a universal connection across humans, and acknowledging of inequality: the historical, structural, invested components which deny the connections across different human beings, and the suffering this causes. I say a little more about humanism in Chap. 2, a discussion which also illustrates how an education in the humanities simultaneously enables an awareness of what "we" share, and of how "we" are constructed according to historically invested differences.

Complicities navigates a familiar tension. There are liberation theories that want to name systems of power and oppression, and the injustices they cause, in order to advocate for material change in real people's lives and in the experience of their communities. And there are deconstructive theories that, in refusing normative and normativizing definitions of personhood, citizenship, morality, wellness, subjectivity and so on, have often been accused of working against material change in their focus on the constructed nature of oppressive phenomena. Such tensions have been evident within feminism and queer theory for decades, as I will discuss in more detail in Chap. 4.

It is important to acknowledge the constructed nature of subject positions, in order to make explicit the politics at play and the investments in presenting as natural what are human systems of meaning, made by people through time and space with something at stake. What it means to be female, or black, or disabled, or Jewish, to name a few examples, is, for the purposes of human systems, entirely located in context. I will continually illustrate this claim throughout this book. On the other hand, strategic essentialisms (Danius & Jonsson, 1993) are often necessary for political work, especially in the context of a rights-based system that needs recognizable groups, endorsed by born-that-way arguments, before rights can be conferred (Bonthuys, 2008; Brown, 1995; Butler, 1993). Essentialism also has psychic value, especially in a Western system based on individualism and individuality. If we understand that subjectivity is made from the systems that structure it, and also feeds back into these systems to continue and to change them, then the "problem" of deconstruction verses essentialism falls away and is revealed as another one of the reductive consequences of binary thinking (Fuss, 1989).

Binary Thinking

Binary thinking sets up a relation, presented as natural, between two ideas (people, concepts, identities) that are constructed as reliant on each other's apparently obvious and immutable meanings. These meanings are assumed to be opposite and are almost always hierarchical. One half of the binary benefits, materially and-or psychically, in other words, from the relation. Accordingly, that half will work to protect the binary structure. One consequence, explored in more detail in Chap. 4, is the way transgender people are so violently policed for threatening the gender binary (male/female).

Binary thinking has been an important part of systems of Western meaning-making and has helped enable the construction of the neoliberal geopolitical global world order of modernity, which has emerged from nineteenth century colonialism, as will be explored in more detail in Chap. 2. Postcolonial theory, among other lessons, illustrated how binary thinking endorsed colonial thoughts and deeds.

Postcolonial theoreticians pointed out how colonizing discourse, the sense that colonizing cultures made of what they were doing, is constructed around a binary system: self/other; good/bad; white/black; master/slave; male/female; subject/object. The terms of these related binaries rely on each other. They are obviously constructed with a hierarchical logic: It is better to be white, master, male and therefore a subject. It is psychologically better, in that it guarantees a specific sense of self, and it is better in terms of access to privilege, resources, authority and power. The disempowered side of the binary, the side of the other/object/slave, is sometimes called the subaltern: the one without the representational and therefore political power in this system (Spivak, 1988). The subaltern is the necessary other to the colonizing self. The relationship across the two sides of the binary is not only hierarchical; it is constituting. The colonizer cannot be a colonizer without a colonized. If we understand this dynamic, we understand what is at stake for the colonizing self in the act of taking power: his very existence. This is the oppressor/victim binary, already embedded in a complicity more complex than the us and them of current identity politics can allow.

Binary thinking is reductive. Cohen (2005) has shown how binary thinking cannot accommodate intersectionality. She argued that queer theory set up a new binary, hetero/queer, which also corresponded to bad/good. She pointed out that, because it relied only on sexuality as the oppression it accounted for, this kind of queer theory overlooked the ways in which someone could be heterosexual and still oppressed, and queer and still hold privilege. She gave the examples of poor women of color on welfare, whose heterosexuality did not fit the required, respectable norm; or enslaved people, whose heterosexuality was denied as part of the denial of their humanity.

Since the beginning of feminist theorizing, from the Combahee River Collective (1983), through the works of Lorde (2007) and into the writings of Hill Collins (2015) and the legal scholarship of Crenshaw (1989), among others (see Moraga & Anzaldua, 1983), the fact of intersectionality has been reiterated by feminists of color (see Nash, 2019). It has been taken up, if inadequately, in some branches of psychology (McCormick-Huhn et al., 2019). But this well-known truth, that people are made up of different parts that impact each other, tells us that you cannot account for someone's experiences by separating out aspects of their identity, and that context affects how we experience ourselves and others. It also tells us that, because binaries artificially impose and reduce identities as constructs, we better serve lived experience and the complex work of liberation from oppression by focusing on the ways we are made together, by each other, and by the systems in which we come into being and which we reproduce and change by being in them.

What's the difference between complicity and intersectionality? Intersectionality can sometimes be used to endorse identity politics, as it can be read as relying on the reification of identity categories in order to make its point. Complicity wants to move us beyond identity politics, in part by challenging the conceptual underpinnings to identity categories. This does most emphatically not mean that I am arguing for an apolitical view of what it means to be person. If I am arguing for a kind of humanist vision, it is a humanism that is first and foremost and always embedded in structural relations of power, since to be human, in this model, is to be complicit in systems. This is one of the ways I am suggesting binary thinking is wholly inadequate to any project of the psychological humanities, of which more below. We have to acknowledge the operations of power and privilege, of history and trauma, of who gets to decide and define who has to be other to the mythical norm (Lorde, 2007). And we have to acknowledge that these operations, as central as they are to the construction of discourses that shape lives and subjectivities and opportunities and violences, are not anywhere near the sum total of what it means to be human. These power dynamics are fundamentally human, and they are also limiting of what it really is to be human. They structure, and in so doing, constrain. We are not, in fact, ineluctably separated from each other by the different ways our lives, experiences and senses of selves are shaped by the structures we inherit, are made by, and go on to perpetuate, challenge or change. As the theories which interrogate the relationship between self and other illustrate, and the insistence these theories enable that we are each dependent on the other, an other, another, we are all complicit in the system (some of these theories are discussed in more detail later in this chapter). We are therefore also all complicit in each other. Not equally, not ahistorically, not to mutual benefit. But nonetheless.

While oppressive systems operate via the construction and violent assertion of artificial binaries (the apartheid regime's attempt to segregate racial identities is one example, Posel, 2001; heterosexuality's construction of homosexuality is another, Katz, 2007), human being is, and always has been, nonbinary. Cultural, systemic and personal meanings are intertwined. And, as attachment theory and the neuroscience of early childhood development illustrate, an individual's sense of self is thoroughly woven into the senses of selves of other humans on a physical level, as well as an emotional one (Bowlby, 1982; Gerhardt, 2004; Mascolo, 2016; Musholt, 2018; Pyne, 2016; Schore, 2003; Siegel, 2003; Stern, 1985). Branches of academic and applied psychology have long been engaging with this reality, as will be explored in more detail below. The image of the fold is also sometimes offered to counter the idea of a self-contained self. The fold, as we will see below, speaks to the ways the idea of an inside is constituted by the outside.

Thus *Complicities* builds on the by-now-apparent insight that humans are embedded in social contexts, that individual subjectivity is shaped by the structures and forces it inherits, and which it perforce responds to. Structural injustice matters to—and in and on—all of us, because we are all complicit in each other. And injustice makes use of binary thinking to construct realities where some are rendered superior because others are rendered inferior, or dangerous, or both.

Binary thinking limits what is humanly possible. To do our best work as therapists, we benefit from a nonbinary view of what it means to be human. This means escaping the model of the individual created for and presented to us by mainstream scientific psychology, of which more below and in the following chapter.

We ourselves are part of the work of helping our clients. We are intersubjectively complicit, a notion that I will return to throughout this book. How we understand what our clients suffer from will inform what version of healthy selfhood we are helping them toward (e.g., Hardy, 2008 and Duran & Duran, 1995 have argued for creating diagnoses that recognize the damage done by racial oppression). A knowledge of the constructed and invested nature of the psychological self, as well as of its real power as a discourse of knowledge creation, is a necessary component of this process. In order to do this, we need a double vision, a both-and: at the same time as we want to resist the binary thinking upon which the Western subject of psychology has been built, we simultaneously have to continue acknowledging that historical forces have created structures which perpetuate systems of inequality.

Part of the work of seeing the systems of meaning at play here is learning about where they come from. The modern subject of psychotherapy, as will be explored in more detail in this chapter and the next, is complicit in the emergence of systems of modernity: liberalism, democracy and the individuality they create and police; capitalism and neoliberalism, and the racism and gender politics they create and profit from, as the chapters which follow will explore.

The self who is the product of the self/other binary is itself an effect of Western history, embedded in culture, economics, politics, gender, race, class, uses of religion, uses and constructions of sexuality, notions of ablebodiedness. This means that both the self and the other on which it depends can be understood not only as starting points for power relations, but also as products of them. Rose (1998, p. 188), following Deleuze, offers the idea of the fold: The self is an effect of the ways in which the forces of the exterior world "form an inside to which it appears an outside

1 Introduction: The Personal Is Still Political

must always make reference." The illusion of depth, the pleats and cavities it causes, "only exist in relation to the... forces... that sustain them." What this means, Rose (ibid) argues, in relation to the subject created by psychology and its related disciplines, is that the

> [S]ubject is assembled... in terms of a problem of "self-mastery": bringing to bear upon oneself—the inside acting upon itself—the power that one brings to bear upon others... [T]he power that is brought to bear upon others is figured as a power relation between this inside of oneself and this inside of the other.

The self's experience of itself is reliant not only on its experience of its other, but on a relation of power with that other. The self/other binary relation is an effect, not only of external, institutional forces providing meanings and allocating resources accordingly, but of the processes of subjectification out of which the modern self emerges. This specific binary relation, which in and out of our systems of power maps on the logic of subject/object, is central to Cartesian modernity; it is the "epistemological hallmark of modern thought" (Coelho & Claudio, 2003, p. 194).

But if the self/other relation emerges out of material, systemic and discursive practices that create the self's sense of itself as well as its need for its other, this is in fact another level of complicity. The binary is artificial. The processes that create it rely on rhizomatic relations between selves and structures as well as selves and others. And as we will see shortly, the idea of complicity I am developing relies on the idea that human subjectivity is folded, not split, that we are enfolded by human being into each other.

We are each of us dependent on each other in many ways. The modern human is subjected by language, by interpersonal neurobiology, by gender and race and age and politics and technology as I explore them later in this book. Human being has also been subjected by binary thinking, which some branches of feminism, queer theory, cultural studies and postcolonial theories have all offered ways to challenge. Rose's (1998) formulation suggests that the binary is not only false because it constructs immutable relations between positions, identities and bodies it sets up as opposite, at worst, or exclusive to each other, at least. It is also false because its very technologies of possibility belie the fact that the self is reliant on another to be itself. Despite the logic the binary seeks to assert, that the self must abjure the other, the Western self is a self because of its other. The imperative to power-mastery that has so far accompanied this truth is what is ensured by the structuring of this relation as binary, which is also a denial of the constitutive complicity of human being.

Rose's (1998) model has an additional consequence for understanding the impact of binary thinking on the modern subject's construction. He describes how the psy disciplines have inscribed a modern subject compelled to have interiority, and structured by the psy technologies (theories and schools of thought, research, institutions, practices of counseling, ideas of wellness and mental illness, psychiatric and penalizing incursions into and onto specific notions of the body, the brain, the soul and so on). This subject is told it is free to choose. As part of this process, the subject is to decide on the self it should be: "To be the self *one is* one must not be the self *one is not*—not *that* despised, rejected, or abjected soul. Thus becoming oneself is a recurrent copying that both emulates and differs from other selves" (Rose, 1998, p. 192). This suggests that binary thinking can be located in the modern self's relationship with its self, too. In needing abjected other selves to help us pick the right, healthy, self, Rose's (1998) process of subjectification articulates an additional role of the binary in helping to internally structure this self. We also see a way the self becomes other to itself, can become its own other, in believing it must improve itself—one of the imperatives of psychotherapy.

The binary, in other words, goes very deep into the Western subject, as well as making that subject reliant on its others. It is perhaps not surprising that theories which suggest human subjectivity does not operate in practice as it is assumed to by binary thinking have not achieved the status of common sense outside of parts of academia.

Complicities

I develop the idea of the complicit subject from the work of Sanders (2002), who examined apartheid as an exemplary complicity-generating system. He argues, using the figure of the South African intellectual, that when you are a product of a system, you cannot avoid collaboration with that system, even when you oppose it. He explores how the Truth and Reconciliation Commission (TRC) sought to make the point that complicity makes us responsible, and that, according to the report published by the Commission, "it is only by recognizing the potential for evil in each one of us that we can take full responsibility for ensuring that such evil will never be repeated" (qtd. in Sanders, 2002, p. 3). The TRC report wanted to focus its readers' attention not only on the large-scale human rights violations that were patently abusive and wrong, but on the daily workings of life under apartheid that helped perpetuate the larger system in countless little ways.

The TRC report, Sanders argues (2002, p. 3), is resisting "the intuition that in order to combat evil one must be, or must proclaim oneself to be, untouched by it." Neither Sanders nor the TRC report engages with the question of evil from a psychotherapeutic point of view, which would want to ask where such dark energy comes from. Binary thinking suggests it is human nature to project our inner darkness outward, onto our others (McWilliams 2020). Thinking complicitously suggests a more complex involvement with the systems of power which help create and shape, and then make use of, the desire to control and hurt others. Thinking complicitously disallows a stance of pure resistance, as Sanders (2002) explores. It suggests that in order to resist, we have to acknowledge our involvement in the system.

This is relevant to a contemporary identity politics that, fed by a divisive political climate, sometimes paints itself into a corner, relying on binary thinking to articulate its objections to oppression. Instead of mobilizing the recognition of structural oppression to enable structural change, it reifies the oppressor/oppressed binary, but flips its moral assignations. Once the othered position becomes saturated with a morally righteous victimhood, it becomes nigh impossible to do anything other than reproduce the binary terms of an oppressive system ad nauseam. One consequence is that human being is reduced to structural markers, where we can never exceed the terms given to us for who we can be (see Brown, 1995; Gamson, 1995). Another is that some subjects are reduced to the status of evil, where privilege and ignorance become, not structural consequences, but markers of individual badness (DiAngelo, 2018). The capacity to engage in structural change is unfortunately and radically foreclosed by this discourse.

McWilliams (2020) offers an analytic point of view on how uncomplicit thinking entrenches the structural positions which perpetuate oppression. Her account helps illuminate some of the dynamics at play in current progressive discourses. She (McWilliams, 2020, p. 184) says the (here naturalized) human tendency to create a self/other binary is at work when someone feels politically enlightened. This is a version of narcissistic entitlement that relies on "a claim of moral authority." Such a position is not only problematic because reliant on the hierarchical thinking of the binary, and an assertion of power over another. It also renders this putatively morally superior woke self particularly vulnerable to shame: "That position of framing myself as among the enlightened… sets me up to be hurt and humiliated whenever I am caught out in some prejudice or microaggression, at which point I tend to resort to paranoid-schizoid defenses against such feelings," which results in an inability to own any of one's own badness, and a need to project it onto the other in the form of an assumption about their destructive intent (McWilliams, 2020, p. 184). This helps explain the white fragility (DiAngelo, 2018) of liberal, well-intentioned white people. It also accounts for the one-upmanship of cancel culture (brown, 2020; Ross, 2019); Butler (1993, p. 311) asks, "Is it not a sign of despair over public politics when identity becomes its own policy, bringing with it those who would 'police' it from various sides?" brown (2020, p. 12) puts it in more recent parlance as a tendency within current movements toward "gleeful othering, revenge, or punishment of others, particularly when these things deepen our belonging to each other, usually briefly, until we too fuck up."

Sanders (2002) says that the notion of complicity extends responsibility from one's relationship to specific unjust systems, or in specific deeds, to one's responsibility as a human to other humans. Etymologically, complicity indicates "a folded-together-ness… in human-being" (Sanders, 2002, p. 5). Furthermore, suggests Sanders (2002, p. 9), following Derrida, the notion of complicit human being contaminates binary positions, by folding together "oppositional pairs," creating "an ethico-political discourse on complicity." Sanders (2002, p. 10) goes on to differentiate between "complicity in the general sense" and "complicities in the narrow sense," the little, daily, thoroughly enmeshed sense of complicities that I wish to invoke as the notion of human being for which I am advocating. I hope it is clear that this model of complicity is also fundamentally "ethico-political." It is intended to acknowledge, not overlook, the consequences of structural oppression and the material use of differences in systems of power (the political awareness), while also arguing for a shared human responsibility which is necessary for a better politics (the ethical part).

The idea of the human subject as made by foldedness, the image of "the basic folded-together-ness of being, of human-being" is also the place "of self and other" (Sanders, 2002, p. 11). In being folded with the other as a condition of human being, complicity is established. And the binary on which self and other structures depend is revealed as actually a relationship of complicity and not a relation of exclusion, opposition and hierarchy.

Sanders (2002, p. 15) also charts how asserting "[a] basic human foldedness" at once functions to deny the commitment to apartness that underlies oppressive systems (like apartheid, literally "apart-ness"), and, in necessarily having to be specific in each articulation of resistance to oppression, must needs be limited by, defined by, the details of the oppressive moment against which it is speaking. It is both a general appeal to human being, and a necessarily limited, partial, materially and historically specific one. In this way, the image of the rhizome (Deleuze & Guattari, 1987) superimposes onto the metaphor of the fold. If foldedness challenges the artificial binary structuring of self and other, the rhizome bespeaks the connections between subjects and structures, within which selves are folded.

The Science of Psychology and the Psychological Humanities

Complicities brings the work of the humanities to the work of psychotherapy. Like the task of articulating a complicit human subjectivity, this is both not a new undertaking, and one that has recently acquired new impetus. It is worth noting that as late as 2019, Marecek was still tracking an uneven application of interdisciplinarity, and feminist, critical and social justice-related concerns in psychology, particularly in the United States.

Psychology as a discipline emerged from philosophy, in the first instance, and from the medicalization of behaviors, some of which became modern identities, in the second (Adriaens & De Block, 2013; Devonis, 2014; Foucault, 1977; Mascolo, 2016). It has what Rose (1998, p. 41) calls "a long past but a short history." Philosophical questions about the nature of perception, how we know what we know, how we know what is real, why we make sense of the world the way we do, how and why our senses work, where and what our souls are and how or if they influence what we think, go back to the ancient Greeks. Psychology as a science began in the late nineteenth century, arguably with a lab experiment tracking response times to aural stimuli (Laubscher, 2015). Psychology emerged together with modern medicine and sexology, as the drive to understand, measure, categorize and rank along biological lines became mainstream in a specific set of political, cultural and economic circumstances. These included colonialism, scientific racism, the consolidation of modern democracies and the early global capitalism implicated in all these; and the invention of the hetero/homo binary along with the consolidation of modern gender and sexual norms (Adriaens & De Block, 2013; Katz, 2007; Saini, 2017; Schiebinger, 2004; Severson & Goodman, 2020; Teo, 2005). Psychology has also always had a metapsychological, critical component (Teo, 2005). The brief account I provide here will focus on the twentieth century, largely British and American, developments.

The process of developing psychology into a scientific field, apparently capable of accounting accurately for human thought and behavior via measurable experiments, was directly implicated in nineteenth century European colonial racism, in American racism, in misogyny and in ableism (Devonis, 2014; Guthrie, 2004; Kendi, 2016; Rippon, 2019; Saini, 2017; Showalter, 2007; Silberman, 2015; Teo, 2005). Or, as McWilliams (2020, p. 181) puts it, "[O]ur track record is replete with malignant othering, from our early enchantment with the eugenics movement, through our enthusiasm for IQ testing…, to our more recent collusion with torture." Psychology has been used to emphasize differences rather than connections, in people and groups, what Devonis (2014, p. 113) calls the, "implicit reinforcement of discrimination via method." And as a discipline, psychology has been implicated in the construction of modern categories of normalcy and deviance which often operated along the lines of social difference and operations of social power; "psychology in fact did not solve problems but produced problematizations in which neutral issues were turned into highly problematized objects" (Teo, 2005, p. 144).

As a result, science's apparent objectivity is not only implicated in human cultural and political systems that belie its claims to truth-telling. It is also implicated in the idea that to be a self is something that can be known, tracked and improved upon. I am not suggesting that science is not real, but I am insisting that science cannot offer us unmediated access to the Lacanian real, the place outside of the symbolic realm within which human subjectivity finds itself. Biological facts exist; physics has laws; numbers can be counted; but the meanings we make will always be structured by the cultures in which we make them. When claims to the absolute truth of human being continue to be made in the name of a science of behavior, it is high time to push back.

Modern academic psychology has relied on a certain notion of the self as "the primary reality and unit of study" (Jordan 1997, p. 9), in the context of a scientifically structured discourse. As a result, it has helped develop the modern version of what it means to be human, begun in the Enlightenment. Today, in the West, "to be human is first of all to be rational individuals, with bodies programed by genetics" (Severson & Goodman, 2020, p. 2). These are the consequences: "At the start of the 21st century,… [e]xpressive individualism reigns supreme in various psychological approaches, promoting individuation and autonomy as primary achievements that facilitate health and wellbeing" (Goodman & Freeman, 2015, p. 5). The colonial inheritances of this psychological discourse of normality remain unspoken within the scientific frame that endorses it (Adams et al., 2015; Adams et al., 2017; Bhatia, 2020; Maldonado-Torres, 2017; Tuhiwai Smith, 2012). This is despite strands of psychology, developed in the twentieth century, that are, variously, humanistic and/or based in phenomenological awareness of meaning-making, or influenced by cultural, political, linguistic, philosophical or psychoanalytic theories. The humanities offers even self-reflexive psychological theories the chance to get outside of the limits of psychology's own discursive constraints (Olson, 2012; Papadopoulos, 2008; Teo, 2005; Teo, 2019).

The psychological humanities (Martin, 2017; Teo, 2017; Teo, 2019) seeks to bring psychology back into more direct and, dare I say it, honest relation to the fields of academic study that focus on the mediated nature of human understanding and meaning-making processes. In 2009, the American Psychological Association asserted that psychology is a natural science (the science of behavior), leading almost immediately to calls to consider psychology a human science instead (Laubscher, 2015, p. 7). The APA's vision of psychology was one of hypotheses, laboratories, equipment, observation, measurements, experiments and the use of scientific method to formulate and test objective facts about human behavior. From a humanities point of view, as I have suggested, science is not a way to access unmediated truth, it is a technology of truth creation. And for practicing psychotherapists, our psychological work's official claims to scientific status—meaning objective, measurable, standardized, manualizable, controllable—cannot hold. "[M]any everyday psychologists know in their hearts that a major realignment of the profession's philosophy of science is desperately needed," Cushman (2019, p. 153) reported, following the audience response to his 2013 address to the APA. As he asserts, "Most of our work as therapists is not the application of universal scientific truths won during long hours of objective research. Therapy, I think, is not scientific… it is a kind of moral discourse, and worse yet, one that has political consequences" (Cushman, 2019, p. 79). Richards (2012, p. 347) insists on the inescapably reflexive nature of psychology as a discipline; it cannot escape being of the situated humanity it wants to talk about: "Psychology's problem in this respect rests in large part on its desperate aspirations to the status of a natural science in quest of universal laws, and psychologists' own self-images of themselves as this kind of scientist."

One method of engagement with the scientification of psychology has been the attempts to assert the scientific nature of the human part of psychology (Brooke, 2015; Freeman, 2019; Sugarman, 2019), to make the claim that while it may not be a STEM science, it should still be taken seriously as a science and can be called upon to account for itself as such ("physics envy," Held, 2020). This is one way to address the anxieties raised in our culture when we argue for psychology's status as contingent, as contingent as the human meanings it seeks to understand. What grounds can it stand on, if its findings are inevitably relative? The million dollar question becomes, "Can psychology as a discipline presume to be both truly scientific and genuinely human?" (Gantt & Williams, 2015, p. 32).

Mascolo (2016) argues that this is the wrong question. Psychology's desire to be considered a science, as it emerged from philosophy, he suggests, has embedded psychology in "methodological fetishism—the privileging of method over theory in the hope that the careful use of scientific methodology would ultimately lead to psychological knowledge" (Mascolo, 2016, p. 544). He suggests that the discipline's concern to understand human experience by solving the objective/subjective dichotomy, through self-definition and focus on method, is misplaced. Psychological knowledge emerges from encounters between people, who bring their own already established knowledges of the construct under scrutiny. These subjective knowledges also have to have a shared dimension in order to be intelligible to all participants in the psychological enterprise. The process is not either objective or subjective. (Notably, binary thinking is inadequate to and reductive of the task at hand). In other words, he (Mascolo, 2016, p. 544) says, psychology is an intersubjectively produced knowledge, and therefore "a genuine psychological science must itself rest on intersubjective foundations." We will return to intersubjectivity below, and in future chapters. For now, it is worth noticing that intersubjectivity is offered here as a solution to the false binary of objective/subjective or science/not science that has helped to structure psychology. He concludes (Mascolo, 2016, p. 553):

> A debate over whether a given discipline is or is not a science would seem to be more of a battle about status and prestige than about identifying alternative pathways to reliable knowledge. A better question might be, given its subject matter, how can we study psychological processes in systematic, reliable and useful ways? If such conditions can be satisfied, the question of whether or not disciplinary practices are "scientific" would be irrelevant.

Implicit in this formulation is a challenge to the meaning of the "scientific." Why is scientific method so reified, why is it endorsed as the best way to achieve knowledge? Mascolo's (2016) exploration of the meaning of the question, "Is psychology a science?" begins by reminding us that psychology emerged from philosophy via the Cartesian separation of mind and body, with the mind being privileged as the seat of rational selfhood. This way of thinking has always been gendered, raced and classed.

Gantt and Williams (2015) reiterate that psychology has emerged out of Enlightenment notions of the individualized and rational self. They also suggest that the humanistic branches of psychology that developed in the 1960s are "Romantic" (p. 42) and a "retreat into subjectivism" (p. 43), in other words, not available to be scientific. They suggest a third option is necessary, where the study of human meaning can be scientific, and can also take seriously the centrality of society and context to human being. They advocate for a model based on a science of understanding, which gives us access to the living complexities of human meaning. They contrast this to the dominant model of scientific explanation, which, in compartmentalizing and seeking authority over, takes the human out of its project altogether. The commitment of all of the contributors to this edited collection (Fischer et al., 2015) is to argue for the scientific validity of an approach to psychology that accommodates social scientific and humanities insights about human meaning and experience.

This project speaks to an ongoing investment in the ability of science to prove things, so that we can rest assured a psychological humanities can still be taken seriously, implicitly by certain people in specific institutions. Such an investment, needless to say, is still operating within a privileged understanding of the realm of "science" as carrying a truth value that no other discourse can be expected to match, and the assumption that such a truth is both necessary and possible. This approach is located on the science side of a science/humanities binary, and limits what the humanities can truly offer in terms of changing the thinking about the responsibility of science in helping to create the world it goes on to reflect, and changing the subject of psychology.

The question of the humanities' knowledge of things that are not facts (often understood in psychoanalysis, which is more welcoming to literature and other cultural artifacts as sources of human truth) and therefore cannot be grasped through scientific method is central to the idea that a psychological humanities can expand the boundaries available to psychology:

> [T]he main problem from the perspective of the psychological humanities is the degree to which reflexivity is able to escape the borders of a given horizon. Clearly this reflexivity cannot be conducted alone in a monologue but requires engagement with the *Other* and horizons that are radically different from one's own... psychologists need to move beyond the natural sciences in order to understand human mental life. (Teo, 2019, pp. 276–7)

Freeman (2019) offers the (from a scientific perspective) radical suggestion that psychology invests more in poetics than in theory. Significantly, he calls for psychology to develop a "poetics of the Other." In this formulation, not only is the other conceived of as more important than the self in the understanding of experience (which is not, in certain quarters, a new idea, as will be discussed below), but poetics are elevated over what Freeman (2019, p. 1) calls "theoretics." Freeman's call is to reimagine psychology away from a "scientific" discursive frame. He advocates for a new kind of psychological thinking, one which takes extremely seriously, even centrally, the wisdom to be gained from "humanizing" (2019, p. 5) the scientific theorizing on which modern psychology as a discipline is built.

Freeman's project is in part to challenge the definition of scientific theory that informs modern psychology's sense of itself. He wants to complicate the idea that the humanist, the poetic, the directly meaningful, is somehow other to the abstraction, deduction and generalizing tendencies of a modern notion of the theoretical. Psychology, he argues, has never been the kind of science it has aspired to be. He argues for the importance of narrative and biography to understanding clinical work (and Martin, 2017 argues for the importance of understanding biography to understand the development of the theories that structure and guide clinical work). Poetry, for Freeman (2019, pp. 9–10), is a place where hidden meaning is revealed, where the world is made visible. Psychologists, he suggests, like artists, share the task of restoring attention to the details of life that habitually slip away from us (see Stern, 2014).

In tracking the work of the poetic, Freeman (2019) gestures to the work that language does. This occurs in the difference between the felt experience of life in the body, and what happens when we humans make sense of experience. In finding the world through words, the subject experiences its own reality: "Something has been realized, made real; and in this making, the world without may be re-found" (Freeman, 2019, p. 13). It is the unknown, made known and thereby experienced as familiar or remembered, that constitutes the poetic otherness of what it truly means to be human. This cannot be captured by theory, Freeman (2019) says. It exceeds attempts to pin it down, to weigh, measure, account for and track it. The poetic cannot be captured and still be poetic. (This reminds me of Kristeva's, 1980 notion of the semiotic). While I appreciate Freeman's valuing of a nonscientific approach, I prefer a more theorized version of "the poetic," reactive as I am to the suggestion that science has concrete, material theory and the humanities has an untheorized, universal realm of art. This is simply a misrepresentation of the highly political, philosophically complex, richly theoretical work done within the discipline of the humanities over the past half century.

Stern (1985) has already offered an explanation for how language, in bringing the child along developmentally, splits her from her bodily experience, from what she can know of herself, at the same time as it enters her into the world outside herself. This underscores Freeman's point that science cannot be a theory of the real because it cannot not leave out the human element of the human experiences it is trying to map; "it is patently unprepared to address the living presence of human reality" (Freeman, 2019, p. 14). Scientific language cannot capture what the poetic (or perhaps the semiotic, which in Kristeva's, 1980 lexicon is where poetic language comes from) lets us know is there prior to our attempts to impose form on it. "[H]uman reality, understood as presence or phenomenon rather than object, eludes the kind of conceptual—and theoretical—containment science generally seeks... [H]uman reality, as living presence, eludes such entrapment" as the provable experiment or the inventory seeks to impose on what it means to be human (Freeman, 2019, pp. 15–16). If we take seriously that the self is reliant on the other—on an other, on another—to be a self at all, we are in the realm of the poetic, according to Freeman (2019). We are also in the realm of the psychoanalytic unconscious, of attachment theory, of literary psychoanalysis, of interpersonal neurobiology and of a notion of human being as complicitous.

Despite its reliance on scientific method to validate its work, psychology has never been an exclusively academic enterprise. Its authority is formulated on its espoused relationship between practice and theory about that practice (Devonis, 2014; Rose, 1998). This allows its pronouncements on human truths to be apparently evidence-based. This, of course, denies the exercises of power that the normative and normativizing energies of psychology have been responsible for (Foucault, 2006; Rose, 1998; Teo, 2005). Authority to know is authority over that which must be known. In the terms of a Western subject that has been shaped by binary logic, what needs to be controlled for is the constituting other.

Self/Other

Disciplines involved with revealing the construction of racial difference, and working in the fields of gender and sexuality, have amply illustrated, both theoretically and materially, the role of the constituting other for the modern self. Whiteness, straightness, maleness, ablebodiedness and Europeanness have all been shown to need their debased binary other halves in order to be themselves (e.g., de Beauvoir, 1997; Dean, 2001; Fanon, 1967; Katz, 2007; Lorde, 2007; McRuer, 2006; Said, 1979).

Some branches of psychological theory and practice, and especially psychoanalytic thought, have long insisted on the importance of the other to the self/other mode of subject constitution (Benjamin, 1988; Churchill, 2015; Coelho & Claudio, 2003; Dean, 2001; Musholt, 2018). And yet in 2015, Goodman and Freeman's (2015) edited collection on psychology and the other begins with the declaration that "the figure of the Other is an... underutilized [...] vehicle for exploring and reconceptualizing classic psychological... issues" (Goodman & Freeman, 2015, p. 5). They (ibid, p. 4) critique modern psychology's construction of "tools and techniques" that "serve... to objectify experience, contain it, render it more... measurable... But in this very objectification and containment, they also serve to take us away from what is truly Other."

In this critique, we can hear an echo of Freeman's (2019) objections to scientific theorizing, which by its nature cannot tolerate the unmeasurable, the unknowable, and also considers these things suspicious by virtue of their "Romantic" or, indeed, subjective qualities. The application of the critical theories of otherness of the last half century seems to have affected psychology very unevenly.

Goodman and Freeman (2015, p. 2) define the other as everything that is not the self: "namely, the world itself." Both the human subject and the subject of psychology, they say, lose the world when we contain the other. And we contain the other because, in its overwhelming otherness, it threatens the boundaries of the self. They characterize the self's relation to the other as necessary: We need it and we reject it. They further suggest that this "perpetual dance" is "ubiquitous" and "universal." "But what happens," they (Goodman & Freeman, 2015, pp. 2–3) ask,

> [W]hen these idol-making and experience-rending tendencies are paired with a social order, philosophical heritage, and economic system that reinforce the centripetal force of the ego?… In this context, the self… becomes an idol of its own… It may be that we have told a story of ourselves—as modern subjects—that… requires us to live in constricted life-spaces, unable to truly attend to the abundance of the world around us… This has left us… ethically depleted, deprived of those existential resources that serve to move us beyond the confines of the hungry ego.

I am uncertain about the assertion that a self/other binary is a universal structure for humanity, being leery of claiming the authority to make my culture's experience true for all. But what is useful about Goodman and Freeman's (2015) presentation of the work of the (Western, late capitalist, neoliberal) self's relation to its other, is their location of the consequences of this relation in our very specific present.

If nineteenth century psychology assumed the Victorian, patriarchal and colonial right to make brutal use of its others (Perry, 2018; and see, e.g., the fate of Sarah Baartman, Crais & Scully, 2009; or the scientific racism espoused by pioneering psychologists, Richards, 2012; Teo, 2005), twentieth century psychology, with the help of feminism, queer theory and critical race studies, noticed this dynamic. For example, Jordan's

(2010) feminist approach helped develop the practice of relational-cultural therapy, which challenges the notion and the valorization of the bounded self (see Miller, 1986). James Baldwin wrote about how twentieth century heteronormative masculinity needed to construct the homosexual as other in order to shore up its own, artificially simple desire, a point Katz (2007) used to show how heterosexuality is a back-formation from its homosexual other. McRuer (2006), in turn, showed heterosexuality's reliance on ablebodiedness, and therefore on the disabled as well as queer other.

McWilliams (2020) details psychoanalytic theory's recognition of the centrality of the other to the modern self, and discusses the idea that we need others to hold the badness we cannot tolerate in ourselves. She identifies four main affects that feed the tendency toward destructive othering: fear, rage, envy and shame. Shame, she (McWilliams, 2020, p. 189) concludes, is above all "the common denominator of most toxic othering." Because shame and the other difficult emotions she identifies are part of being human, she says we cannot prevent ourselves from othering, we can only be vigilant about taking responsibility for what is happening when we do. She (McWilliams, 2020, p. 190) calls this, "the project of owning our own darkness, tolerating the shame it causes, and trying not to project it." This version of the self cannot escape a binary formation with its other, a point I will return to in Chap. 3.

What does a notion of the complicit subject bring to this standard version of the Western self? For one, the arguments made in this book about the relationship between the liberal individual self of current mainstream Anglo-American culture, the traditional project of psychotherapy, and current identity politics and the social injustices they seek to address, problematize the assumption that binary thinking is inevitable. To fully embrace the intergenerational, structurally saturated, rhizomatic, enfolded, complicit self is to reject the power dynamics our world currently depends upon and reproduces. These power dynamics have been presented to us in various ways as inevitable: by Freud's notion of the destructive drives underpinning "the" human psyche, by the "scientific" uses of biology to create gender and racial differences, by capitalism, by colonialism, by neoliberalism, by the assertion that we cannot help but hate and/or fear difference if we are to be human. If we challenge the structuring idea of the binary not as an underlying inevitability of what it means to be human, but as a technology of subjectification for the modern human, we open up different ways of being human. These ways have always existed. And they have been explored in much academic theorizing of the past 50 years or so, if not in mainstream academic (i.e., "scientific") and popular psychology.

Central to my thinking on this, and to the thinking of many others across disciplines, is the work of Judith Butler. For my purposes here, most directly relevant is *The Psychic Life of Power* (Butler, 1997), which explores how to become a subject is to become a self within processes of subjection and subordination:

> [T]o persist in one's being means to be given over from the start to social terms that are never fully one's own. The desire to persist in one's own being requires submitting to a world of others... Only by persisting in alterity does one persist in one's "own" being. (1997, p. 28)

Additionally, Butler's work points out the destructive power of socially inscribed norms to police access to the category of recognizable humanity (see Livingston, 2020). Othered groups are rendered socially unintelligible, their lives unlivable, their suffering ungrievable (Butler, 2003; Butler, 2016). Who gets to define the terms of the system and its performances of proper humanity becomes an important question. As she explores this question, Butler's work offers a detailed exposition of the fact of human complicity, the interdependence of self and other that systems of inequality violently deny (Butler, 2020).

Butler is most well known for her critiques of gender norms and how their reiterations are forged through repetition into apparent truths, endorsed at the expense of those who cannot or do not offer the correct performances (Butler, 1999). But her work also allows us to be suspicious of the norms of healthy psychological subjectivity that have been circulated and enacted by the psy disciplines, and the other discourses of modernity that have emerged together with, and complicit in, psychology. What constitutes the performance of a psychologically good enough subject? Who says?

The Subject of Psychology

Theories of the human in psychology are inevitably metapsychological; they make universal claims about human nature. Atwood and Stolorow (1993, p. 3) were arguing in 1979 that modern psychology had fragmented into different approaches to the question of subjectivity, each approach presenting itself as "the foundation for a science of man." But, as Atwood and Stolorow (1993, p. 4) point out, the different approaches are embedded in their originators' "ideological and conceptual orientations to the problem of what it means to be human," as focalized through their own experiences. The assumptions about and theories of human subjectivity offered by the different psychological schools of thought tell us more about the lives and subjectivities of their proponents than they do about universal humanity, and complicate psychology's claim to objective scientific status. Indeed, preempting many of the more recent arguments in favor of a psychological humanities, Atwood and Stolorow (1993) assert that the problem of metapsychology arises from psychology's attempts to be scientific. They (1993, p. 177), in turn, offer "*a theory of subjectivity itself*... a depth psychology of human experience, purified of the mechanistic reifications of classical metapsychology." Their solution to the problem of subjectivity in trying to understand subjectivity was, of course, intersubjectivity:

> [A] field theory or systems theory... that... seeks to comprehend psychological phenomena not as products of isolated intrapsychic mechanisms, but as forming at the interface of reciprocally interacting subjectivities... From this perspective, the very concept of an individual mind or psyche is itself a psychological product crystallizing from within a nexus of intersubjective relatedness. (Atwood & Stolorow, 1993, p. 178)

Intersubjectivity speaks to one element of the complicities of human being. It is a useful way to help theorize complicity in the therapeutic relationship. Intersubjectivity has a philosophical as well as a psychological tradition (Coelho & Claudio, 2003; Glaveanu, 2019). These tend to be divorced from the scientific branch of psychology, and the idea of intersubjectivity has been most extensively developed in the psy fields by psychoanalysis. The psychoanalytic intersubjective field is defined by the notion of the third, although this third space has been variously characterized as clinicians have sought to name the consequences of cultural and psychic complicities. As I will illustrate in Chap. 6, there are a number of therapeutic modalities that offer ways to apply these ideas in practice.

The notion of the intersubjective third seeks to name what is psychically created between therapist and client when two subjectivities successfully see each other's personhood. The idea of the intersubjective third aims to theorize what is created between the therapist and each client in a way that acknowledges the unique quality of the relationship. The third is excessive to the people involved, because it literally exceeds them. It can be thought of as an unconscious creation between them (Gerson, 2004). Jessica Benjamin (2004, p. 7) has defined the intersubjective third, most broadly, as "anything one holds in mind that creates another point of reference outside the dyad." The third is necessary for each member to get outside of herself, to enable what Benjamin calls mutual recognition between two subjects to happen. Benjamin (2004) describes the third as a fundamental relational principle, which, if surrendered to by the therapist, will enable both therapist and client to move "beyond doer and done to," into a place of reciprocity which undoes the oppressive subject/object dynamic of traditional psychoanalysis, and of a Western world built on binary thinking.

The third, as an external point of reference outside of the dyad, can encompass a range of forces or ideas, such as the cultural third (Gerson, 2004). Alternatively, the idea of the social third names the imbrications of interpsychic and intrapsychic and cultural forces (Benjamin, 2011; Sehrbrock, 2020), what Sehrbrock (2020, p. 291) calls the presence of "ghosts of collective and systemic agents" in the therapeutic encounter:

> [S]ocial thirdness presents a lens that illuminates the socio-political strata of experiences. It crystallizes social meaning that preserves distinctness without collapsing into polarities, extremes, binaries, concretizations of complexity, control, omnipotence, "us versus them," power struggles, splitting, and the phobic hatreds like transphobia, cisgenderism, and lookism, for example. In the context of a therapeutic encounter, social

thirdness is both a lens through which clinicians view and understand the therapeutic process and a position from which clinicians engage with their patients. Social thirdness goes beyond the bounds of dyadic intersubjectivity, focusing on the felt experience of the moment in relation to society and the social unconscious... [T]he social third is like the epigenetic influence of the environment's insignia on the expression of the gene. (Sehrbrock, 2020, pp. 291–292)

The field of intersubjectivity recognizes that the self needs its other in relations of intimacy, not domination (Benjamin, 1988; Glaveanu, 2019).

Benjamin's (2004) notion of recognition articulates the necessity of having a space beyond the binary. In her formulation, it is the collapse into complementarity (that binary energy) that causes dependency to become coercive: When two subjects, relating in a binary way, lose sight of the independent subjectivity of the other, and someone is reduced to a relational object. The binary relation is a relation of power, based on a lack of recognition which causes objectification and contempt (McWilliams, 2020).

In addition to an intersubjective approach, other branches of psychology have also been critical of the mainstream model of human subjectivity as properly independent, intrapsychically constituted, teleologically directed and self-controlled. In the twentieth century, the field paid ever more attention to social context, and to the imbrication of context with the individual (Gough, 2017; Laubscher, 2015; Teo, 2005). Since the second half of the twentieth century, some academic psychologists and psychotherapists have been concerned with hermeneutics, with the ideas of linguistic and social construction, and with the centrality of relationality to human being and to therapy. This is sometimes called the postmodern turn (Anderson, 1997; Anderson, 2007; Teo, 2005). Critical psychology has long been engaged with debates about the nature of selfhood, and aware of the embodied and material constitutive practices in which the psy disciplines have been implicated (Hook, 2007; Papadopoulos, 2008; Rose, 1998).

Here are a few more examples that are by no means exhaustive of the work done in this area: From a hermeneutic perspective, Cushman (2019, p. 9), citing himself from 1990, argues for the historically specific, culturally influenced and political content of any model of the self, in opposition to mainstream psychology's ahistorical individualistic self: "there is no universal, transhistorical self, only local selves; no universal theory about the self, only local theories." Cushman (2019) insists that psychology is a cultural artifact, its version of the self contingent on its own history and place. Furthermore, he argues that the modern self is empty, a result of the policies and politics of the twentieth century, and, crucially, of the liberal individualism that has shaped them. The twenty-first century self, he goes on to suggest, is neoliberally fractured and performative. These ideas are taken up in Chaps. 2 and 5.

Brooke (2015, p. 23), from a human science approach, advocates for a vision of the psychological subject as social: "a human science psychology cannot begin with a notion of the self that is taken for granted and self-originating." Instead, he offers a model of the human subject as embedded in and formed from language, community, history and an embodied identity.

Slaney (2019) suggests theoretical psychology borrows the idea of intersectionality from critical race and feminist theories in order to articulate its plurality. She wants a framework that emphasizes critical inquiry and critical praxis, that is aware of power relations, privilege and oppression, and the imperatives for social justice. Such a discipline would by definition be pluralistic, collaborative and interdisciplinary. McCormick-Huhn et al. (2019) provide an example of what a feminist, intersectional, mainstream psychological practice might look like.

In its turn, cultural psychology has been defined as "an interdisciplinary human science" which recognizes the co-constituted relationship between people and between people and their contexts (Shweder, 1990). However, cultural psychology, like certain branches of feminist psychology, and like multicultural or cross-cultural psychologies, has been criticized for not challenging the Western methodological, empiricist foundations of psychology, which do not acknowledge the material relations of power out of which they emerge and which they perpetuate (Richards, 2012; Teo, 2005). Both transnational and postcolonial and now decolonial psychologies are aware of psychology's responsibility in perpetuating raced relations of power that are also geographical and economic (Boonzaier & van Niekerk, 2019; Collins et al., 2019; Duran & Duran,

1995; Held, 2020; Melluish, 2014; Miller & Miller, 2020; Richards, 2012; Teo, 2005).

Narrative Therapy and other postmodern modalities (Anderson, 1997; Freedman & Combs, 1996; Papadopoulos, 2008; Teo, 2005) have taught psychotherapists to think about the meanings made of and by clients, and have enabled us to learn about the harm done by oppressive systems and the discourses they perpetuate. But almost by definition, we still work with the ideas about the client-as-subject which Rose (1998) points out the psy disciplines have helped create: that they are in search of more authentic personhood, more accurate meanings, greater authenticity. And that they are free to do so, indeed, compelled to do so: it is a sign of their healthy leanings, their personal responsibility and their move toward being better.

So while a critical eye on psychology's meanings and practices has been a part of the discipline, this has not tended to substantially impact the common-sense authority of the psychologized subject, the modern liberal subject of the therapy room and of popular discourses of choice. Fine's (2014) critique of social psychology's engagement with gender difference, including how these often problematic experiments are disseminated in the popular press, gives one example of this. As psychology became disciplinized in the nineteenth century, it participated in alliances with other scientific regimes to establish ways of measuring, knowing, validating, testing and normalizing. What emerges from Rose's (1998, p. 60, 62–65) account of this process is just how woven into modern everyday thought, common sense reality, the subject of psychology is, as a result of this historical process:

> To educate a child, to reform a delinquent, to cure a hysteric, to raise a baby, to administer an army, to run a factory—it is not so much that these activities entail the utilization of psychological theories and techniques than that there is a constitutive relation between the character of what will count as an adequate psychological theory or argument and the processes by which a kind of psychological visibility may be accorded to these domains.... [R]eality becomes ordered according to a psychological taxonomy…

Rose (1998) denotes this a "*techne*" that uses a way of thinking about political power, the creation of authority and authorities, and an ethical requirement to self-knowledge and self-improvement that shapes who we think we are and what we think we should be doing with our lives.

And in 2020, Severson and Goodman were still asserting that Western psychology is failing to locate the human being in context, because of a philosophical focus on the individual and an attempt to mimic the natural sciences (as though these disciplines were not, themselves, saturated with human culture, see Rippon, 2019; Schiebinger, 2004). Severson & Goodman (2020, p. 2) decry the "catastrophic failure to think about human beings as fundamentally social, relational, ethical, historical creatures." They critique the development of a scientific rationalism, a belief in the constructs of objective truth, rationality, individualism, as wholly inadequate to account for the intergenerational transmission of trauma, suffering and injustice. They insist, "to be human is first to be embedded in society, to exist in porous and complex social and ethical relationships" (ibid). What is remarkable about this statement is not its refusal of traditional psychology's "scientific" stance, and its concomitant focus on the individual, the histories of which we have been exploring at length. What is remarkable is that it is asserted in 2020 as a revolutionary statement, as part of a project of leveraging psychology for social justice. Despite decades of theory, in other words, the liberal subject of objective experience and scientific inquiry is still very much the center of psychological meaning.

Thus psychology can be said to be a technique of subjectification still. It is a way of thinking about what it means to be human that creates systems of power, through defining normalcy and deviance (Hook, 2007; Rose, 1998; Sugarman, 2019). It has helped to create an idea of human subjectivity that is self-enclosed and individualized, with the freedom of choice to decide who to be and how to be better. This subject is by definition liberal, and a democratic citizen of the West. The implications of these positionalities will be explored in more detail in Chap. 2, and linked to processes of racialization and gendering in Chaps. 3 and 4, respectively. The latest iteration, post-internet, is the topic of Chap. 5.

Psychology has enormous constitutive power to underwrite a version of reality that entrenches binary thinking, a subject who is based on its other in a culture where institutions shape access to both resources and meanings, and to who can be considered a viable subject or correctly human. What is at stake when we ask psychology to change, to put into practice—in the psychotherapy room, in the pages of newspapers and magazines, as well as in the classroom and academy—the insights that critical psychology has taken from the humanities, is the enablement of new ways of understanding how we might be subjects in relation to each other. In such a world, there is no need to account for a gay gene or the etiology of transness in in-utero hormone exposure. There is no need to invest in the artificial construction of different human races. The logic that underpins structural inequality is revealed as a regime of truth, a construct to enable material gain for the "normal" or normative. And, equally important to my argument, it also means that those who have been constructed as the constitutive other, those whose lives and psyches have been used to enable dominant alliances of the norm, are also obliged to find additional forms of activism. It is not enough to demand or even achieve access to the master's tools. And advocating for revolution, for a complete change, a wiping clean of the slate, is impossible, as the idea of the complicit subject suggests—we are never free to escape where we came from, the terms of how we were made. Social justice change has to be able to hold the complexity of the human, which is not and has never been, binary.

Conclusion

Over two decades ago, as we have seen, Rose (1998) argued that the concept and the ethics of the idea of the modern individual, free to choose his fate, was a discursive construction linked both to the emergence of liberal democracies and to the psy disciplines. He traced the genealogy of this regime of the self, using, as this language suggests, Foucaultian ideas and other theories concerned with deconstruction, discourse and destabilization of the apparently natural and common-sensical. His project was taken up by Hook (2007, p. 8), who also uses Foucault's (1977) idea of disciplinarity to argue that what he calls "a psychological individuality" is central to the emergence of modern ideas, including political systems. This work emerged from the feminist-informed, queering turn in the humanities of the 1980s and 1990s, as is evident in

Rose's (1998, pp. 3–10) account of the academic trajectory underpinning his essays. Despite the intervening decades, psychotherapeutic practice (and many of the institutions that teach and accredit it) has not significantly metabolized the interdisciplinary ideas articulated in 1998 for the discipline of psychology by Rose. Indeed, in 2017, Teo was arguing for the need to include the thinking developed in humanities-based subjects into psychology, and again, in 2019. If Rose's (1998, pp. 1–2) objective was to "question some of our contemporary certainties about the kinds of people we take ourselves to be, to help develop ways in which we might begin to think ourselves otherwise," then my purpose in this book is to argue that this work, so old school by now in the humanities, still needs to be applied to psychotherapeutic practice.

The modern version of the self has been invented through a historical process. It is a macrostructural process, not an individual one. This historical process has everything to do with systems of power and exploitation. These include the economic changes of the industrial revolution and the neoliberal structures that have emerged from the globalization enabled by colonialism, to access to political power and the institutions that enable this access. The mapping of this process is the topic of Chap. 2. And at the same time, all this actual work in the world would not be possible without symbolic structures, without language and the stories it tells us about who is human, who is deserving, who is deviant and so on.

Being human means being complicit. In the systems that shape us all, and that privilege some of us over others. In the language that speaks us into being, the ways we learn to say "I" and "you" and "us" and "them." In the histories that predate us and that set the terms for the world we inherit. In the culture that tells us who we each should be according to the bodies we each have, how we should behave, what we should value and how we should express those values, that behavior, our selves. In the families into which we are born, which hone and focalize the systems, the language, the history and the culture that authorize and shape what it means to be a family, and how a family should function. To be human is to be both-and, not either/or. We can never escape the specifics between us, or the impact of embodiment, and the only way we can be better is to nevertheless allow for a disembodied shared humanness that makes us all possible, and that makes us all responsible for each other. Whether we like it or not.

Works Cited

Adams, G., Dobles, I., Gómez, L. H., Kurtiş, T., & Molina, L. E. (2015). Decolonising psychological science: Introduction to the special thematic section. *Journal of Social and Political Psychology, 3*(1), 213–238.

Adams, G., Gómez, L. H., Kurtiş, T., Molina, L. E., & Dobles, I. (2017). Notes on decolonizing psychology: From one Special Issue to another. *South African Journal of Psychology, 47*(4), 531–541.

Adriaens, P. R., & De Block, A. (2013). Pathologizing sexual deviance: A history. *Journal of sex research, 50*(3–4), 276–298.

Alderman, N. (2016). *The power*. Little, Brown and Company.

Anderson, H. (1997). *Conversation, language, and possibilities: A postmodern approach to therapy*. Basic.

Anderson, H. (2007). A postmodern umbrella: Language and knowledge as relational and generative, and inherently transforming. In H. Anderson & D. Gehart (Eds.), *Collaborative therapy: Relationships and conversations that make a difference* (pp. 7–19). Routledge.

Atwood, G. E., & Stolorow, R. D. (1993). *Faces in a cloud: Intersubjectivity in personality theory*. Jason Aronson.

Benjamin, J. (1988). *The bonds of love: Psychoanalysis, feminism and the problem of domination*. Random House.

Benjamin, J. (2004). Beyond doer and done to: An intersubjective view of thirdness. *Psychoanalytic Quarterly, 73*, 5–46.

Benjamin, J. (2011). Facing reality together. *Studies in Gender and Sexuality, 12*(1), 27–36.

Bhatia, S. (2020). Decolonizing psychology: Power, citizenship and identity. *Psychoanalysis, Self and Context, 15*(3), 257–266.

Bonthuys, E. (2008). The Civil Union Act: More of the same. In M. Judge, A. Manion, & S. de Waal (Eds.), *To have and to hold: The making of same-sex marriage in South Africa* (pp. 171–181). Fanele.

Boonzaier, F., & van Niekerk, T. (Eds.). (2019). *Decolonial feminist community psychology*. Springer.

Bowlby, J. (1982). *Attachment*. Basic.

Brooke, R. (2015). Some common themes of psychology as a human science. In C. T. Fischer, L. Laubscher, & R. Brooke (Eds.), *The qualitative vision for psychology: An invitation to a human science approach* (pp. 17–30). Duquesne University Press.

brown, a.m. (2020). *We will not cancel us: and other dreams of transformative justice*. AK Press.

Brown, L. (2018). *Feminist therapy* (2nd ed.). American Psychological Association.
Brown, W. (1995). *States of injury: Power and freedom in late modernity.* Princeton University Press.
Butler, J. (1993). Imitation and gender insubordination. In H. Abelove, M. A. Barale, & D. Halparin (Eds.), *The gay and lesbian studies reader* (pp. 307–320). Routledge.
Butler, J. (1997). *The psychic life of power: Theories in subjection.* Stanford University Press.
Butler, J. (1999). *Gender trouble: Feminism and the subversion of identity.* Routledge.
Butler, J. (2003). *Precarious life: The powers of mourning and violence.* Verso.
Butler, J. (2016). *Frames of war: When is life grievable?* Verso.
Butler, J. (2020). *The force of non-violence: An ethico-political bind.* Verso.
Churchill, S. D. (2015). Resonating with meaning in the lives of others: An invitation to empathetic understanding. In C. T. Fischer, L. Laubscher, & R. Brooke (Eds.), *The qualitative vision for psychology: An invitation to a human science approach* (pp. 91–116). Duquesne University Press.
Coelho, N. E., & Claudio, L. F. (2003). Patterns of intersubjectivity in the constitution of subjectivity: Dimensions of otherness. *Culture & Psychology, 9*(3), 193–208.
Cohen, C. J. (2005). Punks, bulldaggers, and welfare queens: The radical potential of queer politics? In E. P. Johnson & M. G. Henderson (Eds.), *Black queer studies: A critical anthology* (pp. 21–51). Duke University Press.
Collective, C. R. (1983). The Combahee River Collective Statement. In B. Smith (Ed.), *Home Girls: A black feminist anthology* (pp. 272–282). Kitchen Table Press.
Collins, L. H., Machizawa, S., & Rice, J. K. (Eds.). (2019). *Transnational psychology of women: Expanding international and intersectional approaches.* American Psychological Association.
Collins, P. H. (2015). Toward a new vision: Race, class, and gender as categories of analysis and connection. In S. M. Shaw & J. Lee (Eds.), *Women's voices feminist visions: Classic and contemporary readings* (6th ed., pp. 72–79). McGraw-Hill.
Crais, C., & Scully, P. (2009). *Sara Baartman and the Hottentot Venus: A ghost story and a biography.* Princeton University Press.
Crenshaw, K. (1989). Demarginalizing the intersection of race and sex: A Black feminist critique of antidiscrimination doctrine, feminist theory and antiracist politics. *University of Chicago Legal Forum, 140,* 139–167.

Cushman, P. (1990). Why the self is empty: Toward a historically situated psychology. *American Psychologist, 45*, 599–611.
Cushman, P. (2019). *Travels with the self: Interpreting psychology as cultural history*. Routledge.
Danius, S., & Jonsson, S. (1993). An Interview with Gayatri Chakravorty Spivak. *Boundary 2, 20*(2), 24–50.
de Beauvoir, S. (1997). *The second sex*. Vintage.
Dean, T. (2001). Homosexuality and the problem of otherness. In T. Dean & C. Lane (Eds.), *Homosexuality & psychoanalysis* (pp. 120–143). University of Chicago Press.
Deleuze, G., & Guattari, F. (1987). *A thousand plateaus: Capitalism and schizophrenia*. Trans. B. Massumi. University of Minnesota Press.
Devonis, D. C. (2014). *History of psychology 101*. Springer.
DiAngelo, R. (2018). *White fragility: Why it's so hard for white people to talk about racism*. Beacon.
Duran, E., & Duran, B. (1995). *Native American postcolonial psychology*. State University of New York Press.
Fanon, F. (1967). *Black skin, white masks*. Grove.
Fine, C. (2014). *Delusions of gender: How our minds, society, and neurosexism create difference*. Norton.
Fischer, C. T., Laubscher, L., & Brooke, R. (Eds.). (2015). *The qualitative vision for psychology: An invitation to a human science approach*. Duquesne University Press.
Foucault, M. (1977). *Discipline and punish: The birth of the prison*. Penguin.
Foucault, M. (2006). *History of madness*. Trans. J. Murphy & J. Khalfa. Routledge.
Freedman, J., & Combs, G. (1996). *Narrative Therapy: The social construction of preferred realities*. Norton.
Freeman, M. (2019). Toward a poetics of the other: New directions in postscientific psychology. In T. Teo (Ed.), *Re-envisioning theoretical psychology: Diverging ideas and practices* (pp. 1–24). Springer.
Fuss, D. (1989). *Essentially speaking: Feminism, nature & difference*. Routledge.
Gamson, J. (1995). Must identity movements self-destruct? A queer dilemma. *Social Problems, 42*(3), 390–407.
Gantt, E. E., & Williams, R. N. (2015). Explanation vs understanding in psychology: A human science approach. In C. T. Fischer, L. Laubscher, & R. Brooke (Eds.), *The qualitative vision for psychology: An invitation to a human science approach* (pp. 31–48). Duquesne University Press.

Gerhardt, S. (2004). *Why love matters: How affection shapes a baby's brain*. Routledge.

Gerson, S. (2004). The relational unconscious: a core element of intersubjectivity, thirdness, and clinical process. *Psychoanalytic Quarterly, 73*(1), 63–98.

Glaveanu, V. P. (2019). Being other: Intersubjectivity, allocentrism and the possible. *Journal for the Theory of Social Behaviour, 49*(4), 443–459.

Goodman, D., & Freeman, M. (Eds.). (2015). *Psychology and the other*. Oxford University Press.

Gough, B. (Ed.). (2017). *The Palgrave handbook of critical social psychology*. Palgrave.

Guthrie, R. V. (2004). *Even the rat was white: A historical view of psychology* (2nd ed.). Pearson.

Hardy, K. V. (2008). Race, reality and relationships: Implications for the re-visioning of family therapy. In M. McGoldrick & K. V. Hardy (Eds.), *Re-visioning family therapy: Race, culture, and gender in clinical practice* (pp. 76–84). Guilford.

Held, B. S. (2020). Epistemic violence in psychological science: Can knowledge of, from, and for the (othered) people solve the problem? *Theory & Psychology, 30*(3), 349–370.

Hook, D. (2007). *Foucault, psychology, and the analytics of power*. Palgrave.

Jordan, J. (Ed.). (1997). *Women's growth in diversity: more writings from the Stone Center*. Guilford.

Jordan, J. (2010). *Relational-cultural therapy*. American Psychological Association.

Katz, J. N. (2007). *The invention of heterosexuality*. University of Chicago Press.

Kendi, I. X. (2016). *Stamped from the beginning: The definitive history of racist ideas in America*. Bold Type Books.

Kristeva, J. (1980). *Desire in language: A semiotic approach to literature and art*. Columbia University Press.

Laubscher, L. (2015). Invitation to psychology as a human science. In C. T. Fischer, L. Laubscher, & R. Brooke (Eds.), *The qualitative vision for psychology: An invitation to a human science approach* (pp. 1–16). Duquesne University Press.

Livingston, A. (2020). Inventing nonviolence. *Boston Review* August 31. Retrieved September 9, 2020, from http://bostonreview.net/politics/alexander-livingston-inventing-nonviolence

Lorde, A. (2007). *Sister outsider: Essays and speeches*. Crossing.

Maldonado-Torres, M. (2017). Frantz Fanon and the decolonial turn in psychology: From modern/colonial methods to the decolonial attitude. *South African Journal of Psychology, 47*(4), 432–441.

Marecek, J. (2019). A History of the future: Carolyn Wood Sherif, equitable knowledge, and feminist psychology. *Psychology of Women Quarterly, 43*(4), 422–432.

Martin, J. (2017). Carl Rogers' and B.F. Skinner's approaches to personal and societal improvement: A study in the psychological humanities. *Journal of Theoretical and Philosophical Psychology, 37*(4), 214–229.

Mascolo, M. F. (2016). Beyond objectivity and subjectivity: The intersubjective foundations of psychological science. *Integrative Psychological & Behavioral Science, 50*(4), 543–554.

McCormick-Huhn, K., Warner, L. R., Settles, I. H., & Shields, S. A. (2019). What if psychology took intersectionality seriously? Changing how psychologists think about participants. *Psychology of Women Quarterly, 43*(4), 445–456.

McRuer, R. (2006). *Crip theory: Cultural signs of queerness and disability*. New York University Press.

McWilliams, N. (2020). Finding the other in the self. In D. M. Goodman, E. R. Severson, & H. Macdonald (Eds.), *Race, rage, and resistance: Philosophy, psychology, and the perils of individualism* (pp. 180–197). Routledge.

Melluish, S. (2014). Globalization, culture and psychology. *International review of psychiatry, 26*(5), 538–543.

Miller, J. B. (1986). *Toward a new psychology of women* (2nd ed.). Beacon.

Miller, L. L., & Miller, M. J. (2020). Praxivist imaginaries of decolonization: Can the psy be decolonized in the world as we know it? *Feminism & Psychology, 30*(3), 381–390.

Moraga, C., & Anzaldua, G. (Eds.). (1983). *This bridge called my back: Writings by radical women of color*. Kitchen Table: Women of Color Press.

Musholt, K. (2018). Self and others. *Interdisciplinary Science Reviews, 43*(2), 136–145.

Nash, J. (2019). *Black feminism reimagined: After intersectionality*. Duke University Press.

Olson, R. (2012). Remarks on "Psychology as a STEM Discipline and as Logos of the Soul: The Critical Necessity of the Humanities for Psychological Science". *The Humanistic Psychologist, 40*(3), 270–273.

Papadopoulos, D. (2008). In the ruins of representation: Identity, individuality, subjectification. *British Journal of Social Psychology, 47*, 139–165.

Perry, I. (2018). *Vexy thing: On gender and liberation*. Duke University Press.

Posel, D. (2001). Racial categorisations under apartheid and their afterlife. *Transformation, 47*, 50–74.

Pyne, J. (2016). "Parenting Is Not a Job … It's a Relationship": Recognition and relational knowledge among parents of gender non-conforming children. *Journal of Progressive Human Services, 27(1)*, 21–48.

Richards, G. (2012). *"Race", racism, and psychology: Towards a reflexive history* (2nd ed.). Routledge.

Rippon, G. (2019). *The Gendered Brain: The new neuroscience that shatters the myth of the female brain*. Penguin.

Rose, N. (1998). *Inventing our selves: Psychology, power and personhood*. Cambridge University Press.

Ross, L. (2019). I'm a black feminist. I think callout culture is toxic. *New York Times*, August 17. Retrieved August 9, 2020, from https://www.nytimes.com/2019/08/17/opinion/sunday/cancel-culture-call-out

Rothblum, E. D., & Cole, E. (Eds.). (2018). *Professional training for feminist therapists: Personal memoirs*. Routledge.

Said, E. W. (1979). *Orientalism*. Vintage.

Saini, A. (2017). *Inferior: How science got women wrong – And the new research that's rewriting the story*. Beacon.

Sanders, M. (2002). *Complicities: The intellectual and apartheid*. University of Natal Press.

Schiebinger, L. (2004). *Nature's body: Gender in the making of modern science*. Rutgers University Press.

Schore, A. N. (2003). *Affect Regulation and repair of the self*. Norton.

Sehrbrock, J. (2020). Social thirdness: Intersubjective conceptions of the experience of gender prejudice. *Psychoanalysis, Self and Context, 15(3)*, 289–295.

Severson, E. R., & Goodman, D. M. (2020). Intergenerational strains. In D. M. Goodman, E. R. Severson, & H. Macdonald (Eds.), *Race, rage, and resistance: Philosophy, psychology, and the perils of individualism* (pp. 1–13). Routledge.

Shaw, S. M., & Lee, J. (2015). *Women's voices feminist visions: Classic and contemporary readings* (6th ed.). McGraw-Hill.

Showalter, E. (2007). *The female malady: Women, madness, and English culture 1830–1980*. Virago.

Shweder, R. A. (1990). Cultural psychology: What is it? In J. W. Stigler, R. A. Shweder, & G. Herdt (Eds.), *Cultural psychology: Essays on comparative human development* (pp. 1–43). Cambridge University Press.

Siegel, D. (2003). An interpersonal neurobiology of psychotherapy. In M. F. Solomon & D. Siegel (Eds.), *Healing Trauma: Attachment, mind, body and brain* (pp. 1–56). Norton.

Silberman, S. (2015). *NeuroTribes: The legacy of autism and the future of neurodiversity*. Penguin.

Slaney, K.L. (2019). An intersectionality for theoretical psychology? In T. Teo (Ed.), *Re-envisioning theoretical psychology* (pp. 49–74).

Spivak, G. (1988). Can the subaltern speak? In C. Nelson & L. Grossberg (Eds.), *Marxism and the interpretation of culture* (pp. 271–313). Macmillan.

Stern, D. (1985). *The interpersonal world of the infant*. Basic.

Stern, D. (2014). *The present moment in psychotherapy and everyday life*. Norton.

Sugarman, J. (2019). An historical turn for theoretical and philosophical psychology. In T. Teo (Ed.), *Re-envisioning theoretical psychology: Diverging ideas and practices* (pp. 25–48). Springer.

Teo, T. (2005). *The critique of psychology: From Kant to postcolonial theory*. Springer.

Teo, T. (2017). From psychological science to the psychological humanities: Building a general theory of subjectivity. *Review of General Psychology, 21*(4), 281–291.

Teo, T. (Ed.). (2019). *Re-envisioning theoretical psychology: Diverging ideas and practices*. Springer.

Tuhiwai Smith, L. (2012). *Decolonizing methodologies: Research and indigenous peoples* (2nd ed.). Zed.

Williams, E. F. (Ed.). (1995). *Voices of feminist therapy*. Harwood.

Open Access This chapter is licensed under the terms of the Creative Commons Attribution 4.0 International License (http://creativecommons.org/licenses/by/4.0/), which permits use, sharing, adaptation, distribution and reproduction in any medium or format, as long as you give appropriate credit to the original author(s) and the source, provide a link to the Creative Commons licence and indicate if changes were made.

The images or other third party material in this chapter are included in the chapter's Creative Commons licence, unless indicated otherwise in a credit line to the material. If material is not included in the chapter's Creative Commons licence and your intended use is not permitted by statutory regulation or exceeds the permitted use, you will need to obtain permission directly from the copyright holder.

2

Well-Intentioned White People and Other Problems with Liberalism

Chapter 1 located the notion of the complicit subject within the psychological humanities and the subject of psychology. It argued that the Western notion of human being, which informs the subject of psychology, is based on a binary structure that reflects and reproduces oppressive power dynamics. This binary relationship encodes and enables psychic and systemic power relations (since the two are complicit in each other). The power dynamics enabled by binary logic work through refusing the complicit nature of human being in favor of a relationship between self and other that needs, among other things, a liberal subject formation.

A liberal subject is one who requires sameness in his relationships, who cannot truly tolerate difference. He is born from the Enlightenment's valorization of the rational, self-enclosed individual, a mind who can and should know and control himself—and thus, a subject fundamentally alienated from the capacity to handle encounters with the otherness that is central to what it means to be human. He grew in the soil of capitalism, and the gender and race binaries from which it profited. He eventually fragmented under neoliberalism, as the pressures of capitalism in a globalized economy reached ever further into systems and their subjects.

This chapter provides more detail about the subject of liberalism and its relationship to relations of power. It tracks the move from liberalism to neoliberalism as political, economic and cultural structures of power that have affected the nature of the Western (and Westernized) subject of psychology. It also summarizes the argument that the psy disciplines, and therefore the subject of psychology, are fundamentally implicated in techniques of liberal subjectification. As a consequence, the model of human being on which psychotherapy is built is limited by this history and its effects. Thinking complicitously opens clinicians up to the full potential of intersubjective co-creation with clients, a point which will be fully explored in the final chapter. This entails a commitment to move away from liberal individualism and its ideas about autonomy. It also entails an awareness of the effects of neoliberalism on twenty-first century subjects, which is explored in more detail in Chap. 5.

Liberalism

Before coronavirus, before the racial justice protests sparked by the lynching of George Floyd, before the ugly contentions of the 2020 presidential elections, but right in the middle of the maelstrom of Trumpism, I became a U.S. citizen. My citizenship ceremony took place during the government shutdown at the beginning of 2019, which was caused by a battle over the symbol of a pointless, expensive, destructive wall on the southern American border. Outside the Orpheum Theatre in Oakland, landfill in the shape of little plastic American flags made in China were being sold by a range of people, all of whom were not white. Inside the Orpheum, the very nice staff from the Department of Homeland Security, San Francisco branch, went out of their way to let us know that the majority of the 1000 or so people qualifying for citizenship that day were from Mexico (and then China, and then India). They told us that we were the best of America, and most welcome here. Their political subversion in the context of the Trumpocalypse was clear, and I appreciated it.

They also got a choir of nice elderly people to sing us, "This Land Is Your Land," among other examples of musical Americana. Apparently being inducted into Americanness means being invited to collude with historical amnesia about whose land, exactly, we are on. They showed us a carefully curated slide show of images of immigrants of many ethnicities and colors coming to America over the years. They told us immigrants built America, again indulging in national amnesia. I felt deeply uncomfortable participating in the celebration of nationalism with these necessary omissions. I also felt the privilege of being granted citizenship at a time when some families were being torn apart for trying to get in to this country. I felt very appreciative of being in a country which allowed government representatives to speak out against the government, and appreciative of how they asserted that America is the people in it, not the people in charge. This whole ambivalent event says something, I think, about the liberalism that has built this country and allowed it to continue selling parts of itself for celebrating, while pretending other parts do not exist.

The whitewashed American fantasy is that anyone can achieve anything here, in this land of opportunity, if he just works hard enough. Each person, this fantasy goes, is free to do his best, and entitled by god, law and ethics to the right to be his individual self, make his individual decisions and own his individual stuff. The messy American truth is much murkier, since not everyone has equal access to the opportunities to get ahead. It is also complicated by the larger human and ecological truth that we do not, in fact, each stand alone, that we are implicated in each other's choices whether we like it or not. The exalted ideal of the individual and his rights—the liberal subject, entitled to his land, his guns, his family, his freedom—is not a god-given truth but a construct formed at the cost of a host of others. It also fundamentally disallows the concept of human complicity. Despite even its best intentions, this fierce liberal individualism is profoundly responsible for helping to structure a deeply unequal society, a way of thinking about human being that is inimical to human being (see Davis, 2020). It is part and parcel of systems of oppression, even as it also is deeply committed to discourses of truth, freedom and human happiness.

Liberalism began as both a political and an economic philosophy. It has come to encode the politics of socioeconomic policy as morality. As a political system of thought, it originated in Europe, possibly as far back as the Magna Carta in the thirteenth century, which attempted to limit the monarch's divine right over the individual liberties of the landed gentry. It has thus always been classed. It has come, broadly, to stand for individual rights to, among other things, free will to choose, bodily autonomy and land ownership, none of which can actually be asserted by most individuals in most of the world. Despite what it thinks of itself, there are very real limits to liberalism's claims to universality, to its belief that it encodes values of general human dignity, truth and justice.

Guyatt (2016) has argued that from America's inception, well-intentioned white people recognized that America's founding principle—all men are created equal—was incompatible with genocide and slavery. But they could not accept the differences represented by Native Americans and Africans as equal to their own culture and values. In perhaps the most pernicious blind spot of Western culture, one which arguably builds on a philosophical inability to come to reasonable terms with sexual difference, these early liberal white Americans recognized the humanity of their others but not their innate equality. That could only come if and when They became more like Us. This is the problem with liberalism. Its message is ultimately about the centrality of the whiteness, maleness and classness that birthed it. It looks at others and measures their worth in their willingness to become like itself. It is also terribly, terribly well-intentioned, since it is so obviously the best of what it means to be human that wanting to assimilate others into itself is only a gift, a measure of its generosity. It is a benign Borg. It is bewildered by opposition or resentment from those it wants to help.

It also normalizes the idea that selfhood and ownership are co-constituting. Liberalism, in its insistence on the rights of the individual, encodes capitalist assumptions about the relationship between property and personhood. Part of being a person is the right to own stuff. This inevitably translates into maneuvers for economic and social power, to which other meanings of humanity become subject.

My first understanding of liberalism is through a South African lens. The terms of the debate are different there (see Distiller, 2005). There was a Liberal Party for a while, but it died in the face of apartheid (Rich, 1997). Stephen Bantu Biko (1978), a visionary writer and anti-apartheid activist beaten to death by the police in 1977, made it impossible for any progressive South African to be proud of the epithet. A white liberal, according to Biko, was someone who spoke for black people, who did not recognize their agency. White liberals were (are) products and beneficiaries of racism who were (are) unable to see their own location in the system and how their well-intentioned actions perpetuate injustice, specifically, for Biko, racial injustice.

Post apartheid, liberalism and liberal values continued to be highly contested and racialized (Husemeyer, 1997; Johnson & Welsh, 1998). This is unsurprising, given the class and race tensions the ideology carries in postcolonial times. Liberal ideals fed colonial discourse, in part by circulating a veneer of morality which stitched individual rights (in formations which benefitted colonizers, like the right to own property, without the acknowledgment of the ownership rights of the people who had been there first) to democracy and its institutions. In so doing, it bestowed the state with commitments to dignity and freedom that were, in reality, extremely partial (Mehta, 1999).

As Brown (1995, p. 17) points out, the modern Western state is dependent upon liberalism to authorize its apparently "self-generating" functions: "social repairs, economic problem solving, and the management of a mass population." Liberal ideals helped to create the idea of the modern nation state, whose job it is to manage and protect the rights of the apparently free individual members of said nation. But the state, and the liberal ideas it relies upon and helps to produce, creates the individuals it goes on to protect. And this state, these individuals and the rights to which they are entitled by the law created by the state in the name of its individuals, these things have a very specific history. Perry (2018) has tracked the mutual development of modern patriarchy in the Enlightenment via slavery, colonialism and specific uses of juridical power. This emerging law conflated manhood (meaning legally endorsed, raced, personhood) and the right to property, to create subjects and objects of government.

Perry (2018) shows how economic liberalism, which she tracks to the early expansion of European Empire at the start of the Enlightenment, and which was enriched by the early slave trade, was also a political and a philosophical system. The entire enterprise was enabled by a use of the law to grant ownership rights to those considered people. Thus, economic liberalism is inextricable from "specifically, the doctrine of personhood [which] entails a system whereby the subject before the state or the law was made into either a patriarch, his liege (woman), or someone outside legal recognition, whether slaves or... 'savages' but whom we can also term 'nonpersons' in the juridical sense" (Perry, 2018, p. 21). She shows how the legal personhood granted the gendered, raced, classed liberal subject of emerging modernity was based on the exclusion of those not afforded the legal recognition of their personhood. The right to self-determination, legally and physically, continues to rely on having access to legally recognized personhood and what Perry calls "political recognition."

Rose (1998) has further detailed how individuality and governmentability go together in modern democracy. He adds Foucault's (1977, 1978) insight that the creation of normativity was a crucial part of this process. He details the role of the psy disciplines in creating this normative individuality, which supplements Perry's (2018) explication of the ways that ideas of legal personhood and the patriarchal order it helped establish extended from the public to the private sphere. Before the advent of the psy disciplines, Perry (2018) shows, liberalism was establishing practices of surveillance that penetrated intimate relations and assigned people (and nonpeople) their proper places in the system. In turn, Rose (1998) shows how normative and individualizing technologies of democracy and the emerging discipline of psychology worked together as the Enlightenment continued and into the twentieth century, as we will see in more detail below.

As we will see, too, in its current incarnation, neoliberalism, the imbrication of liberal individualism and capitalism within neocolonial globalization, has specific effects on structures and subjectivities. Liberal subjects, formed through the Law and the law—that is, through both symbolic exercises of power and actual juridical decrees and acts—are part of and parceled with modern race and racism, modern gender binaries, modern democracies, industrial and surveillance capitalism, and the idea of the entitled, enabled individual all these constructs need to do their work of domination. These ideas are illustrated in the chapters that follow.

Williams (1991) writes lyrically about the modern implications of the marriage of liberalism and capitalism in the American legal system. She says that individual rights, that concept so dear to America's sense of itself and the freedoms on which its righteousness depends, were codified by the law to be available only to those who could afford them. Notions of privacy, of intimacy, and the human connection upon which both rely, she shows, have been corrupted by the power of the marketplace to commodify human value. Perry's (2018) exposition of the initial legal construction of American personhood as dependent on commodities and commodity values, as well as on gender and race, provides the historical and ideological underpinning for the sociolegal dynamics, Williams (1991) identifies.

Williams (1991) writes about the valuation of property as something concrete that can be held to legal standards in contract law, standards which can in theory also protect people. Instead, she says (Williams, 1991), value has come to accrue to the curated meaning of a thing, the associations and desires conjured up by an advertising industry that evades legal accountability by relying on the creation of ephemera and selling the idea it associates with the thing instead of the thing itself.

This language was not available to Williams, but she is talking about the brand. When "masque becomes the basis of our bargains," she says (Williams, 1991, pp. 40–41),

> [W]e will create new standards of irrelevance in our lives, reordering social relations in favor of the luxurious—and since few of us can afford real luxury, blind greed becomes the necessary companion… Money reflects law and law reflects money, unattached to notions of humanity.

This is also, not coincidentally, an accurate description of how slavery worked. And slavery is surely the institution which most exposes the investments and limits of a system of thought that wants to declare itself for universal human dignity and rights, thus authorizing its own goodness, while also encoding the right to individual profit as part of what it entitles itself to (see Kendi, 2016). The silently raced component of modern liberalism, and its tendency to not know this, is reflected here.

Williams (1991, pp. 71–71) also writes about liberal good intention. She describes a group of white real-estate developers who are considering entering a church in Harlem during an Easter Sunday service to observe the "show" during a walking tour:

> I wondered what would happen if a group of blue-jeaned blacks were to walk uninvited into a synagogue on Passover…—just to peer, not to pray… Yet the aspect of disrespect, intrusion, seemed irrelevant to this well-educated, affable group of people. They deflected my observation with comments like… "There's no harm intended." As well-intentioned as they were, I was left with the impression that no one existed for them who could not be governed by their intentions.

She adds (Williams, 1991, p. 72), "To live so completely impervious to one's own impact on others is a fragile privilege"—and indeed, fragility is the right frame. It partly explains the defensiveness of well-intentioned white people, in DiAngelo's (2018) term, white fragility. When one's sense of self is based on one's unconscious superiority over the other, wrapped up in one's sense of oneself as therefore obviously a good person, what is at stake when one's intentions are challenged is one's moral goodness. The benefit, the profit accrued from such a positionality of well-intentioned selfhood, for whom the world's goods and meanings are assumed to rightfully exist, is both material and emotional. Both are difficult to give up.

One result is that structures and systems—the law is one of them—which convey rights on the basis of who can be admitted to the realm of the human (Perry, 2018), continue to mete out standards of inclusion through respectability and recognizability (Butler, 2003). This conflicts with any true accommodation of difference, externally, in terms of social structures, and internally, in terms of psychic relations. Liberalism, despite its stated best intentions to accommodate everyone, encodes normativity. It cannot see equally valuable shared humanity across difference.

A Note on the Idea of the Universally Human

If there is one thing my career as a professor of Shakespeare studies taught me, it was to be wary of claims to universal humanity. Shakespeare's texts continue to be sold as valuable because of their "universal themes." The very specific material history behind the selection of Shakespeare as the embodiment of the best of humanity is necessarily excluded from this messaging. There is concerted colonial education policy, linked to a political agenda of "civilization" and cultural conquest, behind the insistence that England's writer has this kind of moral authority over us all. All good literature, arguably, will make use of universal human themes. But it speaks to structural politics that Chinua Achebe's *Things Fall Apart* is made to be an African author speaking to local conditions, for example, where Shakespeare's work, equally embedded in local events, becomes "universal" (Distiller, 2004; Dollimore & Sinfield, 1985; Hawkes, 1992; Holderness, 1988).

The branding of Shakespeare also has an editorial history which is implicated, as all human systems of meaning-making must be, in cultural politics. Just one example is the ways the same-sex eroticism of the sonnets was rewritten by editors, or explained away, while their vicious misogyny was endorsed (Booth, 2000; Duncan Jones, 1997; Fineman, 1986; Halpern, 2002). There is a vast and fascinating academic literature on all these topics: on the construction of Shakespeare's universality via British class and colonial policies; on the editorial history of the works, which helped to invent the idea of the individual genius author out of local writing practices that were much more collaborative and porous; on editorial interpretations and how they built the content for the idea of the universally human; and about how all this played itself out in education systems across the globe during and after high colonialism (e.g., Bristol, 1990; Cloud, 1991; De Grazia, 1991; Distiller, 2009; Erickson, 1991; Howard & O'Conner, 1987; Joughin, 1997; Loomba, 2002; Marcus, 1996; Taylor, 1989). The political nature of any claim to universality is inescapable to a student of these fields.

And yet the European liberalism that emerged in the Enlightenment believed itself to stand for the best in all of us, with the quiet arrogance of a certain kind of white supremacist Christianity. I have often wondered if it is connected to the Ancient Greeks' arrogance: their designation for their outsiders, "barbarians," meant those who did not have language, and therefore culture, because they did not speak Greek (see Mannarini & Salvatore, 2020 for a discussion of the entanglement of citizenship and otherness). This assumption of one's own centrality seems to have carried over into many other aspects of the West's sense of itself, and been a very valuable tool in justifying the work of colonialism. In the world that colonialism made, a certain use of the language of universal human rights has been deployed by neoliberalism to further entrench global economic systemic inequality (Harvey, 2007).

The idea of some universal humanity that we all share, in other words, has all too often been a tool of power and exploitation. The key question, in the face of the very many differences in cultures that a melting pot theory tends to want to not just wish away, but homogenize into the dominant norm, is: who decides? Whose terms for the apparently universal get to define the idea of the human?

As a result of having been a scholar of English Literature in a postcolony like South Africa, I remain profoundly skeptical of any claims to universality. At the same time, I am arguing for a way to conceptualize something we humans all share, something I am calling complicity. This is my attempt to articulate how, being made in systems of power, as we all are, and having very different and unequal lives as a result, as we do, we nevertheless share a human connectedness. This argument is not the same as a statement of support for a universal humanism.

To be human means to be limited and shaped by the world we have no choice but to enter, the world that makes us. Freud (1973) conceptualized this in terms of the Oedipus complex, where every child must submit to an absolute authority and agree to have his or her (those were his gender options) desire directed by what is socially acceptable. This is another way to theorize the operation of normativity in Western modernity.

After Freud's Oedipus, being a person means having to live with deferred desire. Freud's Oedipus assumes that each subject requires the mother-as-object from which to be forced to separate; the other who can never be had but who is necessary to the self's self-constitution. This is one way to authorize a self/other relation. It depends on treating the (m)other as object (Benjamin, 1988). The child's desire, in this model, is to possess her (Freud understood heterosex to be intrinsically about violent male domination and possession of women, see Distiller, 2011; Freud, 1950; Freud, 1946). But the child's desire is blocked because only the father may have her, in a psychic universalization and justification of what is actually a specific value system: monogamous, heterosexual,

Judeo-Christian marriage. In this system, human relations are linked to ownership of property, of mothers as property, of children as property and as the conduits of property through inheritance.

The ownership of women's bodies and therefore of female sexuality is a lynchpin of this system (Rubin, 1975; Saini, 2017; Schiebinger, 2004). Because the system is a system of domination in and through which a child of the West must find their subjectivity, the child must learn to accept the loss of the mother who belongs to another, who is the father's. This psychic loss is enforced through the threat of violence, according to Freud: the threat of castration. In Freud's world view, the threat of castration is embodied in the female. She is the sign, for the boy, of what can happen if you do not obey. For the girl, her body, which lacks the signifier of personhood, is something she must come to terms with in order to accept her proper place (Distiller, 2011). While this is not an accurate description of what it invariably is or should meant to be human, to come into subjectivity, it is an excellent description of the gendered rules of our culture, of the patriarchal, capitalist, colonizing Western world Freud assumed was the whole world.

Freud (1950) told us it was human nature to dominate. He said children want to possess their mothers, and that it is only by submitting to the father's prior claim that they could learn their appropriate place. He said ownership is a foundational element of subjectivity. He told us not only that hierarchy is natural and inevitable, but also that structural power was appropriately male and heterosexual, and implicitly classed and raced through his deployment, throughout his writing, of the figures of "primitives" and the "lower classes" as developmentally akin to children and women. Here is one of the places we see claims to universal meanings reveal their structural embeddedness. So while one answer to the question of why this culture has tended to make the sense it has of difference is, "human nature," I want to continually challenge the politics of that claim. If there is a meaning to "human nature," it is that we are complicit in each other, in all the struggles and power grabs and attempts to cope in this world we have made for ourselves and for each other.

Freud's binary model of subjectivity, which sees the subject as constituted by its difference from the (m)other, enables a liberal politics. This is a politics which facilitated the ideology of imperialism and the practices of colonialism, which is built on misogyny and sexism, and which continues to facilitate the violence, hypocrisies and smugness of white supremacism. It is born from and perpetuates the logic of capitalism as survival of the fittest.

There are other options. Dean (2001) suggests that, instead of developing a theory of the subject based on the self's relation to its other, which is a theory which relies on the binary structuring of difference (and, I add, therefore domination) as its starting point, we should start with an acknowledgment of the way otherness structures our internal relations. To see the self as emerging from the self/other relation is to see it as dependent on its difference from an/other in order to know (or construct) itself. But if I see my own internal unknowability, signified by the unconscious, as the condition of my selfhood, then I am in the realm of my own otherness. I also cannot claim to ever know myself, and therefore to be unitary, and must give up all certainties based on this illusory knowledge.

This undermines the authority of the liberal individualistic self. It has a fundamentally different logic to the system of othering on which our current world order depends. This dependence is psychological, economic, political and social. If we recognize that we are always other to ourselves, that the "self" on which the self/other formulation depends is in fact inevitably alienated from itself, we approach a different ethics, Dean (2001) suggests. This way of thinking about otherness—as within the self—also exposes the binary as a construct. Dean's ethics of self-otherness entails granting recognition to the other despite not being able to see what is familiar and knowable in him, her or them (see Glaveanu, 2019). A liberal morality, on the other hand, demands intelligibility before it will confer humanity. It is thus a coercive, normative politics which reproduces its own terms even as it thinks it is making space for an other.

Dean's is a Lacanian perspective which describes human subjectivity as always already split from itself as a condition of its being (directed away from its desire as it is by the Law of the Father; think of Freud's Oedipus). Freud, of course, is the one whose theorizing of the unconscious makes Lacan's split subject possible. In Freud's own terms, we are all constituted from a loss we cannot know: the loss, in Freud's terms, of the mother we are never allowed to have because she belongs to the Father. But Freud's terms want to convey security through conveying power. Instead, we could consider the ways we are other to ourselves and see what it takes to tolerate the uncertainty this knowledge brings. It is worth noting that a model of psychology as a science, which tests theories based on measurable outcomes to arrive at objective facts, cannot tolerate this kind of radical uncertainty of meaning.

Making room for what we do not know, for the idea that we might be constituted by things we cannot ever really understand, means we also have to let go of the reflexive defense to find certainty by hardening our identities. The retreat into self-certainty (ego, if you like) always comes, Freud's formulation suggests, at the cost of another's subjectivity. It requires the other as object. (The tragedy of identity politics is that, in making space for the other to take back her personhood, to speak in her own voice and to object to her objectification, it has ended up reproducing the system that it wishes to change. If the position of other becomes a place of certainty, it becomes an identity that requires an oppressor. I say more about this in Chap. 6.)

Glaveanu (2019, p. 454) suggests we start with our own otherness in order to prevent an appropriation of the other in the desire to render her into a "self-like structure":

> Starting from the other means recognizing that we are born into a world of others... and that we, ourselves, are other to them. "Being other" is a primary type of human experience with extremely important developmental consequences, particularly if one resists the temptation to destroy the other... or internalize it.

This is a second way to approach otherness in a nonhierarchical manner. We are not only other to ourselves, as Freud's unconscious could have fully taught him if he had not been making meaning from within a binary structure. We are also always others' others. We are complicit in each other's psychic otherness that helps constitute the self, as well as in the material structures and histories that shape subjectivities, and in the discourses that reflect and reproduce these structures and the subjectivities they need. If there is anything universally human, it is this always socially, historically and culturally shaped fact.

Blatant racism, sexism, homo- or trans-phobia and classism are not pretending to inclusivity. These isms are clear about their use of the others they create to shore up their sense of selves. Liberalism's good intentions, its denial of the ways it uses the current system to reinscribe itself as the central subject, is what makes it such a frustrating ideology for its progressive opponents. In the effects of its intentions, liberalism is also alike to the notion of human being endorsed by psychology (see Sugarman, 2019).

The Liberal Subject of Psychology

Rose (1998) argues that Western societies have been freed from religious and political authority only to be enslaved by a liberal individualism enabled by the psy sciences. He (Rose, 1998) details how the techniques of subjectification enabled by the psy disciplines are central to modern subjectivity. Drawing on Foucault (1991), Rose (1998) insists that the modern liberal democratic state cannot be understood as a political formation outside of the regimes of truth about the human subject as citizen that the psy disciplines were central in helping to create. His explanation underscores Brown's (1995), above:

> The disciplinization of psychology is constitutively bound to a fundamental transformation that has occurred in the rationalities and technologies of political power since the last decades of the nineteenth century, in which the responsibility of rulers has come to be posed in terms of securing the welfare and normality, physical and mental, of citizens, and of shaping and regulating the ways in which they conduct their 'private' existence—as workers, citizens, fathers, mothers—such that they enact their privacy and freedom according to these norms of maximized normality. The field of power that is codified as the state is intelligible only when located in this wider matrix of projects, programs, and strategies for the conduct of conduct, elaborated and enacted by a whole diversity of authorities shaping and contesting the very boundaries of the political. (Rose, 1998, p. 46)

What Rose (1998) adds to Brown's (1995) formulation is the role of the psy disciplines as technologies of liberal subjectification in the service of the democratic state. This is what he means when he says, "A psy ontology has come to inhabit us" (Rose, 1998, p. 190. See also Hook 2007).

Foucault (1977) argued something similar when he suggested the panopticon as a metaphor for how a modern regime of power moved from the external imposition of violence as a form of control on the body of the one who transgressed against the ruler, to an internalized, individualized mode of self-control. Modern individuals are formed by self-policing through discourses of normality and deviance that become about who we are as people, what Foucault (2010, p. 145) calls, "the stifling anguish of responsibility… the seals of conscience." This creates an interiority that is made of the psychologized aspect of "self/realization" (Rose, 1998, p. 190), which in turn brings the imperative to freedom: of choice, of political system, of personhood. We liberal Western subjects internalize the rules for who and how to be, and the process of psychotherapy, while it can help to identify and restructure some of these internalized narratives of selfhood, also participates in reiterating the technologies of self-understanding which reproduce the creation of the free, autonomous subject who consents to her own subjectification (Butler, 1997).

As we saw in Chap. 1, the subject of psychology is, first and foremost, individualistic. As we have seen in this chapter, this individualism cannot be separated out from Western political structures. Rose (1998) details how, with the help of individual and social psychology, individualism becomes a regulatory device in tandem with the development of modern democratic ideals. Democracy entails commitment to notions of "liberty, equality, and legitimate power" (Rose, 1998, p. 118), in other words, which ensure that a citizenry is ruled by people to whom it conceded control of its own free will. The unified self, while it presents itself as obvious and natural, is instead a socially inscribed production, a construction in time and space and power relations, including economic relations (see Papadopoulos, 2008). I have been suggesting it is dependent on a binary relation of being with otherness which is not only a false message about human being, but one that is responsible for perpetuating systemic oppression.

Rose (1998) shows how technologies like the scientific definitions and explorations of attitudes, the poll and public opinion were invented in America and enlisted as scientific endorsements of government. Government, in this formulation, is not in fact freely chosen by the people, but is a mode of control that develops from feudal rulers into modern democracies. Following Foucault, from the eighteenth century control of a population entailed, "not just control of a territory and its subjects, but the calculated administration of the life of the population, of each and of all" (Rose, 1998, p. 119). This requires knowing your subjects, who they are and what they want.

It also, as Rose (1998) goes on to show, enables the development of the realization that, just as attitudes can be polled, so they can be affected and changed by communication techniques and the manipulation of messages. This was one locus of Trump's control: the understanding that twenty-first century democratic America, as the culmination of these related technologies of individualization, public opinion and governmentability through discourses of liberty, freedom and choice, runs on the logic not of "the objective characteristics of the situation, but the subjective relation of the individual to his or her situation" (Rose, 1998, p. 130). It is not the facts or the alternative facts that matter, but how a political leader can leverage people's attitudes to the facts.

Talking about liberalism in this way becomes "a series of reflections on government that stress[…] its limits" (Rose, 1998, p. 69). In order for a liberal government to know how much governing of its free citizens is the right amount of intervention into and structuring of private lives, Rose (1998) says, it needed to know its citizens. The psy disciplines were a way to know people so as to know how to govern them (see Foucault, 1978; Foucault, 2010). And as we have seen, this required individualizing human being.

In contradistinction to the production of the liberal, modern, individual self, who knows itself through its responsibility to govern itself according to rules of putative normality, a theory of the subject as complicit suggests that it is never free to be only itself. Such a model undoes the liberal subject at the heart of Western modernity, the center of an invisibly raced, classed and gendered reality.

These modern inventions also rely on binary thinking. Governmentability relies on the construction of norms. These norms, as we have seen, were produced in tandem with—indeed, helped to produce—the individual liberal subject, free to choose, and apparently therefore self-governing. The requirement for norms against which to measure individual persons required the invention of deviance (Foucault, 1977; Foucault, 1978). The regulatory power of the mythical norm (Lorde, 2007) specifically produces an otherness designed to be exploited. Political, psychic and material gains are all wrapped up in, and reliant on, each other, and in a binary system.

From Liberalism to Neoliberalism

The taken-for-granted notions which underpin the American dream not only help deny the reality of structural oppression that has in fact built this country. They also have helped, in this great American age where everything, including human connection, is for sale, to commodify identity. This will be discussed in more detail in Chap. 5. In part to pave the way for that discussion, I will now turn to the characteristics of the economic, political and psychic order enabled by the world set in place by Enlightenment-formed liberalism: neoliberalism.

Sugarman (2020) points out that the neoliberal turn of the late twentieth century exacerbated the blind spots of liberalism: by emphasizing the fantasy of free choice while removing governmental responsibility for the social and economic structuring of life, neoliberalism puts the individual even more at risk of being responsible for his own failure, with specific consequences for the psychologization of the subject (see also Melluish, 2014).

Neoliberalism intensifies the atomizing individualism of liberalism, and its relationship to commerce as a naturalized aspect of personhood. It elevates further the celebration of and commitment to freedom of choice, as a personal and an economic imperative. Free market economics and the subject free to choose its participation in this market, together with the advances in technology that lead to social media, created a way to brand identity as and for profit, as we will see in Chap. 5.

As a political response and an economic system, neoliberalism began in earnest in the 1980s. Neoliberalism is an economic response to a political understanding of human nature and society. It emerged in reaction to the idea of the social welfare state, and to economic stagnation and political threats to liberalism in the 1970s. It took the terms of liberal individualism—that people should be free to make what choices they want—and applied it to institutional frameworks and the market economy. It sought to remove any constraints that the "embedded liberalism" of the postwar world order built into social, political or economic structures (Harvey, 2007, p. 11; see Chap. 2). It set in place policies intended to deregulate global industry, support a free market economy, encourage competition through privatization, enable flexibility through short-term contracts and worker mobility (and disposability), and discourage the role of government in corporate structures. The market, not the state, should set the terms, neoliberalism says; this will ensure the greatest freedom of choice (Harvey, 2007; Melluish, 2014).

Neoliberalism has been remarkably successful at reshaping social contracts and at reaching into private spheres with the logic of the market. It has reformulated institutions, "divisions of labor, social relations, welfare provisions…, ways of life and thought, reproductive activities, attachments to the land and habits of thought" (Harvey, 2007, p. 3). Along with technological advances, it has intensified, commodified and made ever more literal the use of information about people to help construct subjectivities (see Zuboff, 2019). It has also thus had the consequence of "reformulating personhood, psychological life, moral and ethical responsibility, and what it means to have a selfhood and an identity" (Sugarman, 2020, p. 74). As the state recedes, "Social control is primarily performed through the colonization of previously regarded private areas of individual experience: the body, health, fashion and well-being, sexuality, your living room" (Papadopoulos, 2008, p. 153; see Davies, 2016). When one of the architects of neoliberalism, Margaret Thatcher, declared that society was to be replaced by individual men and women, she said, "Economics are the method… but the object is to change the soul" (qtd. in Harvey, 2007, p. 23).

Zuboff (2019) argues that this is exactly what has happened. Zuboff (2019) says that neoliberalism broke the social contract liberalism made with capitalism. While the postindustrialized Western individual was promised mass-produced access to a goods-based life by what she calls the first modernity, neoliberalism fragmented and atomized connections between people and their institutions, by its hyperindividualizing of commodified desire. The individual of the second modernity is the owner of an iPod, programming their ever-changing unique playlist, rather than the purchaser of a mass-produced CD, released by a music industry that tells us what we like. This second modernity, working together with neoliberalism's dehumanizing "economic violence" (Zuboff, 2019, p. 37), enabled the advent of what she calls surveillance capitalism, where consumer behavior is, first, mined for its commercial value. When the technologies that enable this process are left unchecked, behavior is then manufactured and produced. The industrial revolution that created modern capitalism and its liberal individual entitled to the things capitalism makes has almost cost us our planet, she says. And, she warns, the surveillance capitalism produced by neoliberalism is on the brink of costing us our humanity, as our souls are ever more curated by technology:

> Surveillance capitalism operates through unprecedented asymmetries in knowledge and the power that accrues to knowledge. Surveillance capitalists know everything *about us*, whereas their operations are designed to be unknowable *to us*. They accumulate vast domains of new knowledge *from us*, but not *for us*. They predict our futures for the sake of others' gains, not ours… surveillance capitalism is a rogue force driven by novel economic imperatives that disregard social norms and nullify the elemental rights associated with the individual autonomy that are essential to the very possibility of a democratic society. (Zuboff, 2019, p. 11)

For Zuboff, modernity's necessary creation of liberal individuality, and the democratic state that needs it, is threatened by neoliberalism's enabling of surveillance capitalism. The characteristics of liberalism, especially its moral character, remain for Zuboff the markers of something admirable, necessary and good.

Liberalism created "self-regulating individuals" who, under neoliberalism, have become "networked actors who actively forge the structures necessary" for their atomized modes of regulation (Papadopoulos, 2008,

p. 153). Liberalism taught us to be individuals with rights that were implicitly linked to ownership, to accumulation, and therefore, I am arguing, in contradistinction to Zuboff's characterization of liberalism, to the exploitation of others. While it may think itself noble, liberalism's intentions do not excuse its impacts. It taught us to take responsibility for ourselves in order to forge compliance with a norm that was used to govern us all. Neoliberalism lifted these values out of the remit of the state and gave them to the deregulated market economy. The result, along with a vastly increased wealth gap, was, "The Commodification of Everything" (Harvey, 2007, p. 165).

One consequence has been the experience, at the level of the individual, of the need to be adaptable and superficial (Cushman, 2019). The self is under immense pressure to constantly consider and reinvent itself in order to stay economically and, for certain classes of Western subjects, socially relevant.

At the same time, neoliberalism intensifies liberalism's problems with otherness. Sugarman (2020) argues that neoliberalism as an ideology of freedom and profiteering discourages the ethical recognition of otherness and difference, and as such is a further technology of ever more toxic, ever more intense individuality. The neoliberal subject, then, is no more able to come to terms with complicity. This is despite its location in networks of connection that are ever more global, and ever more globalized, in world where people and places are, in Melluish's (2014) rephrasing of Giddens (1991), intensely connected, and affect each other across large spatial distances. We will return to this in more detail in Chap. 5.

Complicit Intersubjectivity

What does a theory of complicity bring to the historical, economic and ethicopolitical processes that have helped to shape the subject of psychology and that psychology has helped to shape? What does it mean to reject the liberal individual in favor of a complicit subject in the therapeutic encounter? The next three chapters will provide details, by exploring both theoretical and practical implications for thinking in a nonbinary way, along specific axes of difference (race, gender and generation). And psychotherapy already has a modality that seeks to think about the non-binary therapeutic use of difference. Other approaches, which may not use these same terms, nevertheless provide ways of practicing that fit within them, as will be explored in Chap. 6.

Intersubjectivity is a therapeutic approach which understands that binary thinking, based on a way of relating that requires the other to be constituting object for the subject, cannot enable mutual human recognition or connection. Instead, it seeks to name a third, which breaks the binary, and where two subjects can meet as subjects, not pressurizing the other subject into object status. In its classical psychoanalytic definition, it is:

> [A] field theory or systems theory… [that] seeks to comprehend psychological phenomena… as forming at the interface of reciprocally interacting subjectivities… It is not the isolated individual mind,… but the larger system created by the mutual interplay between the subjective worlds of patient and analyst… that constitutes the proper domain of… inquiry. (Atwood & Stolorow, 1993, p. 178)

The suggestion that the analyst is not in objective control of the interaction, is actively participating in what is being made with a client and is fully implicated in all her personhood was unsettling at first to established analytic orthodoxy. There were objections that the approach invited "structureless chaos," "the surrendering of one's personal reality" and "anarchy in the analytic relationship" (Stolorow et al., 1994, pp. 203–208). The challenge to liberal individualism and the illusion of mastery it provides was clearly threatening to the analytical version of the traditional subject of psychology.

The notion of the third undermines the security of the liberal subject, because it requires it to stop using the other's difference to constitute itself. Thinking in terms of the intersubjective third requires a movement into a mutually constituted space where meaning is made in the complex interplay between subjects. This also means by definition that the contexts and systems each subject brings as part of itself must be included as well. If we add a complicit understanding of human being to this approach, we have the potential to meet each other in full recognition of our co-constituting influence on each other, structurally (politically, culturally), and interpsychically. We become ourselves because of each other, and it is only in this space that meaning is made, any meaning, but also including therapeutic meaning.

This is what is at stake when we think complicitously as therapists: We are undoing the notion of the individual human we are trying to help. In the process, we also undo our own scientifically-endorsed authority, because this authority is created by and based on the liberal version of the subject it helps to produce. This version of the psy disciplines (authoritative, objective) is a version of the subject that denies complicity. It wants control, boundedness, for the other to be rendered knowable for the sake of the self. As such, it participates in overpowering discursive and material systems of power and inequality, creating, policing and punishing deviance, constructing diagnoses that it passes off as absolute truth in tandem with medical and pharmaceutical industries who go on to profit, underwriting ideas about norms of race, gender and sexuality that have reinforced intersecting oppressions. This is not to suggest that there is no value in seeking patterns or generalizations for diagnostic purpose, or that medication is a conspiracy. But it is to reject the often absolute and objectifying claims made in the name of diagnosis and pharmaceuticals, and to insist that these apparently objectively scientific tools have cultural histories and political implications (some examples include the development of the paraphilias, see Adriaens & Adriaens & De Block, 2013; or the understanding and treatment of autism, see Silberman, 2015: gender dysphoria will be addressed in Chap. 4). The complicit therapist's job becomes a question of how to hold containing authority in a nonbinary interpersonal mode.

The achievement of an intersubjective space that is complicit is no simple matter. Complicity suggests shared humanity, and shared responsibility. But equality between participants in an intersubjective therapeutic encounter cannot be wished into being. Indeed, if the therapist cannot acknowledge her structural privilege—according to her social markers, if relevant, and according to her role—then she will fail to know her own complicity in the systems in which both she and her client are subjected. This, too, is taken up in Chap. 6. Knowing, itself, is no easy matter, and nor is naming what we might be able to know. Language itself comes burdened with complicity.

In her famous essay of postcolonial theory, "Can the subaltern speak?", Spivak (1988) argued that some of the great poststructuralist theoreticians of the academy (Althusser, Deleuze, Foucault, and Guattari) were guilty of effacing their own social, economic and intellectual power in the process of speaking for and about those who did not have the power to represent themselves, either politically or in the languages of, and cultures formulated by, neocolonial institutions. She said that in the context of concrete power relations, the oppressed (subaltern) subject has no way to speak for herself; the available language cannot be hers. In the context of a binary structure, the subaltern cannot speak in the language given to her by a regulatory system that seeks to both define and control her, as its other.

As I have been suggesting in this chapter, this power dynamic is denied by the very liberalism that constitutes the modern subject, in its inevitably binary formation. And the economic, political, cultural and ideological workings of colonialism are at the start and the center of Western liberal ideals, and underlie the twenty-first century globalized and neoliberal world. While I have also been suggesting that the notion of human being as complicit renders all language problematic if what we want is authentic self-representation (there can be no such thing), Spivak's point reminds us of the necessary both-and of human being in the world today. It is necessary to acknowledge real systems of privilege and inequality that structure people's daily lives as well as their senses of self. And in order to move beyond a social system which uses binary thinking, self/other modes, subject/object power dynamics, enabled by a social symbolic which does the same, we would do well to acknowledge that what makes us all human is our embedded complicity in each other. Postcolonial theory's examinations of cultural hybridities and creolizations help to make this point, that human being is responsive and adaptive and absorptive, even in the face of destructive and oppressive forces (Bhabha, 1994; Distiller, 2005).

Those of us who benefit from privilege, bearing in mind intersectional complexity, are also wounded, if differently, when our constitutive others are hurt so that we may feel whole. For example, there are several consequences for white people of living in an oppressive structure even as we benefit from it. Alexander (2012) and Wise (2012) both show how racist impulses in working-class whites served to break possible class alliances and enable the development of economic and social structures that hurt some whites, too. While she wants to make visible the unearned benefits of being in the center of power, MacIntosh (2008) also wants to make the point that "privilege" as a noun for something that confers assets and power at the expense of others is a misnomer. To have this kind of "privilege" is to be morally and psychologically weakened by the unearned advantages we accrue simply by being born. DiAngelo (2018) addresses this white fragility directly, explaining the ways in which whiteness is invisible to most white people, and the consequences of white people's inability to talk about race and the racism in which we white people are all complicit. Humanity suffers when binary thinking is allowed to define our scope of possibilities, an idea which will be expanded upon in more detail in Chap. 4. Allowing this, that human being connects us all, allows us also to share something, even with those whose subjectivity has been rendered other by the systems we share—including therapy.

Swartz (2013) has written about the intersubjective field between white therapist and clients of color in postapartheid South Africa. She says that in the context of historical and ongoing inequality, where racial difference is painful to acknowledge because of all it means in the dyad, naming becomes a very powerful tool:

> The challenge is to make a co-constructed intersubjective space, an analytic space in which naming is an occasion for curiosity, and where difference in identity is used not as a final recognition, but as a signal to go beyond—towards a shared humanity. Naming will be a shared, not a unilateral, activity. (Swartz, 2013, p. 20)

This reaching toward mutuality through speaking together, specifically in the recognition of unequal power, counteracts Spivak's subaltern's unspeakable position. It is a reaching toward complicity in human being, where our names for each other become conversations, not labels. In the therapeutic encounter, it is the therapist's responsibility to establish the possibility for this space. This is the art of psychotherapy, which cannot be manualized or scientifically measured.

In her case examples, Swartz (2013) spends most time interrogating her own internal fractures and fears as the only way in to engaging with her clients, to take responsibility for the ways in which they could too easily become her constituting other. This work can only occur with the therapist knowing her place in the system, in the encounter, and when privilege has been acknowledged.

Sehrbrock (2020), using intersubjective vocabulary, describes social thirdness, the space made of the collective and the cultural as well as the interpsychic. He describes what happens when what he calls prejudice causes collapse of the social third into the binary: two subjects locked in their own positionality with regard to each other, unable to see the other's point of view. For Sehrbrock, too, in order for the therapist to allow the social third in the intersubjective space, she must be able to tolerate knowledge of her own privilege.

I am aware of how easily this kind of work can recenter whiteness, and other forms of privilege, in the therapeutic encounter. I am also aware of how easily discourses of universal humanity reinscribe the dominant paradigm as the standard for that humanity. However, by locating this work within the intersubjective field, specifically in the analytic third space, Swartz (2013, p. 28) is hoping to use her awareness of her privilege, together with her own intersectionalities, to create a space of true recognition: "Intersubjective theory foregrounds mutual recognition and survival of difference and, paradoxically, in this is contained the possibility of negotiation beyond the dynamic of domination." If we are thinking complicitously, then the survival of difference is more than resisting a dynamic of domination. Difference becomes part of what we share, and the dynamics of domination become a simplified and simplistic reduction of what is possible between us.

Sehrbrock's (2020) examples of working with the social third in therapy are about gender, sexuality, homophobia and misogyny. Swartz's example (Swartz, 2013) is about race. In the next two chapters, I will explore in more detail what a complicit approach—a nonbinary vision, which enables a vision of shared human being—does to race, gender and sexuality as markers of identity, as constructs and as perpetuators of oppression in modern liberal structures which construct and value individualism, commodity value and neoliberal performances of personhood. Chapter 5 picks up this last point and focuses on some of the consequences of a subjectivity reliant on social media for younger clients of Western psychotherapy.

Spivak denotes the ability of those in power to define the social/economic/racialized other as epistemic violence. This is the violence made possible by ways of knowing that construct the meanings they go on to find. When a 17-year-old boy can be murdered for walking down the street with a bag of Skittles because of what he is presumed to mean, and when this presumption is endorsed by the jury that found his killer innocent, the epistemic violence at work in American constructions of race and gender is clear to see. In the next chapter, I take seriously the epistemic violence of raced identities in America, while also exploring what a model of complicity has to offer for a way forward.

Works Cited

Adriaens, P. R., & De Block, A. (2013). Pathologizing sexual deviance: A history. *Journal of Sex Research, 50*(3–4), 276–298.

Alexander, M. (2012). *The new Jim Crow: Mass incarceration in the age of colorblindness* (Rev. ed.). New Press.

Atwood, G. E., & Stolorow, R. D. (1993). *Faces in a cloud: Intersubjectivity in personality theory*. Jason Aronson.

Benjamin, J. (1988). *The bonds of love: Psychoanalysis, feminism and the problem of domination*. Random House.

Bhabha, H. (1994). *The location of culture*. Routledge.

Biko, S. (1978). *I Write What I Like*. Ed. A. Stubbs. Bowerdean.

Booth, S. (Ed.). (2000). *Shakespeare's sonnets*. Yale University Press.

Bristol, M. D. (1990). *Shakespeare's America, America's Shakespeare*. Routledge.

Brown, W. (1995). *States of injury: Power and freedom in late modernity*. Princeton University Press.

Butler, J. (1997). *The psychic life of power: Theories in subjection*. Stanford University Press.

Butler, J. (2003). *Precarious life: The powers of mourning and violence*. Verso.

Cloud, R. (1991). 'The very names of the Persons': Editing and the invention of dramatick character. In D. S. Kastan & P. Stallybrass (Eds.), *Staging the

Renaissance: Reinterpretations of Elizabethan and Jacobean drama (pp. 88–96). Routledge.

Cushman, P. (2019). *Travels with the self: Interpreting psychology as cultural history*. Routledge.

Davies, W. (2016). *The happiness industry: How the government and big business sold us well-being*. Verso.

Davis, W. (2020). The unravelling of America. *Rolling Stone*, August 6. Retrieved September 28, 2020, from https://www.rollingstone.com/politics/political-commentary/covid-19-end-of-american-era-wade-davis-1038206/

De Grazia, M. (1991). *Shakespeare verbatim: The reproduction of authority and the 1790 apparatus*. Clarendon.

Dean, T. (2001). Homosexuality and the problem of otherness. In T. Dean & C. Lane (Eds.), *Homosexuality & psychoanalysis* (pp. 120–146). University of Chicago Press.

DiAngelo, R. (2018). *White fragility: Why it's so hard for white people to talk about racism*. Beacon.

Distiller, N. (2004). "We're Black, stupid": uMabatha and the new South Africa on the world stage. In N. Distiller & M. Steyn (Eds.), *Under Construction: "Race" and identity in South Africa today* (pp. 149–162). Heinemann.

Distiller, N. (2005). *South Africa, Shakespeare, and post-colonial culture*. Edwin Mellen.

Distiller, N. (2009). Begging the questions: Shakespeare in post-apartheid South Africa. *Social Dynamics, 35(1)*, 177–191.

Distiller, N. (2011). *Fixing gender: Lesbian mothers and the Oedipus complex*. Farleigh Dickinson University Press.

Dollimore, J., & Sinfield, A. (Eds.). (1985). *Political Shakespeare: New essays in cultural materialism*. Manchester University Press.

Duncan Jones, K. (Ed.). (1997). *Shakespeare's sonnets*. Thomas Nelson.

Erickson, P. (1991). *Rewriting Shakespeare, rewriting ourselves*. University of California Press.

Fineman, J. (1986). *Shakespeare's perjured eye: The invention of poetic subjectivity in the sonnets*. University of California Press.

Foucault, M. (1977). *Discipline and punish: The birth of the prison*. Trans A. Sheridan. Random House.

Foucault, M. (1978). *A history of sexuality volume 1*. Random House.

Foucault, M. (1991). Governmentality. In G. Burchill, C. Gordon, & P. Miller (Eds.), *The Foucault Effect: Studies in governmental rationality* (pp. 16–49). Harvester Wheatsheaf.

Foucault, M. (2010). The birth of the asylum. In P. Rabinow (Ed.), *The Foucault reader* (pp. 141–167). Vintage.
Freud, S. (1946). *Civilization and its discontents.* Hogarth.
Freud, S. (1950). *Totem and taboo.* Norton.
Freud, S. (1973 [1905]). Three essays on the theory of sexuality. In *The standard edition of the complete psychological works of Sigmund Freud, Vol. 7: A case history of hysteria, three essays on sexuality and other* works, S. Freud, ed. and Trans. J. Strachey (pp. 125–245). Hogarth Press & The Institute of Psycho-Analysis.
Giddens, A. (1991). *The consequences of modernity.* Polity Press.
Glaveanu, V. P. (2019). Being other: Intersubjectivity, allocentrism and the possible. *Journal for the Theory of Social Behaviour, 49*(4), 443–459.
Guyatt, N. (2016). *Bind us apart: How enlightened Americans invented racial segregation.* Basic.
Halpern, R. (2002). *Shakespeare's perfume: Sodomy and sublimity in The Sonnets, Wilde, Freud, and Lacan.* University of Pennsylvania Press.
Harvey, D. (2007). *A brief history of neoliberalism.* Oxford University Press.
Hawkes, T. (1992). *Meaning by Shakespeare.* Routledge.
Holderness, G. (Ed.). (1988). *The Shakespeare myth.* Manchester University Press.
Hook, D. (2007). *Foucault, psychology and the analytics of power.* New York: Palgrave Macmillan.
Howard, J. E., & O'Conner, M. F. (Eds.). (1987). *Shakespeare reproduced: The text in history and ideology.* Methuen.
Husemeyer, L. (Ed.). (1997). *Watchdogs or hypocrites? The amazing debate on South African liberals and liberalism.* Friedrich-Naumann-Stiftung.
Johnson, R. W., & Welsh, D. (Eds.). (1998). *Ironic victory: Liberalism in post-liberation South Africa.* Oxford University Press.
Joughin, J. (Ed.). (1997). *Shakespeare and national culture.* Manchester University Press.
Kendi, I. X. (2016). *Stamped from the beginning: The definitive history of racist ideas in America.* Bold Type Books.
Loomba, A. (2002). *Shakespeare, race, and colonialism.* Oxford University Press.
Lorde, A. (2007). *Sister outsider: Essays and speeches.* Crossing.
MacIntosh, P. (2008). White privilege and male privilege: A personal account of coming to see correspondences through work in Women's Studies. In M. McGoldrick & K. V. Hardy (Eds.), *Re-visioning family therapy: Race, culture, and gender in clinical practice* (pp. 238–249). Guilford.

Mannarini, T., & Salvatore, S. (2020). The politicization of otherness and the privatization of the enemy: Cultural hinderances and assets for active citizenship. *Human Affairs, 30*, 86–95.

Marcus, L. (1996). *Unediting the renaissance: Shakespeare, Marlowe, Milton*. Routledge.

Mehta, U. S. (1999). *Liberalism and empire: A study in nineteenth-century British liberal thought*. University of Chicago Press.

Melluish, S. (2014). Globalization, culture and psychology. *International Review of Psychiatry, 26*(5), 538–543.

Papadopoulos, D. (2008). In the ruins of representation: Identity, individuality, subjectification. *British Journal of Social Psychology, 47*, 139–165.

Perry, I. (2018). *Vexy thing: On gender and liberation*. Duke University Press.

Rich, P. B. (1997). A new South African liberal conscience? *Current Writing, 9*(2), 1–20.

Rose, N. (1998). *Inventing our selves: Psychology, power, and personhood*. Cambridge University Press.

Rubin, G. (1975). The Traffic in Women: Notes on the "Political Economy" of Sex. In R. R. Reiter (Ed.), *Toward an anthropology of women* (pp. 157–210). Monthly Review.

Saini, A. (2017). *Inferior: How science got women wrong – And the new research that's rewriting the story*. Beacon.

Schiebinger, L. (2004). *Nature's body: Gender in the making of modern science*. Rutgers University Press.

Sehrbrock, J. (2020). Social thirdness: Intersubjective conceptions of the experience of gender prejudice. *Psychoanalysis, Self and Context, 15*(3), 289–295.

Silberman, S. (2015). *NeuroTribes: The legacy of autism and the future of neurodiversity*. Penguin.

Spivak, G. (1988). Can the subaltern speak? In C. Nelson & L. Grossberg (Eds.), *Marxism and the interpretation of culture* (pp. 271–313). Macmillan.

Stolorow, R. D., Atwood, G. E., & Brandchaft, B. (Eds.). (1994). *The intersubjective perspective*. Jason Aronson.

Sugarman, J. (2019). An historical turn for theoretical and philosophical psychology. In T. Teo (Ed.), *Re-envisioning theoretical psychology: Diverging ideas and practices* (pp. 25–48). Springer.

Sugarman, J. (2020). Neoliberalism and the ethics of psychology. In D. M. Goodman, E. R. Severson, & H. Macdonald (Eds.), *Race, rage, and resistance: Philosophy, psychology, and the perils of individualism* (pp. 73–89). Routledge.

Swartz, S. (2013). Naming and otherness: South African intersubjective psychoanalytic psychotherapy and the negotiation of racialised histories. In C. Smith, G. Lobban, & M. O'Loughlin (Eds.), *Psychodynamic psychotherapy in South Africa* (pp. 13–10). Wits University Press.

Taylor, G. (1989). *Reinventing Shakespeare: A cultural history from the Restoration to the present.* Oxford University Press.

Williams, P. (1991). *The Alchemy of race and rights.* Harvard University Press.

Wise, T. (2012). *Dear White America: Letter to a new minority.* City Lights.

Zuboff, S. (2019). *The age of surveillance capitalism: The fight for a human future at the new frontier of power.* Profile.

Open Access This chapter is licensed under the terms of the Creative Commons Attribution 4.0 International License (http://creativecommons.org/licenses/by/4.0/), which permits use, sharing, adaptation, distribution and reproduction in any medium or format, as long as you give appropriate credit to the original author(s) and the source, provide a link to the Creative Commons licence and indicate if changes were made.

The images or other third party material in this chapter are included in the chapter's Creative Commons licence, unless indicated otherwise in a credit line to the material. If material is not included in the chapter's Creative Commons licence and your intended use is not permitted by statutory regulation or exceeds the permitted use, you will need to obtain permission directly from the copyright holder.

3

Wakanda Forever

Racism is a system whose function is to confer privilege. That privilege has two main components, economic and psychic. Racism as a system is fundamentally reliant on binary thinking in order to build the symbolic meanings on which its material practices are erected. Historically and philosophically, racism is an implicit part of the well-intentioned liberalism which has crafted the individualized subject of Western psychology. As Perry (2018) has shown, the processes of the Enlightenment, together with the genocide and slavery that accompanied the colonialism which made modernity, needed a category of nonpersons in order to authorize and enrich the gendered and classed person who was a product of these historical forces. These processes of person production were as much economic and legal as they were psychological, showing once more the imbrication of all these forces.

Racism, of course, makes use of the construct of race to authorize itself. There is no scientific validity to the construct of race. There is only one, human race, although there are geographically regional genetic variants of humans. All the scientific and psychological work on race and putative racial differences in the nineteenth and twentieth centuries was research done on "something which *was not there*" (Richards, 2012, p. 19;

see Posel, 2001; Richeson & Sommers, 2016). Or, as Oluo (2019, pp. 11–12) puts it, race is "a lie told to justify a crime" (see also Kendi, 2016). The historical shaping of the idea of race helps to reveal it as a human political event, shaped by economic relations of power, colonial dynamics, law and citizenship rights, and so on. This will be explored in more detail below. The biological underpinnings of race thinking has shifted in the later twentieth and the twenty-first centuries to become more complexly cultural (Fernando, 2017), but the attachment to the idea of fundamental, defining differences, always constructed by hierarchical assumptions, remains in place and remains available to perpetuate oppressions.

Like gender difference, racial difference is embedded in and produced by human culture. Race and gender cannot really be understood in isolation from each other, as their meanings inform and rely on each other. Nor can class, location, ethnicity, ablebodiedness or religion be taken out of the meanings made of bodies that are raced and gendered in systems of modernity. Each identity category co-creates the others. Each has an interrelated material history that tends to pass itself off as natural and inevitable. And racial difference has been a specific focus of psychology, most problematically in its early contributions to scientific racism and eugenicist practices. In the late twentieth and in the twenty-first centuries, other psychologies have evolved with commitments to social justice and decolonial practices, which seek to counter the ways notions of racial difference have informed the work of early mainstream psychology, including in its early social and cultural variations. This later work is made possible because of the contributions of people other to psychology's developmentally white, Western, male and middle-class beginnings.

In this chapter, I offer a framework for understanding race and racism in the America I found when I arrived here as an immigrant a decade ago. Because I am a white South African who grew up under apartheid, the relations of racism between whites and Black people of African descent were most in focus for me. I have come to learn of the other flavors of racist oppression in which America specializes, against Latinx people, against indigenous Americans and against Asian Americans. The intersection of my theory of complicity and the complexities of racialized experiences is illustrated in this chapter via my engagement, as a white South

African immigrant to America, with the film *Black Panther*. For this reason, this chapter will focus on the racism built by and from American slavery. I acknowledge that racisms extend and multiply, and have different historical trajectories and investments (Richards, 2012). My argument here, about how racial difference functions, can be applied to all symbolic uses of binary thinking imposed on human bodies.

Below, I offer more detail for a structural definition of racism, in order to continue to illustrate the connections between modernity, binary thinking and systems of oppression. I hope to show we can acknowledge the historical and ongoing operations of oppression, which work through creating binary differences, *and* nuance the ongoing subject positions such oppression produces. By now, in a world made impossibly complicated by the hybridizing, fracturing and commodifying realities produced by neocolonialism and neoliberalism, we need to recognize the extreme systemic inequalities within which the postmodern world resides, and also acknowledge that human being is not binary. We need to be able to think complicitously.

Race

The invention of modern notions of race and the racial difference it produces is rooted in historical practices of modernization, emerging capitalism and liberal individuality. It begins with slavery and proceeds through colonialism (Fernando, 2017; Kendi, 2016; Perry, 2018; Richards, 2012). Colonialism was not just a military enterprise. It was cultural and psychological too (Fanon, 2005; Wa Thiong'o, 1986; Wa Thiong'o, 1993), which postcolonial, liberation and decolonial psychologies continue to address (Adams et al., 2017; Fernández & Gutierrez, 2020; Hook, 2012; Maldonado-Torres, 2017; Mignolo, 2011; Miller & Miller, 2020).

As we saw in the last chapter, Perry (2018) shows how enslaved and colonized people were made to be the constituting others for emerging liberal capitalist modernity. Indigenous and enslaved people were legally and culturally conferred with nonpersonhood in order to help define the modern liberal subject. She also argues that public violence was enacted on the body of the racialized other long after Foucault (1977) denoted the end of public violence as a means of sovereign social control for white citizens. These very specifically racialized "mechanisms of domination" (Perry, 2018, p. 35) are part of what we are seeing in the ongoing violence publicly enacted by the state against Black and brown bodies on the streets of America today. This suggests the structural need modern American democracy has for the dehumanization of its constitutive others, and helps explain the apparent intractability of race as a necessary construct within a system built on the binary of self and other.

Teo (2005) adds to this historical picture the role of science as a system of classification, also developed through the Enlightenment and nineteenth century colonialism. The emerging discipline's obsession with grouping and measuring,

> [W]as consequently applied to human populations… From a sociohistorical standpoint, the concept of "race" allowed for the justification of colonialism, domination, and slavery, because non-European groups (and certain European populations) were not just constructed as different, but also as inferior. (Teo 2005, pp. 155–6)

Here again are the invested hierarchical aspects that binary thinking brings to human differences, many of which are written on the body, for the purposes of psychic and economic gain.

Thus, as Perry (2018, p. 21) also shows, there have always been connections between abjected racialized bodies and bodies gendered female (see also Haraway, 1989; Richards, 2012):

> The position of the nonperson is a fundamental supplementation of the idea of gender as produced by disciplinary power (essentialized concepts and rules for men and women) and the naturalization of binary gender categories that were, and continue to be, applied to citizenries.

The idea of racial difference requires binary gender difference as a conceptual underpinning. It is built on it and cannot be understood separate from it. Both make use of the body, and of regimes of inclusion and exclusion, normality and deviance, acceptability, policing and power (see Hook, 2012). By the same logic, sexuality and definitions of ablebodiedness are equally relevant to the construction of race (Cruz, 2016; McRuer, 2006; Stephens & Boonzaier, 2020).

Since all of these identities are cultural constructs made from embodied differences, Rose (1998, p. 184) argues that the body is in fact "a body-regime" constructed by the linkages of "surfaces, forces, and energies." The body is not an absolute truth underlying experience, but a contingent effect of the experience we are allowed to have. The body is a "relationship." This is another view of human being as complicit: Our very bodies are formed in relation to each other and to the systems that make us as individuals and groups, and which we, in turn, continue to make, albeit differentially (this argument implicitly draws on Butler, 1999 too, and is applied to therapeutic modalities in Chap. 6).

Our raced bodies exist in relation to each other in an additional and very specific way. The centuries of horror inflicted on bodies and subjectivities raced not-white by Western culture have enabled the whiteness assembled on the bodies and in the behaviors of people invisibly raced white. The raced self/other relation on which the dominant modern mode of human subjectivity depends may be a construct, but it is a construct with devastating embodied force (see Hook, 2012; Salter & Haugen, 2017).

To view a complicit way forward is to challenge the thinking on which white supremacy depends. And by white supremacy, I mean to invoke not only blatant white violence against racialized others, but the well-intentioned liberalism charted in the previous chapter, which enacts its own pernicious forms of epistemic and material violences on raced bodies. To continue to advocate for a complicit model for human being is not to attempt to deny the damage racism has done and continues to do, on subjectivities and bodies that may be co-constructed, but whose oppression and suffering are no less real for all that. Because of the ongoing effects of modern racism, it is sometimes necessary to talk of race as though it were real, in order to reach a point of being able to insist that it is not, while holding on to subjects and bodies formed by racial difference and respecting their experiences as such.

I acknowledge what race has been and continues to be in this country: one of the largest, most important, most profitable building blocks of America. After the initial colonization and the genocide of Native

Americans it perpetrated, this country was built through slavery. This historical fact continues to affect everyone, and in specific ways, indigenous peoples and Black Americans. Jung (2015) understands racism as operating on a civic level, to define who may be part of the nation and its resources, and who should be excluded and exploited for the furtherance of those resources and those who benefit from them. This argument correlates with Perry's (2018) explication of the development of the American subject via colonialism and slavery. And George (2020) says that since America's very sense of its civilization is grounded in slavery, instead of civilization functioning to restrict instinctual aggression, as Freud suggested, in America's case, it facilitated it. The impulses that drove slavery are not past, "but a savagery essential to the modern" (George, 2020, p. 110).

The slave is used by the master, George (2020) shows, to make up for the master's subjective Lacanian lack. The slave is the jouissance of a modernity founded on racism and capitalism, and their unholy union. "Being was actively siphoned from the person of the slave in order to… grant the master access to whiteness as a master signifier of being" (George, 2020, p. 115). Being, here, indicates Lacan's formulation for the place of the subject (George, 2020, p. 111). George (2020) shows how the white American subject's sense of self was built on, at the expense of, the slave, providing a psychological correlative to Perry's (2018) legal and cultural history. This Lacanian symbolic structuring underpins American society, "founded… upon a brutal expression of base instincts that then root white identity in its signal notions of freedom and independence" (George, 2020, p. 117). One consequence is the importance of racial identity for African Americans, George (2020) says, which came to function as a place in which Black people could find their denied selves, in part through community. A result has been the development of a strategy "to fight racism with race" (ibid, p. 124).

To talk about this is to engage another complexity of the topic. We need to insist on the material and psychic consequences of this very specific history while remaining cognizant of one of its tropes, the "damaged negro" stereotype (for more on the history of this stereotype, see Richards, 2012, p. 172; Fernando, 2017, pp. 65–69; Griffith, 1977). Often well-intentioned white psychologists and sociologists, offering liberal accounts of the effects of oppression, created a version of Black family values and concomitant inner Black life and personality that offered new ways to reduce and stereotype Black people. Instead of nineteenth century biology-based arguments, the mid-twentieth century offered "cultural" reasons for Black inferiority (e.g., see the discussions about *The Mark of Oppression* by Kardiner and Ovesey [1951], or Moynihan's [1965] *The Negro Family: The case for national action* in Fernando, 2017 and Richards, 2012).

Psychology's twentieth century concern with the effects of racism tended to reinscribe the notion of the damaged oppressed Black person bearing the pathologizing "mark of oppression": culturally deprived, with low self-esteem, a destroyed and/or debased family structure, and no internal psychic resources to help himself, albeit through no fault of his own. Well-intentioned white psychologists helped underwrite this stereotype: "With friends like this …" (Richards, 2012, p. 281). In America, Black psychologists have refuted this stereotype for as long as they have existed, since the 1930s (Guthrie 2004; Richards, 2012, chapter 11).

This is a complicated topic for a well-intentioned white woman to broach, as illustrated by Oluo's (2019, chapter 3) painfully funny account of her discussion about race with her white mother. I wish to properly acknowledge the complex process of surviving and speaking back to dehumanizing violence that is both actual and symbolic, without presenting victimhood as a constituting element of Black subjectivity under white supremacy, or reductively stereotyping Black people because we have a racist history of stereotyping Black people.

Binkley (2020) helps to theorize this problem by suggesting the raced subject is read through the double vision of generalized abnormalities assigned to a racialized type. Even with the mid-twentieth century shift of focus in psychology away from racial inferiority and toward racial oppression as a shaping factor on raced subjectivities, "the same assumptions concerning the radical alterity of the emotional and psychological lives of racial minorities remained intact," but this time cast as a cultural problem, not a biological truth (Binkley, 2020, p. 98). Racial categories are reorganized, but not fundamentally changed or addressed. Binkley (2020, p. 99) addresses the stereotype of Black emotionality, and especially Black rage, through this lens, which encompasses the racist idea of the "damaged negro." In current liberal psychologized contexts, Binkley

(2020) says, the frightening specter of this angry, "damaged negro" is contained through white listening, a process whereby "the normal had to co-emotionalize with and listen to the abnormal... [which] served the ends of both criminalization and critique" (Binkley, 2020, pg. 100).

Binkley (2020) suggests also that, via the imperatives of neoliberalism, listening for the purposes of containment has become a corporate strategy for managing race. Binkley (2020) discusses the limits this model places on white empathy: whites must listen, but can never truly know the Black rage they must witness, and if they claim they can, they are revealing their failure of understanding, their as-yet-unredeemed racism. Hidden Black rage,

> [B]ecomes precisely the second body it seeks to dispel... This is a second body whose eruptions bring powers of illumination that disrupt but also silently restore that other second body that is necessary for the racial contract to remain in place: the second body that constitutes whiteness itself. (Binkley, 2020, p. 104)

This is why, he says, institutionalized discussions about race largely fail to disrupt the status quo. He suggests that engaging with race through the emotions race gives us, each in our raced position, reinscribes race. Binary logic at work.

Binkley's (2020) attempts to account for the ongoing intractability of racist othering in well-intentioned spaces speak to the mess we are in. Many writers (e.g., Oluo, 2019) address how hard it is to talk about race in America today. DiAngelo (2018) engages in detail with the aspects of whiteness that defend against real conversations about the centrality of white privilege to structural racism, and the psychological fragility that is the consequence of inheriting a self made out of unearned privilege (see MacIntosh, 2008).

DiAngelo's book received national attention after the racial justice protests of 2020, following the police murder of George Floyd. A consequence has been a backlash against her attempts to hold white people accountable for the workings of white supremacy. One pertinent objection is similar to the problem we have tracked above, that her focus on the power of whiteness to perpetuate structural oppression demeans and disempowers Black people (McWhorter, 2020). Another is that she generalizes about white people (The Conversation, 2020). Trying to advocate for current accountability from white people (all white people, because the political, economic, educational, legal, psychological and cultural systems that have been built do create a starting point where personhood is assumed to be linked to whiteness, among other markers of human being), and acknowledge that oppression shapes lives, while also arguing that to be human is to be more than all these things, is a difficult business. Perhaps more than any other current issue, race makes clear the complicated inheritances of binary thinking woven into material practices.

In addition to the work of enslaved people themselves and those that came after, like W.E. du Bois, James Baldwin, Maya Angelou or Audre Lorde, there is a highly contemporary American literature that celebrates survival and documents the ongoing consequences of systemic racism for Black people, and for the society that continues to marginalize them. Here are a few examples: DeGruy (2005) offers an account of the effects of slavery on African American identities, providing psychological explanations for cultural adaptions. She offers the concept of Post-Traumatic Slave Syndrome to destigmatize survival responses to being Black in America. Boyd-Franklin (2006) writes about the psychology of Black families with a sensitive and nonhomogenizing lens. Brewster and Stephenson (2013) write about families, the education system and selfhood. Williams (2001) and Alexander (2011) penned stunning indictments on the legal system. Hardy (2006, 2008) has written and talked about racism in family therapy and as a developmental trauma. Tatum's (1997) *"Why Are All the Black Kids Sitting Together in the Cafeteria?" and Other Conversations About Race* remains a beautifully written and compelling account of the mechanisms and costs of racism. Adichie (2013) dealt with it through fiction. In the last few years, Coates (2015), Kendi (2016), Morris (2016), Dyson (2017), Menakem (2017), Cooper (2018) and Bryant (2020) have all spoken urgently about the ongoing experiences of black Americans, counting the ongoing costs of racism, emphasizing strength and resilience, and insisting on the structural elements of racism in America.

Racism

Racism is not best defined as a psychological quality held by individuals. Psychological explanations miss the larger point of how and why racism operates. Racist structures do not only enable individuals to believe hateful things or behave hatefully. They also allow certain groups to act on this hatred, in ways that substantially and structurally affect others. Racist structures allow some to accrue privileges of all sorts, psychological and material, over others, by taking things away, psychological and material, from those others. Racist structures then justify and perpetuate that system of privilege. So while it may also be a personal attitude, racism operates and perpetuates structurally. As beneficiaries of the system, white people are implicated in racist oppression, whether we like it or not, and whether we think we mean it or not.

It is often said that the human brain cannot help but rely on group differences to make snap judgments (Hewstone et al., 2002; Richeson & Sommers, 2016; Rippon, 2019). The arguments are not only neurobiological. A recent psychoanalytic article on otherness, for example, begins with the assertion, "There is an emotional/cultural need to define oneself in relation to otherness, manifesting clearly in racial, ethnic, national, religious, sexual, and gender identities" (Molofsky, 2019, p. 49. See also McWilliams 2020). And a recent social psychology-informed article, which explores the role of otherness to the idea of the citizen, suggests that human beings have always needed enemies in order to be able to define their friends (Mannarini & Salvatore, 2020). The authors also make the point that neoliberal fragmentation has resulted in more intense cleaving to local and national identities that are therefore more reactive and more insular.

Current conditions may well have exacerbated binary thinking. But if it is inevitable that human beings will use groupthink to develop identities in a way that makes binary othering necessary, then we are very close to legitimizing racism. It is more historically and psychologically accurate to trace the ways that racial difference has been constructed and imposed on bodies, and to name the purpose of these activities: profit. Cushman (2019, pp. 41–43) also makes the point, following W.E.B. Dubois, that if we legitimize racism with a psychologized endorsement that humans neurobiologically cannot help but use binary thinking, then we miss the material, economic benefits to institutionalized oppression. Racism, a system which privileges some at the expense of others, is not an inevitable part of human nature. It is highly specific, invested, historical event. Binary thinking obscures this fact. It also, not coincidentally, thereby naturalizes the systems of thought that underpin colonially formed, capitalist-saturated modernity, with all its rules about who deserves to be on top and why: Darwinism, patriarchy, Freud's idea that it is human nature to dominate, and that domination is properly male and so on. Thinking of humans as complicit in the systems that structure us and which we, in turn, participate in and may sometimes alter accordingly, allows us a much more realistic and complex entry into how and why we oppress each other, how systems convince people to participate and collaborate, sometimes even in the process of resisting, and what the consequences are for human being in these systems, albeit with different people paying different prices.

Hook (2012, p. 4) offers the notion of the "psychopolitical" to fully account for the interactions of psychology and the complex interacting contextual forces which help to shape the psyche, and which are in turn shaped by psychological needs and pressures. In other words, to talk about racism we need more than a psychological vocabulary. We need to be able to combine insights about psyches with knowledge about systems of power, about historical forces and the events they shape, with understandings that are material as well as existential. We need, in other words, a psychology informed by knowledge from the humanities as well as the social sciences, because we need to be able to see how discourses shape what is humanly possible. Only then can we properly account for the historically specific, psychically invested, inscriptions of raced differences (and the gendered, classed, abled or disabled, sexually normal or perverse meanings they accompany) on human bodies and being.

Making sense of difference is a part of human being. But Western modernity's specific tactics are embedded in relations of power: economic, legal, nationalist, embodied, gendered and raced. They also make use of a morality of the good and the normal (which are sexually inflected); this is part of liberalism's inheritance. Binkley (2020, p. 96) suggests, via

Foucault's ideas of normalization and the medicalization of the abnormal, that racism involves "a reading through" of the subjectivity of the raced other, to find the abnormality of the raced subject. He points out how scientific racism, which helped invent modern racial difference, used the idea of deviation from the implicitly white, European norm to classify racial others as inferior (see Teo 2005). Thus, again, racial difference has played a central role in the construction of modern relations of power, and racism is a product of the evolution of Western norms of personhood.

Hook (2007) explores how the processes of modern subjectification both and he and Rose (1998) detail can help us think about racism and racialized subjectivity. He (Hook 2007, p. 217) suggests we need to acknowledge that the processes of racialization which produce race and endorse racism demonstrate "affected subjectivity," that is, "a level of penetration and consolidation within subjects that is reducible neither to the terms of psychological explanation, nor to sociological critiques of determining social structures." Racism and the processes of racing it relies upon cannot be reduced to politics or economics or psychological gain. It saturates the structures into which we are born and which therefore shape us. It affects subjects on all complicit levels, interpersonally and intrapersonally. And it also requires access to the self/other binary in order to make its own hateful sense of things. If we are to dismantle racism and the structures that enable it, we have to be able to both acknowledge the profoundly personal implications of raced identity and ask for a new model which would undo the binary structure on which raced identity depends. Race structures this world, and is therefore central to human subjectivity and experience. It is also an artificial construct. In a real sense, it does not exist. As we have seen, it was brought into apparent being by systems of modernity, of which the psy disciplines are part.

Race and Racism in and Through Psychology

If the psy disciplines have been central to the emergence of modern, liberal democratic, states and subjects (and states of subjectivity), then they have also been central to the emergence of modern race and racism. Ideas about what constituted scientific method and proof, and the questions asked about human being via these formats, linked the emerging psy disciplines to emerging processes of racialization. Historically specific Western notions of scientific truth, liberal individuality, democratic governance and racial (and gender and sexual) difference are complicit in each other.

Evolutionary theory, which was a foundational colonial ideology, helped shaped the way psychology was used as it emerged as a discipline in the late nineteenth century. This impacted how apparent biological differences were used to construct differences in human being in order to create cultural, intellectual, moral and spiritual hierarchies. "The 'biologisation' of human diversity was thus consolidated; not only physical appearance but also temperament and culture reflected a people's innate evolutionary status" (Richards, 2012, p. 15). We have already explored the role of psychology in developing methods for producing individuality and the means for assessing these; Richards (2012, p. 22) makes the point that since psychometrics were developed in the service of eugenics, as a way to measure differences that were sought in order to be hierarchically ranked, "[s]tudying race differences is thus but an extension of the study of individual differences."

It is thus no surprise that psychology played a central role in the development of modern scientific racism. As is well-documented, psychology was enthusiastically involved in the development of theories of eugenics and of IQ testing which "proved" racial differences and white, European racial superiority (Fernando, 2017; Guthrie, 2004; Richards, 2012; Teo, 2005). And psychology's initial framing of empirical differences as biological set up the long-standing and extremely damaging "problematization" of Black people, in Teo's (2005, p. 173) term, in ways specific to how Blackness was raced (see Kendi, 2016; similar processes happened with other racialized groups). The effects on the practice of the psy disciplines have been recently charted in a series of essays published in response to the American cultural moment of 2019. This work explores the problems of well-intentioned whiteness, of structural racism and of the history of psychology in helping to shape these forces (Williams et al., 2019).

Richards (2012) says that psychology, as a discipline that emerged from America and Europe, could not *not* be racist and Western-centric (see also Fernando, 2017). He also suggests that there exists alongside the racism in psychology a "constant cycle" (Richards, 2012, p. 348) of antiracist intention that often fell short, being of its time and of its discipline. He asks that psychology's self-reflexive engagements with its constituting racist energies be acknowledged, along with the tools the discipline has developed to combat racism. For example, he argues that the process of engaging with the racism of the Race Psychology of the early twentieth century (see Fernando, 2017) helped make white psychologists aware of racism, and helped make racism a topic outside of psychology. To this we must insist that while we might be able to trace in psychology an academic trajectory from finding and ranking racial differences, to a concern with why people are racist and the effects of racism on people of color, the shortfalls cannot be overlooked in the name of good intentions. As a discourse born of white, European, male power and initially very committed to finding the scientific evidence for the rightness of that power, traditional psychology struggled, and arguably still struggles, to exceed its constitutive underpinnings. It has often ended up in the camp of well-intentioned whiteness that cannot see its own privilege and therefore perpetuates the structures of oppression it simultaneously disavows (Dovodio & Casados, 2019; Richards, 2012; Salter & Haugen, 2017).

Since the 1960s, psychology's constitutive others (Black people and people of color, the colonized, women, the neurodiverse, sex and gender perverts) have begun to speak back en mass, and from within. There are those newer psychological fields concerned with social, geographical, racial, economic and gender justice and their intersections, as more psychologists and psychologies from other places and othered identities have begun to establish voices in the field (e.g., Boonzaier & van Niekerk, 2019; Collins et al., 2019; Ebersohn, 2019; Montero, 2017; Salter & Haugen, 2017; Smith et al., 2013; Williams et al., 2019). More complex and important questions have become possible. Still in 2020, Bhatia (p. 263) was asserting that while we may acknowledge that, "Whiteness and white identity have played a dominant role in producing normative psychological knowledge in the U.S," the psy disciplines still do not acknowledge "the explicit ways in whiteness as privilege, power, norm, and an oppressive force acts as a dominant cultural norm and shapes the identities of both white people and non-white migrants [the focus of her article]."

In part because of the ongoing unacknowledged operations of structural racism, "Unfortunately mainstream psychiatry and psychology have so far failed on the whole to fully take on board the insights offered by the progressive thinking that flooded the British and American scene at the end of the twentieth century" (Fernando, 2017, p. 85). Fernando (2017) details the regressive shift back toward racism in West in the twenty-first century. He attributes this to an inattention to structural matters in the previous century, as well as to racism's ability to shapeshift. He also specifically traces the rise of Islamophobia as a new incarnation of racism in America and Britain. He concludes that the psy disciplines may be too implicated in racist thinking and racist structures to be able to offer anti-racist solutions in their current forms. And from a decolonial point of view, Miller and Miller (2020, p. 382) argue that psychology cannot be decolonized within the structures that exist, because the psy disciplines, colonialism, modernity, the state and individualism are all constitutive elements of the modern subject: "decolonization will take the end of the world, and… decolonization is the end of the world as we *know* it" because, "The very way in which we go about 'knowing' itself is entangled in colonial/modern ways of thinking that cannot but reproduce the violences at the core of their construction."

From this perspective, psychology's subaltern, by definition, still cannot speak. We need to approach the issue rather from a complicitous perspective than a binary one. Psychology, like English literature, can and has been changed in the hands of those whose enforced otherness helped to make both disciplines what they are. But a binary model, which locks in place oppressors and oppressed, cannot deliver any of us out of the self/other mode of being and knowing. This is another way the humanities, through postcolonial and cultural studies, can offer productive frames to psychological theories. But it does require relinquishing an exclusive commitment to scientific method, which cannot accommodate the philosophical complexity or the conceptual fluidity of complicity. We cannot operationalize or statistically demonstrate the complexities of mimicry and hybridity, the inevitably complicit agency of talking back in what started out as the master's language, of knowing and acting on what cannot be seen by systems of power. Nevertheless, all these ways of human being exist.

I learned from studying postcolonial and neocolonial uses of and responses to Shakespeare, as an icon of universal humanity and cultural genius, that oppressed groups metabolize epistemic abuses and, even as they are changed by them, change them in turn. Oppressive forces destroy, but oppressed people also reclaim them, make them exceed their original intentions (Distiller, 2012a). People find all kinds of ways to fight back, ways that are also always complicit, as in the Hollywoodization and commodification of "Africa" in *Black Panther* that is also an act of highly overdue recognition and valuation by the systems that make us all.

Complicities: *Black Panther*

People of color continue to suffer from systemic oppression, and African Americans carry specific historical burdens in America today regardless of class affiliation. Black Americans cannot be sure of being safe as they walk down the street, or listen to music as they fill their cars with gas, or pray in their churches, or speak on their cellphones in their families' yards, or sleep in their own beds in their own apartments, free from a race-based denial of their very right to exist in their own country. Their citizenship rights are not assured in a place whose definition of human being began in racialized binary thinking. Perry (2018) has pointed out how the legal definition of Western personhood developed out of the deployment of the category of nonperson assigned to the slave, and Alexander (2011) has detailed the legacies of this system for Black and brown people in America today (see Williams, 1991). As I have been arguing, the implications run deep: into Western modes of individuality, linked to state and institutional belonging and the legal systems that allow or disable these; into capitalist imperatives to value and devaluation, of owning and ownership that confer human being and withhold human being; and in the complex constitutive connections between and among these systems. This legacy for Americans of African descent is what the 2018 Marvel superhero film *Black Panther* is speaking back to.

For those who have had no contact with popular culture in the last three years, here is a very brief summary of some key plot points: T'Challa (Chadwick Boseman) is the prince of the fictional African nation

Wakanda, which has kept itself and its technological sophistication hidden from the world, pretending to be the expected African "third world country." T'Challa becomes the king and superhero Black Panther when his father, T'Chaka (John Kani), the king and the previous Black Panther, is killed. His antagonist in the film is an American special ops soldier nicknamed Killmonger (Michael B. Jordan), who is also his cousin, abandoned in Oakland as a child by T'Chaka. With the exception of a white CIA officer (Martin Freeman) who helps them, the other main characters are all powerful Black women, among them Shuri (Letitia Wright), T'Challa's genius sister, and Nakia (Lupita Nyong'o), his activist lover, who is a Wakandan spy in the outside world. In some really critical ways, *Black Panther* is a representational revolution, centering Black people as actors, characters, producers and makers of mainstream media. It depicts an Africanness that is deliberately created in opposition to the debased or demeaned version of neocolonial Africa which passes for Western knowledge of the continent, its people and its diaspora.

In 2014, Gay complained about the reductive and stereotyped depictions of Black experience in American movies. She asked for a cinema that went beyond the struggle narrative, that stopped fetishizing the broken Black body and reiterating Black victimhood as the only kind of subjectivity available to Black people in mainstream culture. With *Black Panther*, released four years later, I wager she got her wish. Directed by Ryan Coogler, released by Disney in February 2018, the movie was a revelation to the box office: a movie by and about Black people that made a whole lot of money. According to the Brookings Institute, *Black Panther* made $427 million, placing it second only to *The Avengers* in terms of profits, and second only to *Star Wars: The Force Awakens* for opening profits (Sims, 2018; Sow & Sy, 2018).

This was more than a commercial moment though, it was a moment of empowerment and visibility for Black people wherever Hollywood movies are sold:

> The importance of seeing black people for the first time depicted in a major movie as kings, queens, inventors, and diplomats, rather than slaves, thugs, dealers and thieves, has given the movie a real-world political engagement not seen in other superhero films. The journalist Shaun King even went as

far as to argue that it is a cultural phenomenon equal in importance to Dr. King's "I Have a Dream" speech and Rosa Parks refusing to give up her bus seat. (Faramelli, 2019, n.p.; see Faithful, 2018)

Offering a regal Black superhero to the world, *Black Panther* did something important for American culture and the subjects who inhabit it (González-Velázquez et al., 2020). As part of its centering of Black people, the film was as bold as it could be in addressing race and racism, given its conditions of production. It offered mainstream audiences a serious, unapologetic engagement with Black rage and Black power. It is remarkable that this conversation was even allowed to happen in a Disney blockbuster.

The film's exploration of possible responses to Western epistemologies of race and the centuries of colonialism thereby enabled focuses on Black experience and references African philosophies. Its central commitment is to exploring the politics of racial liberation (Newkirk, 2018; Orr, 2018). Faramelli (2019) sees *Black Panther* as resolving the dialectic it presents between different kinds of revolutionary theory, isolationism ("black sovereignty," represented by T'Challa) versus a radical engaged "black solidarity" (represented by Killmonger). It offers, he says, the option of a Sojan Thirdspace via the character of Nakia, not coincidentally a woman in a patriarchal culture (Wakanda is an absolute monarchy, with patriarchal lineage).

The Thirdspace is a hybrid space of dialogue and negotiation, not unlike the intersubjective third. For Faramelli (2019), this results in the film's embrace of a responsible, international form of Pan-Africanism, a rejection of Wakanda's traditional exceptionalism and an equal rejection of the cultural nationalism enabled by an essentializing, and therefore Manichean, negritude which "only reinforces the hegemony of colonial power." This last is evidenced in Killmonger's desire to create and rule a new world empire, won and held through military might.

Instead, T'Challa uses Wakanda's resources to begin a process of global outreach, starting in Oakland—implicitly a location which invokes the racialized struggles of African Americans, the birthplace of the real-life Black Panthers and the site of Killmonger's childhood trauma and radicalization. For Faramelli (2019), *Black Panther* rejects a business-as-usual liberalism for a new kind of radical engagement, led by Black women, as T'Challa decrees that Shuri and Nakia will run the Wakandan International Outreach Center. He concludes, "This Thirdspace position has the potential to create new spaces and transform the Oakland housing project where T'Chaka kills Killmonger's father into a space of liberation."

Not everyone loved, or agreed on, the film's message. Its heteronormativity has been critiqued (Meyer, 2020), as has its centering of African American needs to the exclusion of transnational and Islamic Africans (Alaoui & Abdi, 2020). It has been faulted for its reiteration of African royalty as the model for African subjectivity, an objection made against other African American engagements with the continent (Rickford, 2020; Semphere, 2020). Zizek (2018), in his review of the film, calls it an "empty vessel containing antagonistic elements." He notes that the film's enthusiastic reception spanned the political spectrum. Black power advocates loved it, as did liberals who liked the "education and aid, not struggle" conclusion to the film's exploration of options for racial justice. And right-wing commentators found in the nationalist refrain "Wakanda Forever" a version of Trump's isolationist "America First" (see Faramelli, 2019; Varda & Hahner, 2020).

There has been criticism from African writers of the film's valorization of an idealized Africa at the expense of engaging with the continent. While it offers "a rich embodiment of African culture,... [*Black Panther*] is surprisingly removed from the reality of today's African social issues and its politics" (Garside, 2018, p. 109; see Faramelli, 2019; Zizek, 2018). The film's use of other African countries as foils to Wakanda has been criticized as Western stereotyping, and its solution to the question of Wakanda's responsibility to Black people has been found to be, variously, and relatedly, neoliberal and Western development-oriented (Hanchey, 2020; Johnson & Hoerl, 2020; Varda & Hahner, 2020). Varda and Hahner (2020) argue that representational diversity alone is not enough to guarantee revolutionary representation, and Johnson and Hoerl (2020) accuse the film of maintaining whiteness despite its centering of Black bodies.

Despite also not being convinced that the ending was not endorsing a form of repurposed Western aid, albeit more community-minded and

African-led (see Hanchey, 2020), I was profoundly moved by this film, and I felt profoundly ambivalent about my affective reaction to it. It is precisely an instantiation of complicity when I do not have language that is able to convey the full range and responsibility of what I mean: every time I see this film I am moved to tears by the vision of an independent, proud, empowered African nation that is greater than the West (and I know the problem with white women's tears, DiAngelo, 2018, and I am a white woman and I am also a colonially produced kind of African white woman); I ache for an Africa that has not been brutalized by colonialism and I know that to reduce the entire continent to a Western developmental discourse of abjection is not an accurate description of Africa or Africanness, and certainly does not see the humanity of Africans; as a white South African, my right to access Africanness is forever mediated by the racialized structures erected in my favor and from which I benefitted. But all this is who and what I am. As a white South African, I am the product and the beneficiary of colonialism and apartheid. And as a white, middle-class citizen of the global South, I sit at an angle at the table of neoliberalism and neocolonial cultural imperialism. As someone now living in America, I have all the privileges of American whiteness, and also stumble as an older immigrant through a place that does not value my origins, my experience or my age.

O'Loughlin (2020, p. 357) uses postcolonial notions of mourning to theorize the cost of the mimicry at work in trying, as in Irish immigrant, to be white in America. She invokes her "own autobiography, in which the acquisition of Whiteness is confounded by my origins in a colonized nation" to "suggest[…] that the encounter with the discourse of American Whiteness is troubled for those, like me, who, while we may pass as White—something Asian Americans and other persons of color cannot do—still experience a… splitting."

As a white South African, my whiteness is not partial, as O'Loughlin's Irishness renders her in a British context. Nevertheless, *Black Panther* confronted me head-on with the complicitous contradictions that make me. I too, experience a splitting. The difficulty speaking authentically from these multiple, fractured, contradictory positionalities is not only about my own struggle with my Good White Personhood. It is not only about my awareness of what it means to have grown up under apartheid and benefitted from it. It is also at least in part about the way identity functions in America as I have found it today. It seems to me that one of the rules of identity politics is that you cannot speak except of what you know from your own embodied experience, and only to others who are exactly like you. So where does this leave me? What am I authorized to speak about here?

Black Panther is a discussion between African Americans and continental black Africans. As Rickford (2020, n.p.) puts it, "African American imaginings of Africa often intermingle with…. intimate hopes and desires for Black life in the United States… [F]or African Americans,… Africa remains an abiding source of inspiration and identity." He writes of

> [A] venerable African American tradition of crafting images of Africa that are designed to redeem the entire Black world… a retort to the contemptuous West and its condescending discourses of African danger, disease and degeneration… those tattered, colonialist tropes.

I felt a little like an eavesdropper, watching this movie, even as I also reveled in its reclamation of Africa from the typical, abjected Western depictions of the continent and its peoples, *and* as I felt myself a white African watching mainstream America claim a version of Africa as though it has just realized the continent has something to offer. I felt my fractures, my foldedness, my complicities.

The African aesthetic of *Black Panther* (see Faramelli, 2019), and some of its landscape, is deeply familiar to me, is in my bones and is embodied in me in complicated processes of subjectification and racialized domination. Some of it was filmed in my homeland. The cadence of the English of many of the African characters is one of the textures of my life. Some of the characters spoke isiXhosa, the hearing of which, in my current location, made me insider (South African) and outsider (white South African) and another kind of outsider (white person in America). I know also that it is my class-race-educational privilege that allows me to be a global citizen, to be in America legally, to afford the film. I also know that it is no uncomplicated feat for a white South African to claim a love of Africa and a relation to Africans, let alone a familiarity with a land and with people the exploitation of whom funded and nursed my very being.

My childhood was structured by the incredibly complex and contradictory experiences of being surrounded, and care for, by Black women and men who were denied access to their own children and families so they could serve mine. The relationships were relationships of power that I could experience as relationships of connection. And yet they were also relationships of connection, however mediated and compromised. This cracked and damaged social, emotional, cultural reality is my South African version of the neocolonial world. It's fucked up, and it's also real and true. It is partial and compromised, and it is all I have. In *Black Panther*, I recognize South African cadences and artwork and languages and landscapes in ways that most Americans will not. And that is as much mine as the privilege and violence and horror that is my white Africanness. This is my embodied complicity.

As a student of early modern English literature, I had the chance to experience being treated as a subject of the colony, as an always inferior wannabe by the center of this particular power when I was a graduate student at Oxford University. One result of that experience was to shape my initial academic career around the question of colonial cultural politics, and of who might make what use of the cultural capital that is "Shakespeare." Since my field included South Africans and Shakespeare, I had repeated occasion to view, teach and write about the work of John Kani. His remarkable, revolutionary portrayal of Othello in apartheid South Africa, which I saw as a high school student at the time, is a key text for postcolonial Shakespearians (see Distiller, 2012b). The last production I saw before leaving South Africa starred the elder Kani as Caliban and his son, Atandwa, as a breathtaking Ariel, in *The Tempest*. Seeing them both in *Black Panther* (Atandwa Kani plays a younger version of King T'Chaka) felt personal to me. I feel proud of Atandwa Kani, as though he were my son's friend. I feel like I am watching a kinsman age when I feel grief at how old John Kani is looking. The passing of his years feels linked to the passing of mine, because of what we share in being South African as we share Shakespeare. There is a complicity at work here, which is comprised not only of the connections across colonialism and Englishness, but also by the fractures of South Africa's settler colonialism and apartheid histories. Kani and I are both of that web, and it connects us in powerful—power-full—ways. I know that my whiteness gave me a totally different experience of being South African to Kani's, and one that I had at the expense of Kani and his children. The challenge of speaking about any of this, here in America, is the challenge to navigate not only my history and the legacy of my late twentieth century (settler colonial, neocolonial) whiteness, but also the challenge of finding a speaking position within American identity politics in the present.

Black Panther's conversation with the aspects of Africa it uses to help set its scene is also a conversation about America's position in global networks of power. A constructed "Africa" is given valence, authority, legitimacy, as well as recognition, when it is valued by Hollywood in this way. This is both a victory and a collusion in, or co-option by, a system of valuation where worth is bestowed by a specific kind of circulation in a specific kind of public sphere, and authorized by commercial success. Thanks to *Black Panther*, "Africa" is now a successful brand. Here, too, is complicity.

Black Panther is overdue, and necessary, in the context of the ongoing devaluation of Africa and Black Africans, continental or diasporic. It is an important cultural corrective for America specifically and for the colonizing West. And it also indicates America's complicity in discourses of race and power transnationally. America's capitalist neocolonial power is part of what authorizes and conveys value on the version of Africanness that *Black Panther* so lovingly depicts. As I sit at the intersections of so many of these positions, as I try to hold my various complicities, I feel these splits as the only place any of us have from which to start trying to connect with each other.

In his beautiful exegesis of decoloniality, Mignolo (2011, p. 280) writes,

> [F]or a white European body to think decolonially means to give; to give in a parallel way to the way a body of colour formed in colonial histories has to give if that body wants to inhabit postmodern and poststructuralist theories.

Mignolo has already explained why Western epistemologies cannot ever see the humanity of the West's others, and how the imbrications of colonialism and slavery with methods and institutions of knowledge creation mean that a new, delinked, decolonial way forward is the only option for what he calls Third World people. It is not what is enunciated that matters, he says, it is the always political fact of the enunciation that creates possibilities in the world. In this context, the white European body has to give up its liberal individuality, its good intention. It has to be willing to be changed, if it wants to enter the third space, beyond the either/ors of Western modernity, made possible by decoloniality. But what of the body that is not either white European or marked as colored by modernity? What of the white body born, because of modernity's systems of oppression, in the so-called Third World, into positions of power locally and of partial otherness globally? The complicities embodied thus, as I have been suggesting, need their own enunciative acts.

Humans unspeakably exceed the structural positions allocated to them by history, by systems of power, by tradition and by white supremacy and patriarchy. This place beyond language where something crucially human happens is detailed in Chap. 6. As much as we are trapped and determined by the structures in which we find ourselves, our capacity for complicity allows for sometimes unexpected, perhaps always partial, possibilities to find ourselves in new, unexpected, Thirdspace, intersubjective, terms. This is not to deny the brutalities of history, and it is to recognize the agency of those who survive it every day. It is also an attempt to understand the complicated, complicit work of racial justice that is done by *Black Panther* which is also the work of capitalism, and of American cultural colonialism, in the context of the possibilities and limits of identity politics.

A week after the movie's box-office-smashing opening, The Brookings Institute published, "Lessons from Marvel's Black Panther: Natural resource management and increased openness in Africa" (Sow & Sy, 2018). The article draws lessons for "Africa," imagined as a singular place, from the movie, for example:

> [W]hile oil and diamonds are not as versatile as vibranium [Wakanda's alien super-metal that is the source of its power] and cannot be used individually to promote the technological advancement of resource-rich African countries, there exists a space for the revenues they generate to be reinvested in technology and manufacturing, among other sectors. (Sow & Sy, 2018, n.p.)

This rather slick correlation, between the power that the fictional vibranium conveyed on the fictional Wakanda and the power of oil and diamonds to bring money and technology to Africa, overlooks the brutal history of Western exploitation of African resources. The article notes that some countries in Africa, unlike Wakanda, tend to export their riches, and blames this process for "misaligned exchange rates, the decline of non-resource sectors, political authoritarianism, conflict, and economic inequality" (Sow & Sy, 2018, n.p.). This is a gross oversimplification, to say the least.

Oil and diamonds—and ivory, and gold, resources plundered from The Congo and from South Africa, to name two specific additional examples—have not been underutilized by Africans because they did not think of developing those resources. They do not need the (American created) example of vibranium to remind them of what they might do by helping them to imagine the possibilities. And this easy vision of reinvested African resources pays no attention to neoliberal global economic systems which actively disempower Africa, or to the local and continental political aftermaths of colonialism.

The article concludes by hoping for more positive depictions of Africa in the movies (presumably American, since there is a thriving industry in Nigeria and a growing industry in South Africa). It calls into being through the existence of a fictional place the possibility that Africa's potential might be more fully respected and realized in the real world:

> [F]ictional Wakanda provides an image of the prosperity and technological advancement, which awaits properly managed resource-rich countries. The subsequent technological proliferation and increase in global trade will hopefully be featured in the Black Panther sequel. (Sow & Sy, 2018)

The representational power in imagining a different world, and thereby a different world order, does matter, as we have seen. But this cannot stand in for responsible mapping of why Wakanda is a fiction and not a reality. And feeling good about what we see on a Hollywood screen is not the same thing as actually engaging with what needs to change if we do want to see a more globally empowered African continent.

Furthermore, a year later, Brookings returned to *Black Panther* in their "Africa in Focus" section in February of 2019, in an article entitled, "From Wakanda to reality: Building mutual prosperity between African-Americans and Africa" (Signé & Thomas-Greenfield, 2019). The authors called hopefully for the possibility of cultural heritage tourism for African Americans, which it contrasts to the holiday tourism for whites that it says comprises the bulk of the industry in Africa today. African Americans, say the authors, "may" be more interested in reconnecting with "Africa" than in "riding camels in the Sahara" like white tourists do. They suggest African American visitors use National Geographic to select places to visit (where, presumably, they will not see pictures of camels in the Sahara). The possibility of these new kinds of tourists opens up new commercial pathways, they suggest, and is a way for African Americans to "invest" in Africa's growth (Signé & Thomas-Greenfield, 2019, n.p.).

"[D]uring the hype of 'Black Panther,'" the authors recount, "we both were giving talks on how to unlock Africa's potential." They continue:

> Many of… the African-American professionals, community, and business leaders… asked us how they could help make Africa as successful as the imaginary Wakanda. In other words, where are the opportunities to develop mutually beneficial relations between Africa, African Americans, and the United States?

I value and respect the connections being made between Black Africans in different places across the globe. But I cannot help but notice the normalization of a Western, American model of economics that has everything to do with *Black Panther*, the brand. The authors are entrepreneurially riding the wave of possibility opened up for their careers by the movie's success; they are accurately noticing the ways global power relations currently work as they also seek to help empower "Africa." This empowerment, as I have been suggesting, is needed across spheres, from the material to the discursive. And yet the overarching value system that is accepted and continued by this entire exchange, by this conflation of the fictional and the real, by the assumption that a comic book can uplift the reductively constructed place "Africa," simplified into an idea by the (important) work of identity, all of this takes for granted and perpetuates

American cultural dynamics that are very much part of the problem. Here is another example of complicity made visible by *Black Panther*. The cultural imperialism does not cancel out the representational empowerment. The connections between continental and diasporic Africans are not invalidated by the complex economic power dynamics at play. The yearning for African upliftment is not less important because there is also some Western-centric economic thinking at play here. It all works together to articulate some of the complexities and complicities of being human and being raced and being placed in this global time.

In this context, Newkirk's (2018) comments and question seem prescient, and to be speaking about complicity:

> But the film will likely garner much of its earnings and generate much of its cachet from members of a mobile black middle class, centered largely in America, that have carved out some political and media prominence, both individually and as a group. Those viewers have rightly applauded the film for its incredible gains in representation, and will perhaps use it as a rallying cry for increasing diversity, often among their own ranks as a class. But Killmonger's question seems as pointed through the fourth wall toward them as it is to Wakanda: What will they do with the power they do have to make the world livable for those without it?

The question of how structurally oppressed groups of people have power differentially in relation to each other is a central one for the next chapter, which examines the dynamic between feminism, queer theory and transgender rights. In this example, too, I hope to show how binary thinking cannot serve and to suggest ways of working with psychotherapy clients who want or need to talk about their gender that opens up models of human being for us all.

Works Cited

Adams, G., Gómez, L. H., Kurtiş, T., Molina, L. E., & Dobles, I. (2017). Notes on decolonizing psychology: From one Special Issue to another. *South African Journal of Psychology, 47*(4), 531–541.

Adichie, C. N. (2013). *Americanah*. Random House.
Alaoui, F. Z. C., & Abdi, S. (2020). Wakanda for everyone: An invitation to an African Muslim perspective of Black Panther. *Review of Communication*, *20*(3), 229–235.
Alexander, M. (2011). *The New Jim Crow: Mass incarceration in the age of colorblindness* (Rev. ed.). New Press.
Binkley, S. (2020). Black rage and white listening: On the psychologization of racial emotionality. In D. M. Goodman, E. R. Severson, & H. Macdonald (Eds.), *Race, rage, and resistance: Philosophy, psychology, and the perils of individualism* (pp. 90–107). Routledge.
Bhatia, S. (2020). Decolonizing psychology: Power, citizenship and identity. *Psychoanalysis, Self and Context*, *15*(3), 257–266.
Boonzaier, F., & van Niekerk, T. (Eds.). (2019). *Decolonial feminist community psychology*. Springer.
Boyd-Franklin, N. (2006). *Black families in therapy: Understanding the African American experience* (2nd ed.). Guildford.
Brewster, J., & Stephenson, M. (2013). *Promises kept: Raising black boys to succeed in school and in life*. Spiegel & Grau.
Bryant, H. (2020). *Full dissidence: Notes from an uneven playing field*. Beacon.
Butler, J. (1999). *Gender trouble: Feminism and the subversion of identity*. Routledge.
Coates, T. (2015). *Between the world and me*. Spiegel & Grau.
Collins, L. H., Machizawa, S., & Rice, J. K. (Eds.). (2019). *Transnational psychology of women: Expanding international and intersectional approaches*. American Psychological Association.
Cooper, B. (2018). *Eloquent rage: A black feminist discovers her superpower*. Picador.
Cruz, A. (2016). *The color of kink: Black women, BDSM, and pornography*. New York University Press.
Cushman, P. (2019). *Travels with the self: Interpreting psychology as cultural history*. Routledge.
DeGruy, J. (2005). *Post Traumatic Slave Syndrome: America's legacy of enduring injury and healing*. Uptone Press.
DiAngelo, R. (2018). *White fragility: Why it's so hard for white people to talk about racism*. Beacon.
Distiller, N. (2012a). *Shakespeare and the coconuts*. Wits University Press.
Distiller, N. (2012b). Authentic protest, authentic Shakespeare, Authentic Africans: Performing Othello in South Africa. *Comparative Drama*, *46*(3), 339–354.

Dovodio, J. F., & Casados, A. T. (2019). The science of clinician bias and (mis)behavior. In M. Williams, D. C. Rosen, & J. W. Kanter (Eds.), *Eliminating race-based mental health disparities* (pp. 43–59). Context.

Dyson, M. E. (2017). *Tears we cannot stop: A sermon to white America*. St Martin's Press.

Ebersohn, L. (2019). *Flocking together: An indigenous psychology theory of resilience in Southern Africa*. Springer.

Faithful, G. (2018). Dark of the world, shine on us: The redemption of Blackness in Ryan Coogler's Black Panther. *Religions, 9*, 304.

Fanon, F. (2005). *The Wretched of the Earth*. Trans. R. Philcox. Grove.

Faramelli, A. (2019, September). Liberation on and off screen: Black Panther and Black Liberation Theory. *Space, Place, and Identities Onscreen, 43*(2). Retrieved October 13, 2020, from https://doi.org/10.3998/fc.13761232.0043.202

Fernández, A. T., & Gutierrez, M. C. (2020). Colonialism, gender and mental health in psychology: A view from Eastern Cuba. *International Review of Psychiatry, 32*(4), 340–347.

Fernando, S. (2017). *Institutional racism in psychiatry and clinical psychology: Race matters in mental health*. Palgrave Macmillan.

Foucault, M. (1977). *Discipline and punish: The birth of the prison*. Penguin.

Garside, D. (2018). Ryan Coogler's film Black Panther. *South African Review of Sociology, 49*(2), 107–110.

Gay, R. (2014). *Bad Feminist*, New York: Harper. is cited l. 559.

George, S. (2020). Jouissance and discontent: A meeting of psychoanalysis, race, and American slavery. In D. M. Goodman, E. R. Severson, & H. Macdonald (Eds.), *Race, rage, and resistance: Philosophy, psychology, and the perils of individualism* (pp. 108–131). Routledge.

González-Velázquez, C. A., Shackleford, K. E., Keller, L. N., & Vinney, C. &. Drake, L.M. (2020). Watching *Black Panther* with racially diverse youth: Relationships between film viewing, ethnicity, ethnic identity, empowerment, and wellbeing. *Review of Communication, 20*(3), 250–259.

Griffith, M. S. (1977). The influence of race on the psychotherapeutic relationship. *Psychiatry, 40*, 27–41.

Guthrie, R.V. (2nd, Ed.) (2004). *Even the rat was white: A historical view of psychology*. Boston: Pearson.

Hanchey, J. (2020). Decolonizing aid in *Black Panther*. *Review of Communication, 20*(3), 260–268.

Haraway, D. (1989). *Primate visions: Gender, race, and nature in the world of modern science*. Routledge.

Hardy, K. (2006). Psychological residuals of slavery. DVD. Psychotherapy.net
Hardy, K. (2008). Race, reality and relationships: Implications for the re-visioning of family therapy. In M. McGoldrick & K. V. Hardy (Eds.), *Re-visioning family therapy: Race, culture, and gender in clinical practice* (pp. 76–84). Guilford.
Hewstone, M., Rubin, M., & Willis, H. (2002). Intergroup bias. *Annual Review of Psychology, 53*, 575–604.
Hook, D. (2007). *Foucault, psychology, and the analytics of power*. Palgrave.
Hook, D. (2012). *A critical psychology of the postcolonial: The mind of apartheid*. Psychology Press.
Johnson, J. L., & Hoerl, K. (2020). Suppressing Black Power through Black Panther's neocolonial allegory. *Review of Communication, 20*(3), 269–277.
Jung, M. (2015). *Beneath the surface of white supremacy: Denaturalizing U.S. racisms past and present*. Stanford University Press.
Kendi, I. X. (2016). *Stamped from the beginning: The definitive history of racist ideas in America*. Bold Type Books.
MacIntosh, P. (2008). White privilege and male privilege: A personal account of coming to see correspondences through work in Women's Studies. In M. McGoldrick & K. V. Hardy (Eds.), *Re-visioning family therapy: Race, culture, and gender in clinical practice* (pp. 238–249). Guilford.
Maldonado-Torres, M. (2017). Frantz Fanon and the decolonial turn in psychology: From modern/colonial methods to the decolonial attitude. *South African Journal of Psychology, 47*(4), 432–441.
Mannarini, T., & Salvatore, S. (2020). The politicization of otherness and the privatization of the enemy: Cultural hinderances and assets for active citizenship. *Human Affairs, 30*, 86–95.
McRuer, R. (2006). *Crip Theory: Cultural signs of queerness and disability*. New York University Press.
McWhorter, J. (2020). The dehumanizing condescension of *White Fragility*. *The Atlantic*, July 15. Retrieved October 4, 2020, from https://www.theatlantic.com/ideas/archive/2020/07/dehumanizing-condescension-white-fragility/614146/?gclid=CjwKCAiAv4n9BRA9EiwA30WND-v_CdXagEBVzAogh4D6JtOl1wiqwNdl6IEkM8blOts09B95ntoyRxoC8mcQAvD_BwE
McWilliams, N. (2020). Finding the other in the self. In D. M. Goodman, E. R. Severson, & H. Macdonald (Eds.), *Race, rage, and resistance: Philosophy, psychology, and the perils of individualism* (pp. 180–197). Routledge.
Menakem, R. (2017). *My grandmother's hands: Racialized trauma and the pathways to mending our hearts and bodies*. Central Recovery Press.

Meyer, M. (2020). *Black Panther*, queer erasure, and intersectional representation in popular culture. *Review of Communication, 20*(3), 236–243.
Mignolo, W. (2011). Geopolitics of sensing and knowing: On (de)coloniality, border thinking and epistemic disobedience. *Postcolonial Studies, 14*(3), 273–283.
Miller, L. L., & Miller, M. J. (2020). Praxivist imaginaries of decolonization: Can the psy be decolonized in the world as we know it? *Feminism & Psychology, 30*(3), 381–390.
Molofsky, M. (2019). Co-opting the body of the identified other: The hysterization of otherness in relation to self. *Psychoanalytic Review, 106*(1), 49–71.
Montero, M. (2017). Psychology of liberation revised (A critique of critique). In B. Gough (Ed.), *The Palgrave handbook of critical social psychology* (pp. 147–161). Palgrave Macmillan.
Morris, M. W. (2016). *Pushout: The criminalization of black girls in schools*. New Press.
Newkirk, V. R. (2018). The Provocation and power of *Black Panther*. *The Atlantic*, February 14. Retrieved October 28, 2020, from https://www.theatlantic.com/entertainment/archive/2018/02/the-provocation-and-power-of-black-panther/553226/
O'Loughlin, M. (2020). Whiteness and the psychoanalytic imagination. *Contemporary Psychoanalysis, 56*(2–3), 353–374.
Oluo, I. (2019). *So you want to talk about race*. Seal.
Orr, C. (2018). *Black Panther* is more than a superhero movie. *The Atlantic*, February 16. Retrieved October 28, 2020, from https://www.theatlantic.com/entertainment/archive/2018/02/black-panther-review/553508/
Perry, I. (2018). *Vexy thing: On gender and liberation*. Duke University Press.
Posel, D. (2001). Racial categorisations under apartheid and their afterlife. *Transformation, 47*, 50–74.
Richards, G. (2012). *"Race", racism, and psychology: Towards a reflexive history* (2nd ed.). Routledge.
Richeson, J. A., & Sommers, S. R. (2016). Toward a social psychology of race and race relations for the twenty-first century. *Annual Review of Psychology, 67*, 439–463.
Rickford, R. (2020). The pitfalls of African consciousness. *Africa is a country*. Retrieved September 25, 2020, from https://africaisacountry.com/2020/09/the-pitfalls-of-african-consciousness
Rippon, G. (2019). *The Gendered Brain: The new neuroscience that shatters the myth of the female brain*. Penguin.
Rose, N. (1998). *Inventing our selves: Psychology, power and personhood*. Cambridge University Press.

Salter, P. S., & Haugen, A. D. (2017). Critical race studies in psychology. In B. Gough (Ed.), *The Palgrave handbook of critical social psychology* (pp. 123–145). Palgrave Macmillan.

Semphere, T. (2020). Beyond African royalty. *Africa is a country*. Retrieved October 3, 2020, from https://africasacountry.com/2020/09/beyond-african-royalty

Signé, L., & Thomas-Greenfield, L. (2019). From Wakanda to reality: Building mutual prosperity between African-Americans and Africa. *Brookings Insitute*. Retrieved October 1, 2020, from https://www.brookings.edu/blog/africa-in-focus/2019/02/14/from-wakanda-to-reality-building-stronger-relations-between-african-americans-and-africa/?utm_campaign=Brookings%20Brief&utm_source=hs_email&utm_medium=email&utm_content=69969587

Sims, D. (2018). The game-changing success of *Black Panther*. *The Atlantic*, February 20. Retrieved October 28, 2020, from https://www.theatlantic.com/entertainment/archive/2018/02/the-game-changing-success-of-black-panther/553763/

Smith, C., Lobban, G., & O'Loughlin, M. (Eds.). (2013). *Psychodynamic psychotherapy in South Africa: Contexts, theories and applications*. Wits University Press.

Sow, M., & Sy, A. (2018). Lessons from Marvel's *Black Panther*: Natural resource management and increased openness in Africa. *Brookings Institute*, February 23. Retrieved May 2, 2019, from https://www.brookings.edu/blog/africa-in-focus/2018/02/23/lessons-from-marvels-black-panther-natural-resource-management-and-regional-collaboration-in-africa/

Stephens, A., & Boonzaier, F. (2020). Black lesbian women in South Africa: Citizenship and the coloniality of power. *Feminism & Psychology, 30*(3), 324–342.

Tatum, B. D. (1997). *"Why are all the black kids sitting together in the cafeteria?" and other conversations about race*. Basic.

Teo, T. (2005). *The critique of psychology: From Kant to postcolonial theory*. New York: Springer.

The Conversation. (2020). Robin DiAngelo's *White Fragility* ignores the differences within whiteness. August 27. Retrieved October 4, 2020, from https://theconversation.com/robin-diangelos-white-fragility-ignores-the-differences-within-whiteness-143728

Varda, S. J., & Hahner, L. A. (2020). *Black Panther* and the alt-right: Networks of racial ideology. *Critical Studies in Media Communication, 37*(2), 133–147.

Wa Thiong'o, N. (1986). *Decolonizing the mind: The politics of language in African literature*. James Currey.
Wa Thiong'o, N. (1993). *Moving the centre: The struggle for cultural freedoms*. James Currey.
Williams, P. (1991). *The alchemy of race and rights: Diary of a law professor*. Harvard University Press.
Williams, M., Rosen, D. C., & Kanter, J. W. (Eds.). (2019). *Eliminating race-based mental health disparities*. Context.
Zizek, S. (2018). Quasi duo fantasies: A Straussian reading of "Black Panther." *Los Angeles Review of Books*, March 3. Retrieved October 27, 2020, from https://www.lareviewofbooks.org/article/quasi-duo-fantasias-straussian-reading-black-panther#!

Open Access This chapter is licensed under the terms of the Creative Commons Attribution 4.0 International License (http://creativecommons.org/licenses/by/4.0/), which permits use, sharing, adaptation, distribution and reproduction in any medium or format, as long as you give appropriate credit to the original author(s) and the source, provide a link to the Creative Commons licence and indicate if changes were made.

The images or other third party material in this chapter are included in the chapter's Creative Commons licence, unless indicated otherwise in a credit line to the material. If material is not included in the chapter's Creative Commons licence and your intended use is not permitted by statutory regulation or exceeds the permitted use, you will need to obtain permission directly from the copyright holder.

4

Thought Bodies: Gender, Sex, Sexualities

> [B]odies are always 'thought bodies' or 'bodies-thought'—and perhaps one day we will look back on the 'sex-thought-body' that has so exercised our own century, our own repetitive and wearying anxiety about our sexual bodies, our commitments to the difference of gender that marks us so indelibly… with a certain wry amusement. (Rose, 1998, p. 183)

This chapter offers an exploration of the limits of binary thinking, and the multiple kinds of damage it causes. It offers three illustrations of complicitous situations that complicate a view of gender, sex and sexuality as understandable through binary thinking. Each illustration offered here has been rendered additionally difficult and painful by categorical thinking, the kind of thinking that the scientific method often depends upon and that the psy disciplines often perpetuate.

Thinking complicitously means getting outside of binary structures to conceptualize subjectivity as implicated in, not bounded from, otherness. It also means acknowledging we are implicated in the systems of power and meaning that make use of otherness. If race, as we have seen, is one constructed place where fixed identities emerge in response to histories of oppression authorized by binary thinking (which also means by ways of thinking that assert hierarchies of value for material profit), then gender is another.

One of the urgent border wars being fought in the West at the moment is the struggle for transgender and nonbinary human being. As with the development and pathologization of racialized differences, psychology has had a central role to play in establishing meanings for and treatments of transgender and nonbinary people, as it has for sexual queers and for femininity and femaleness, all related (but not coterminous) histories of constructed meanings which gave rise to real, lived identities and material conditions of being. The first illustration provided here is an exploration of how transgender human being has been thought about in Western systems, including both the scientific and medical establishments, and feminist and queer theories.

I use the term "transgender" to refer to all people who occupy a gender identity different to the one assigned to them at birth, from within a binary system, on the basis of their perceived anatomy. Transgender people may or may not require hormonal or surgical gender affirmation. Some transgender people may occupy standard or standardized gender locations for "male" or "female." Some may identify as trans men or trans women, and some may identify as women or men who happen also have a transgender trajectory.

I use the term "non-binary" specifically to indicate those people whose gender identities cannot be accommodated within the gender binary. Sometimes nonbinary people need to enact a nonbinary embodiment with the help of medical interventions. Some nonbinary people will also be transgender. There are many other terms for noncisgender identities, and the list changes as the culture makes room and new iterations emerge. For the purposes of brevity, I include identities such as genderqueer or agender within the rubric of nonbinary. All of these markers are gender markers, and do not denote anything about sexuality or sexual orientation. Some transgender and/or nonbinary people will also be queer, which in this context means members of the LGBQ+ sexuality umbrella.

In the second illustration explored here, I move from gender to sexuality, and some of the structuring dynamics of normative heterosexuality. Another urgent conflict, sometimes conceptualized as equivalent to war (Faludi, 2006; Herman, 1997; Ward, 2020), is the struggle for sexual agency experienced by girls and women—in the terms of this discussion, this usually means those assigned female at birth (AFAB), although it can

4 Thought Bodies: Gender, Sex, Sexualities

and should include those who are otherwise female or feminized—in this patriarchal culture.

Finally, I look at what emerges when genders and sexualities in another place have to make sense of themselves within neocolonial conditions. By examining the transnational complexities of Western LGBTQ ideas and identities in South Africa, I offer a third illustration of complicitous thinking about both gender and sexuality, as they can be taken together.

The topics of gender and sexuality offer a crucial opportunity for practitioners of the psy disciplines to see what theories developed in the humanities can offer us. Psychology has been implicated in the assertion of binary thinking, in the reinscription of science and biology as technologies for proving gender in always already gendered cultures in the name of objective truth. It has helped develop and perpetuate notions of sexual normativity (Drescher, 2015a) that are also, inevitably, deeply raced and classed (Carter, 2007). It is high time for the psy disciplines to think differently about gender, sex and sexuality, and to stop perpetuating norms as natural.

This chapter offers what I hope are useful, currently relevant insights into discussions that are at least as old as feminism itself, about the relationship between sex and gender, and about at least some aspects of normative (hetero)sexuality. In the evolving realms of transgender mental health, of sexuality studies and of decolonial imperatives within a transnational frame, these discussions are both urgent and in flux, the more we listen and learn.

All three of the examples presented here illustrate a problem with language. Each of the areas of human being explored in this chapter (transgender being; heteronormative female being; transnational queer being) demonstrates that language has shaping power, and that language gives or disables agency. If you do not have the words to describe an experience, it cannot be recognized by others, and it is much harder to make sense of it for yourself. If you do know your own meaning, but your words are dismissed or derided, your experience cannot be acknowledged or addressed. Each of the examples under discussion here tracks a struggle to find the words to articulate versions of human being that are othered within current systems of power. This is evidence of the importance of language as a human system, and of the symbolic as providing primary access to human subjectivity and processes of subjectification.

Starting with a brief overview of the evolution of gender within Western culture, this chapter offers comprehensive illustration of the constructed nature of apparently natural meanings, and how binary thinking shapes difference. In this way, it extends the arguments of the previous chapter, that apparently common sensical categories are historical formations, informed by the psy disciplines, among other disciplinary matrixes. We need to bring this thinking to our psychotherapeutic practice, in order to hold space in a way that can manage the complicities that are always at play within a client's sense of self, and between therapist and client. The question of practice is the main topic of the last chapter. Let us begin by reviewing what is perhaps the most powerful binary structure underlying Western culture.

Binary Gender

In practice, gender is complicated and personal, informed by each person's cultural and family dynamics as well as by their intimate experiences of themselves, both before and after language has had a go at shaping them. For example, Harris (2009) writes powerfully, from within a relational psychoanalytic frame, about gender's fundamental complexity, which is denied and reduced by a binary logic. She shows that gender is material, relational, actively assembled and contextual. It is made up of developmental events that may or may not directly relate to gender and/ or sexuality. It is both personal and collective; "It is as though gender were often the point of maximal psychic vulnerability, a flash point for the construction and maintenance of subjectivity" (Harris, 2009, p. 175). This is indeed a psychoanalytic understanding, which sees gender identity, achieved through sexuality, as instantiating the child's move into personhood via an encounter with the family, representing social rules, through the Oedipal process. Implicitly, therefore, gender is a key place where inherited social meanings enter subjectification.

Doan (2010) explores how, in addition to carrying interpersonal social meanings, gender is an interaction between a person and the kind of space that person moves through. Other people's presence in space helps bring different expectations and behaviors depending on the place that is shared. This is a visual, embodied geography of complicity to add to Harris's psychoanalytic one. If there is a place where the personal, the social, the historical, the embodied and the familial obviously combine to construct complicity—the place, the subject and their context cannot be delineated from each other—it is gender. This is so, even as gender often feels like the most personal of places, where we find our inner selves: complicity at work, making the subject.

As we will see, Western culture, assisted mightily by scientific thinking which wants categories, has a deep investment in denying the complicit content of gender. Patriarchy needs a gender binary. As discussed in Chap. 1, binary thinking enables a dynamics of psychic and material power.

Binary gender is also a Western attempt to make sense of sexual difference under patriarchy. This use of sexual difference has been theorized, by psychoanalytically informed thinkers, as productive of misogyny and sexism (Benjamin, 1988; De Lauretis, 1987; Dean & Lane, 2001; Rose, 1986), as well as heteronormative heterosexuality (Butler, 1999). While this process has historical nuance (Perry, 2018), there is a larger theoretical point to be made here about some of the formative energies of the culture as a whole (see Gilmore, 2001).

Ward (2020) and Carter (2007) add the important point that the heteronormative gender binary, as it developed in America, is also raced. As I suggested in the previous chapter, this is inevitable, since gender and race co-constitute, as feminists of color have always said. Modern American heterosexuality was formed in and shaped by the early twentieth century (Katz, 2007). Eugenicist practices fundamentally informed the development of discourses of healthy heterosexuality, as circulated by the psy disciplines as well as medical and sexological interventions. Whiteness became the implicit human norm in part through these processes (Carter, 2007; Ward, 2020). Camminga (2019), too, shows connections between eugenics, sexology, racism and binary heteronormativity in early twentieth century South Africa, a site of interest to the eugenics movement in the North because of its highly racialized colonial dynamics.

There is a long genesis to binary gender logic in Western cultural and political systems, where people, in the first place white people, born with penises, have unmediated access to subjectivity, and everyone else has additional work to do. This assumption is Freud's starting point, as we saw in Chap. 2. Freud articulated overtly, in a discourse that became psychology, what up till then Western culture had taken for granted.

We can start tracking this with the first scientist of Western culture, Aristotle. Biologically, AFAB women cannot do what men do, produce semen, and this, for Aristotle—and especially for the early modern era which "rediscovered" him—was evidence that they were incompletely human, "nothing else but an error or aberration of nature… yea the first monster in nature," as a 1615 summary of his position put it (Aughterson, 1998, p. 464; see Schiebinger, 1989). Nature therefore endorsed women's inferior social position in ancient Greek culture. Aristotle helped lay the groundwork for the idea that biology is destiny. Even apologists of Aristotle's views on women concede he takes for granted that men and women have different, complementary, biologically endorsed roles to play in society. Of course, this means women are not cut out for civic life, but are designed by nature to have, raise and stay with children as their *raison d'etre* (Dobbs, 1996). There are several familiar patriarchal assumptions at play here, which structure gender difference along the lines of different innate essences. These naturally give rise to different, complementary abilities: public and private capacities; intellect or mind versus body; or as Aristotle put it, form (the male) versus matter (the female).

These assumptions and structuring principles built on themselves (see Coole, 1988; Gilmore, 2001). The Greeks knew women were inferior to men, not able to think clearly or execute good judgment. In line with this, the sin of Eve came to contaminate women's meaning in medieval and early modern culture (see Distiller, 2008). The cultural story is that women cannot be trusted because they are penetratable (symbolically, by the snake's words, a sign of their constitutional and co-constituting physical, intellectual and moral weakness; women are, as the early modern period put it over and over, "leaky vessels"). Their bodies are the sign of their inferiority. Their bodies are also the source of their power over men. They can and, so goes the common cultural narrative, do use their bodies to tempt men, as Eve convinced Adam to fall. This suspicion of female sexuality remains powerfully present in the treatment rape survivors continue to receive today. Women are made responsible for eliciting men's desire, and ruthlessly punished for being desirable (see Gilmore, 2001; Ward, 2020). There is a logic of domination in this understanding of heteronormative desire (see Distiller, 2011). Binary thinking structures this dynamic, where the difference and otherness signified by the woman's body are simultaneously attractive, threatening and debased. This terrible, destructive difference must be controlled, or the gendered subjectivity which depends on keeping it out risks dissolution.

In the sixteenth and seventeenth centuries in Europe, there were vigorous debates over the nature of women, which tried to determine their proper social place (Beecher, 2005; Laqueur, 1992). Much of the debate concerned policing what they could wear, where they could occupy space and with whom. It was important to know what kept women's bodies in their proper place, since there was much cultural anxiety about loss of social distinction if women were allowed to dress like men, or vice versa (Levine, 1994; Orgel, 1996). There were, in fact, stories circulating at the time about women behaving inappropriately and thus turning into men (Laqueur, 1992). The control of women's bodies, then as now, was implicitly linked to the control of their public speech (Boose, 1991; Distiller, 2008; Jones, 1986; Vickers, 1981; Wall, 1993). It would make a fascinating project to compare the cultural texts that responded to Queen Elizabeth I, who, at the point of emergence of early modernity, brilliantly navigated the impossible contradiction of occupying a position of male authority with her female body, with the treatment of Hillary Clinton in the 2016 elections, as postmodernity seems poised to fracture under the representational pressures of social media (see Berry, 1989; Marotti, 1982; Solnit, 2018).

With the Enlightenment and the development of modern science, including psychology, came the cultural and economic idea of the individual as we now know him, as we have seen. In this time, drawing on colonial racism as well as centuries of sexism, Linnaeus developed his taxonomy of all things. He chose the term *homo sapiens* (meaning "man of wisdom") to emphasize the ways in which men are different to primates. He chose the term *mammals*, referring to the body part shared by only the females of all the species he was connecting, to denote what joined humans to animals (Schiebinger, 2004). The old binary meanings continued to influence new discourses, including Darwin's (see Saini,

2017), where female bodies continued to be tied to lower, earthy, realms; to the apparent imperatives of (hetero)sexuality and their consequences (rape, pregnancy); to an emerging concept of "nature"; and to the reduced capacity for intellect and therefore personhood that started with the Ancient Greeks (see Schiebinger, 1989). French writer Gustave Le Bon, interested in both psychology and anthropology, opined in 1879:

> [Women's] inferiority is so obvious that no one can contest it for a moment; only its degree is worth discussion. All psychologists who have studied the intelligence of women, as well as poets and novelists, recognize today that they represent the most inferior forms of human evolution and that they are closer to children and savages than to an adult, civilized man. They excel in fickleness, inconstancy, absence of thought and logic, and incapacity to reason. Without doubt there exist some very distinguished women, very superior to the average man, but they are as exceptional as the birth of any monstrosity as, for example, of a gorilla with two heads; consequently, we may neglect them entirely. (Qtd. Fisher 2011, p. 10)

Articulating for the first time the language of the unconscious of Western culture, Freud (1973) also said biology should be destiny, and since women self-evidently had nothing where the signifier of subjectivity should be, they needed to come to terms with their proper receptive place in the world, for the sake of the reproductive security of the race. Freud heteronormatively assumed that babies can only be made by heterosexuals in monogamous pairings (see Distiller, 2011), and require the unpaid labor of female bodies to survive, as a consequence of natural imperatives. Any other configuration, because to the Victorian mind unnatural, threatens proper human development, which finds its best expression in the creation of more monogamous heterosexual pairings. This assumption has structured the discipline of psychology and most of its offshoots until recently, and still exists as a powerful cultural norm. In this version of proper gender, linked to sex and sexuality, people assigned female at birth and who remain so are required to internalize and embody specific qualities and meanings. As always, race layers onto these pressures, adding meanings and rules (Cooper, 2018; Cruz, 2016; Perry, 2018; Ward, 2020), as does ablebodiedness (Drummond & Brotman, 2014) and class (Yeskel, 2015).

Binary gender is a core structural component of the self/other power dynamic that informs Western modernity and which enabled the colonial enterprises that gave us our twenty-first century global systems. It unconsciously drives much of what dominant institutions assume to be true about nature, about gender roles, about sexuality and about how they each inform the other.

Transgender Complicities

Despite the shaping assumptions of Western science, dominant culture and heteronormativity that gender is essentially binary in structure, gender is in fact made of a complicit structure. It is not, in lived reality, formed out of complementarity, where your gender is kept in place because it is not like the "other" gender. The very instability of this apparently natural and obvious relation gives it the lie; there are too many instances in history and in science of additional options for gender to be based in binary logic, or to be based on binary sex (Fausto-Sterling, 1993). Gender is complex, intertwined with heteronormative systems of oppression, as well as with histories of resistance and whatever personal assertions take shape in the contexts available to any given subject. There is not one original source of gender. Gender is put together by subjects of culture, language, history and family, and by the mediated sense we each make of biology, of how our bodies feel to us through the network of options made available to each of us by the worlds of possibilities and of limits we inherit.

Then there is the matter of how gender, after it is internally felt, is expressed, and what the relationship is between the two. Queer theory was partially built on the argument that the iterative social performance of gender helps to create the way it feels to be gendered (Butler, 1999). The implications are not only for the social meanings of gender or the subjective interpretations of gendered selfhood. Butler also famously asserted that gender is a performance which effects help to ensure that sex is always already gendered, and not the other way around (see also Butler, 1993); binary sex is not the bedrock of gender, but a consequence of it. The apparently unidirectional causal relationship between sex—genitals, hormones, chromosomes—and the social identities "male" and "female" is thereby broken. Gender and sex both exist through the doing of the socially sanctioned rules of gender which go on, as feminist historians of science and feminist scientists continue to show, to inform and shape our "scientific" understandings of sex and gender, and the biological meanings we make of sexual difference (e.g., Fausto-Sterling, 1992; Fausto-Sterling, 2000; Fine, 2014; Fisher, 2011; Haraway, 1989; Rippon, 2019; Saini, 2017; Schiebinger, 2004).

This gets complicated when we apply the queer and feminist thinking that opens up binary gender assumptions to the lives and self-narratives of some transgender people. As Prosser (1998, p. 43) puts it in his brilliant interrogation of the relationship between feminist and queer theories and transgender lives (he is writing in the period where transsexual and transgender were still sometimes being used interchangeably, and before nonbinary was a publicly recognized identity),

> The transsexual doesn't necessarily *look* differently gendered but by definition *feels* differently gendered from her or his birth-assigned sex. In both its medical and its autobiographical versions, the transsexual narrative depends upon an initial crediting of this feeling as generative ground. It demands some recognition of the category of corporeal interiority (internal bodily sensations) and of its distinctiveness from that which can be seen (external surface): the difference between gender identity and sex that serves as the logic of transsexuality.

Many of us experience what it means to be a cisgender woman or man as natural, but queer theory teaches that that feeling is created through our participation in the repeated signals and signs that society provides us as the correct ways to be (also raced, classed, ablebodied or disabled) women or men. For many transgender people, and certainly for the medical and psychological discourses that authorize their being, the natural imperative comes directly from the body, and is at odds with the social rules being imposed on the body. As Prosser (1998, p. 67) shows, "transsexual autobiography challenge's theory's cynicism over identity's embodiment" (see also Califa, 1997; Serano, 2016).

4 Thought Bodies: Gender, Sex, Sexualities

It is my assertion that the fact of transgender human being is perhaps the best case study we have so far in the complicit nature of gender. The embodiment of identity cannot be separated into constructed or performed gender, and sexed objective truth. The theoretical conundrum only arises if we remain committed to the binary formulation, where sex and gender are either/ors of each other, as has informed the debate about gender theory and transgender personhood. Each construct (sex, gender) draws on inherited systems of meaning and structures of expression to establish their intelligibility to themselves and each other. They inform each other. Each will have a personal meaning for each subject, whose pure epistemology we can never recover from the tangle of complicities that make us all. Thus trans does not need to remain in binary relation to cis. Following on from this, if we (the cisgender establishment) can accept trans personhood as within the realm of the human, we do not need to account for it. We can accept it, and learn from it.

I say this without wanting to reproduce the objectifying and instrumentalizing of trans personhood that has been committed by queer theory (see Prosser, 1998; Pyne, 2016). Transgender people are not theories or ideas, and their lives are often made much more difficult by the positions of otherness they are often forced to occupy (Grant et al., 2011). Transgender people are also not a coherent or homogenous group. There are as many different possibilities for transgender personhood as there are transgender people, even before intersectionality is added to the account. In theory, this is true for cisgender people too, if we can get beyond the strictures of the binary that wants to structure both our gender identities and our sexualities (Butler, 1999; Garber, 2005).

The theoretical conundrum that transgender personhood apparently presents to the queer and feminist theories that both enabled and used versions of transgender emergence is one example of complicity at work: sex versus gender is a binary construct, even as the psychic investments in asserting the truth of sex over gender were crucial for the emergence of transgender human being.

The structuring principle available for transgender emergence, which sets the terms for transgender human being to become intelligible, is another example of complicity. This latter set of terms, and the options they enabled for speaking transgender human being, is implicated in the psy technologies, as well as in sexology, endocrinology and surgery. Below, I will address these complicities in more detail.

First, there is a political point to be made. Sadly, the invocation of feminism in the context of a discussion about transgender personhood requires contextualization, given the deployment of putatively feminist arguments that are transphobic (starting, perhaps, with Raymond, 1979). Some people who call themselves feminist, relying on essentialized definitions of femaleness, would deny transgender people, especially trans women, the right to assume their correct gender. Building on a second wave logic which looked to reclaim the debased meaning of femaleness that was a result of the marriage of biology and gendered destiny, for these thinkers, being born and raised in a body with a vagina is the bottom line—and only legitimate—experience of femaleness. This reductive approach to the complex relations between the social rules for gender, embodiment, and victimhood or suffering overlooks the true gift of feminism: that none of us need be bound by a constructed relationship between gender and sex which strives to limit who we can be or how we can feel about our bodies.

Perry (2018) argues that the limitations of modern feminism are a result of the political processes of the twentieth century. These processes brought feminism into the mainstream, and thereby also into liberalism, whose politics of representation limited what was possible. Neoliberalism's fracturing of the social contract worked together with liberal commitments to affirmative action, so that as the twentieth century proceeded, "Rather than sharing prosperity, prosperity was made more competitive, exclusive, and slightly more diverse" (Perry, 2018, p. 91). The result, she says, is that in asking for a seat at the table, feminism had to align with the definitions of personhood that were available. The underlying necessary existence of the nonperson, discussed in the previous chapter, what Perry (2018, p. 93) calls the "monstrosity," was overlooked by these feminist strategies of inclusion. This was "a product of how we arrived at the institutional spaces where we have the conversation" (Perry, 2018, p. 93). In other words, participation requires complicity.

An investment in suffering—a way to find profit in one's sense of self—as the authorizing maneuver for access to both political and moral identity is one result of the neoliberal processes Perry (2018) tracks and discusses (see also brown 2020). This will be explored in more detail in the following two chapters, but it is worth noting here, as we explore why some people who know what gendered oppression is might seek to oppress other genders in turn.

Perry (2018) is theorizing how only certain categories of human being have been accommodated by mainstream feminism, that is, feminism that has achieved institutional recognition. Her larger project is to show how the legal category of human being in the West was historically constituted from practices which needed nonpersons as the constitutive other. To expand the terms of Perry's (2018) theory, trans and nonbinary persons are the unacknowledged nonpeople underpinning binary gender's rules for human being. "To embrace the monstrosity is to wrestle with the world from the status of the outside" (Perry, 2018, p. 97), as feminists of color did by "centering the position of the woman who existed outside personhood and theorizing from there" (ibid., p. 91). If there is one lesson to be learned from this, surely it is that our feminist work begins and ends with all those placed outside of the world. Apartheid, as a specific instantiation of white supremacy, imposed a racial hierarchy on people of color as a way to divide and conquer. This encouraged collaboration with the system. People who call themselves feminists but refuse transgender people's human being seem to me to be collaborating with the patriarchy that oppresses them, when they want to construct a hierarchy of access based on arguments about who has the right kind of bodies to deserve activist attention. There is more than enough patriarchally induced suffering to go round. Transgender justice is not a threat to cis women. It is the path to our liberation.

And, as we have started to see, just like trans-excluding "feminists," transgender being has typically been expressed through language that ties gender to the body. There has historically been an institutional investment in essentializing transgender experiences, reinscribing a narrative of wrong-body-based subjectivity that renders the trans person in need of binary-based medical transition to correct the biological error.

The coercive practices of the medical and psy disciplines that have constructed transgender people so as to interact with them have been well-documented. In the early days of transsexual emergence in the 1950s, heteronormative and binary gendered performances were mandatory for those transgender people who needed to seek access to transition-related interventions (Bettcher, 2014; Califa, 1997; Denny, 2004; Pyne, 2016; Stryker, 2008; Tosh, 2016). Namaste (2000) has detailed how this history skews access to any evidence-based theories of trans "authenticity": Studies that inform diagnostic categories and best practices have traditionally been formulated from work done in gender clinics where trans people have been coerced into performing heteronormative binary gender before being allowed access to treatment.

This situation helped to create a cisnormatively-mediated discourse through which transgender subjectivity continues to be viewed (O'Shea, 2020; Spade, 2003). Since the 1990s, the experiences, languages and subjectivities of transgender, nonbinary and other differently gendered people have vastly expanded (Valentine, 2007). But there largely remains a nonnegotiable focus on the body that is an important element of being transgender (Bettcher, 2014; Langer, 2019; 2013; Pyne, 2016; Saketopoulou, 2014; Serano, 2016). Trans people continue to have to assert their knowledge that they exist in their own bodies.

It would be arrogant and dismissive of much carefully argued and important work to suggest that such narratives, of being in the wrong body, or of transgender being emerging from uncontestable body-based feelings and knowledge, were merely manipulation, at best, or false consciousness, at worst. Many transgender writers invoke this discourse to authorize themselves. Autobiographical writing (see, e.g., Califa, 1997; Feinberg, 1993; Prosser, 1998; Serano, 2016) and qualitative studies of the last two decades (see Levitt & Ippolito, 2014) comprehensively document experiences of initial estrangement from self because of a core, but initially unexpressable, sense of one's gender identity, which can be exacerbated by negative responses to one's gender presentation. Wilkinson (2015) describes a process where personal, body-based truth intersects with social expectation and public treatment to create a necessary gender transition process. Thinking complicitously allows us to believe transgender speakers: they may be using what tools are available to them, socially and intrapsychically. But since we all do this, as a function of being human, and since we no longer assume binary thinking is necessary, we require no evidence from transgender people regarding the legitimacy of their existence, either in theory or in biology.

This helps resolve the tension between queer theory and autobiographical felt truth. Kaufmann (qtd. in Pyne, 2016, p. 55) recounts,

> Jessie, a self-identified male-to-female transsexual, was dismayed after reading a completed study in which I examined the narrative construction of her gender. Wiping tears from her eyes, she said, "You have taken away the identity I have worked all my life to build"… [M]y desire was to deconstruct gender, not erase her identity… How did I make such a mess?

Or, as Buckner (2016, p.76) shows, "While a social constructionist framework is empowering, it can also foster contempt, resentment, and critique of transgender embodiments that rely on essentialist, binary models of gender expression." One of Buckner's therapist respondents said,

> *Sometimes I get a little judgy when I hear people just, trans people, just stuck in that binary, you know?* "I have to be a woman", *you know?* "I was born a man but I've always felt like a woman and I've got to be a woman and I'm going to be a woman"… *and sometimes I get judgy and I think, why can't you just be you? … Like why couldn't this person just be genderqueer? Or genderfluid? Or gender-something? Why did they have to be a woman?*" (Buckner, 2016, p. 76)

This clearly denies the transgender client's experience of herself, and refuses her right and ability to articulate her gender and her body's relationship to it. And at the same time, there is a problematic history to the use of biology in the psychological understanding and treatment of trans people, where transgender identity has to come from a biological source.

Seeking to understand the etiology of transgender identity, in order to account for it, in a move which assumes it needs to be accounted for (to be legitimized? To be normalized? To be prevented?), there has been work on *in-utero* hormone exposure or prenatal gender developmental pathways which might have caused a transgender identity (e.g., the plenary lecture given at the WPATH conference by Dr. Karissa Sanbonmatsu, on November 7, 2020, titled, "Understanding gender identity: From DNA to the brain"; Zhou et al., 2007; Erickson-Schroth, 2013). Here, we once more see science believing it has answers to questions that are more correctly, more complexly, more complicitously, cultural—which is to say, both and always already constructed *and* biological, since our human experience of the biological must always be mediated, especially in a realm as fundamentally made of human being as gender. Thinking complicitously allows it all to be true: that many transgender people have a body-based truth which no-one, especially not an institutional gatekeeper, has the right to contest; and that transgender people, like all other people, can only put narrative constructions together from the symbolic histories available even as many of them also alter the available symbolic language as they use it, creating something new that is also real and legitimate (in a process akin to postcolonial processes of hybridity, and maybe even mimicry, theorized by Bhabha, 1994; see Distiller, 2012 for a cultural example of these ideas in practice).

And it is clear that transgender and nonbinary people have had to fight for symbolic space within the languages and the institutions that make us human. Writing about searching for space and speech as a differently gendered human within the confines of a scientifically-structured discipline (speech pathology), Azul (2018, p. 121) asks,

> How to emerge from a condition of not-being-able-to-speak-and-not-being-heard-with-what-one-has-to-say if the nature of one's voice-lessness cannot be explored with the methods of knowledge production in which one has been trained and if the promises of one's coming to voice cannot be accommodated within the constraints of the worldview according to which one has been raised?

Azul (2018, p. 122) critiques speech pathology definitions because they locate the problem in the speaker:

> This is a form of voice-lessness… that does not appear in speech-language pathology dictionaries and text-books because its cause cannot be attributed to a malfunction of the speaker's psyche or their vocal folds… In fact, it appears unrelated to the voice producer as they are commonly understood, namely, as an entity from which that which we call "voice" emerges. Rather, this condition of voice-lessness seems to be imposed by the phonees,

those who/which are exposed to vocal productions that have originated from elsewhere. Such phonee-imposed voice-lessness is characterized by the phonees' inability or refusal to acknowledge the presence and relevance of an utterance, by the phonees' lack of capacity or willingness to make sense of vibrations that have reached their senses.

Azul's (2018) notion of vocal productions that have originated from elsewhere which partially constitute the experience of nonbinary personhood through their refusal to allow it, to hear it speak its truth, is a perfect example of the foldedness, the outside-insideness of the subject of complicity (see Chap. 1). It also speaks to systems of oppression which plague the subject seeking to make language for itself or to assert its existence. The binary structures at work here cannot accommodate a nonbinary human speaking. And yet that human exists, and is speaking.

Azul (2018, p. 122) concludes, "research approaches are needed that seek to attend to the complexities of the participants' sociocultural positionings and to their preferences regarding how they wish to be perceived and addressed by others in encounters." The assertion here, in keeping with respecting the individual truth of gender's relation to the body, is that the gender outlaw (Bornstein, 1995; McKenzie, 2010) be allowed to vocalize/authorize/author themself, using and in so doing altering the available discourse. Azul (2018) offers an account of their own journey. They recount the damaging long-term psychic consequences of working in a scientific field which operated by categorizing bodies and their voices according to binary gender norms as part of its recognition of healthy human being. One of their points is the limitations of binary thinking. Another is that scientific or standard academic language cannot adequately account for this experience, this kind of knowledge. The call for a new model is clear.

In a special issue of the *Journal of Gay & Lesbian Psychotherapy*, Denny (2004) worried about some of the negative consequences of rejecting the binary gender model intrinsic to the old medical model of transsexuality. He wondered if protection against discrimination and hate crimes would be extended to a nonspecific, "ambiguous or alternating" group, and about additional possible legal losses that would follow from depathologizing transgender identity (Denny, 2004, p. 32). In our identity-focused, liberal rights-based system, you have to be part of a recognizable group in order to be entitled to protections. There is also the risk that medical treatment will not be authorized if someone is not conceptualized as sick (Ettner, 2007).

Indeed, "[M]ost of the successful legal claims for trans equality have come through strategic use of the medical model of transsexuality" (Spade, 2003, p. 30; Spade demonstrates the disciplinary and formative relationship between medical systems, the law and gender intelligibility). Legal protections require not only assertions of group identity, but an alliance with the psy and medical disciplines that render transgender being intelligible and acceptable within the terms of a cisnormative symbolic.

In the psy disciplines, transgender personhood is indicated currently by the diagnosis of gender dysphoria. This controversial diagnosis has a telling history. It emerged from the perversions, later paraphilias and the struggle to remove homosexuality from the DSM (Bryant, 2006; Butler, 2004; De Bloch & Adriaens, 2013; Drescher, 2015a; Drescher, 2015b; Lev, 2006; Wiggins, 2020). In other words, gender dysphoria has evolved through the long, convoluted history of the medical and psychological establishments' attempts to classify and pathologize gender and sexual deviations from the binary hetero norm. In the past few decades, activism from transgender and nonbinary people, clinicians and clients (Markman, 2011; Spade, 2003), has resulted in some changes for the better. In 2022, the World Health Organization's manual, the International Classification of Diseases (ICD) 11, will do away with its previous diagnosis of "transsexualism" and instead have "gender incongruence," which is a sexual health and not a mental health diagnosis (Atienza-Macías, 2020). This is progress. However, the requirement for transgender and other gender diverse people to have a diagnosis before being legible to the system and able to access interventions if they are needed remains problematic.

In line with an increasing call to have cisgender people step away from the policing of trans lives, Wiggins (2020) suggests that the medicalization of transgender distress be turned on the largely, and historically, cisgender clinicians who wield it. The investment in categorizing trans suffering (as gender dysphoria) as the new diagnostic replacement for the older frame of perversion is itself a perversion: a sign of cis disavowal of the anxiety caused by an encounter with gender difference. Because "the more a gender is assumed to be static, ciscentric, and knowable, as is encouraged in most Western medical, colonial contexts, the more foreboding would be a confrontation with its variance" (Wiggins, 2020, p. 66). In truth, the "traumatizing reality" is that "gender is uncertain, its affects and genealogies are unclear" (ibid, p. 69). This is a beautiful extension of the old feminist investigations into sexual difference as a constituting problem for patriarchy's symbolic work. It is also a logical extension of the queer deconstruction of the body as the underlying source of gender, where gender becomes sex. Gender difference, instead of sexual difference, becomes the destabilizing force that binary thinking needs to control. If we allow transgender experience into the realm of the human, the body is always real, even as it is also malleable and constructed. Sex is available to be a felt truth and a construct reliant on gender *at the same time*, because this is what human being is. This is complicity in action. Or, as Buckner (2016, p.53) puts it, the "stark divide" between transgender narratives of essential biological truth and queer theories of gender as socially constructed and reified through doing, "implodes in practical application."

Wiggins (2020, p. 69) suggests that the psy disciplines' manifestation of perversion is the fetished object of the DSM, the diagnostic manual whose evolution of definition for transgender being controls access to medical interventions and also grants cultural meaning to transgender being. *Pace* Freud, Wiggins argues,

> A perverse defense uses the fetish object to purchase certainty and control in the face of variability and lack. And although this object may allow for the fantasy of knowing, it does so at the expense of possibility and of a receptiveness to difference.

This is a turning back on the psychological establishment of the frame used to understand, assess and approach transgender people. Wiggins (2020) suggests that perversion can be used as a structure of thought, freed from Freud's Oedipal, biology-based and culturally specific meanings. By this argument, the clinical requirement of transgender distress is the perverse fetish at the heart of Western and psychological culture.

This is not to deny the burden borne by transgender communities, and especially by poor trans women of color: "That we live and die unliveable lives is not an academic abstraction but the brute reality of an often transphobic contemporary society" (O'Shea, 2020, p. 2). But it is to challenge the fact of transgender life as the source of the suffering, and to place it instead on transphobia. Such a move, taken to its full potential, would obviate the need for a diagnosis for transgender experience. If transgender humanity were accepted as such, without othering from a cisgender norm, the rigidity of binary gender and the connections to sex underneath, it would be broken once and for all. Sex could be gender without bodies being rendered irrelevant. A new culture would be possible. This is not an attempt to symbolically use the fact of transgender personhood to argue for a queering of the gender binary. It is an attempt to take seriously the lived realities of transgender people, to accept that embodied subjectivity is a right belonging to all humans regardless of the source, since embodied subjectivity is the complicit heart of our complicit being (and the key to therapy, as explored in Chap. 6). It is to argue that trans exclusion from the realm of the healthily human is a result of binary gender rules.

So what should cisgender clinicians do? The gender affirmative model (Hidalgo et al., 2013; Keo-Meier & Ehrensaft, 2018) has developed in response to the medicalization and pathologization of transgender people. It marked what Pyne (2014, p. 1) calls "a paradigm shift: from disorder to diversity, from treatment to affirmation, from pathology to pride, from cure to community." As Denny (2004, p. 34) says,

> There is a world of difference when both the therapist and the patient believe the patient to be mentally ill and in crisis, and when both the therapist and the client believe the client to be healthy and self-actualized and contemplating a life-altering decision [such as transition].

In addition, the purpose of therapy is no longer assumed to be to consider transition, or only one form of transition. The gender affirmative approach normalizes gender fluidity as an aspect of human diversity, and places any pathology on the culture's response to the trans person. It defines gender as being the result of a complex interweaving between biology and socialization, and one that has a culturally specific component as well (Hidalgo et al., 2013).

As Lev (2004, p. 4) puts it, "clinicians need to ask what it means to be a healthy, functioning gender-variant person within an immutable, dual-gendered world." It means, in part, owning the almost inevitable misattunement that will follow, as cisgender clinicians have to explore their own formation within symbolic systems that did not consider trans humanity as a norm, or at all. It means knowing that biology is not destiny and gender is culture, and that the person you are sitting with may have an embodied, unarguably physical experience, empirical and not discursive, which needs to be believed. We have to hold that gender is a construct, a highly invested, artificial projection onto, or use of, the difference that exists in kinds of bodies on the human spectrum. Certainly, the fiction that gender, and the sex on which it is supposedly based, can only be an either/or is not even scientifically true. And in the structures of the world, which enable human being, there are many transgender people who experience their gendered selves as unarguably embodied, sometimes "across" binary gender. It really does not matter why, unless we need to find reasons to underwrite transgender humanity instead of just accepting it.

A theory of complicity allows for all the both-ands at play here. Gender identity and gender experience are highly personal and also totally mediated, including through medical and psychological discourses that seek transgender causality in the body. Theories of core gender are located within scientific and clinical models that legitimate transgender personhood through biological arguments. Deconstructive theories want to free gender from biology, in the first place for the emancipation of people born with vaginas and usually also uteruses in a culture that has always wanted to control and delimit them accordingly.

Heterosexual Consent

The question of whether women can truly consent to sex with men within a patriarchal world order is not a new one in feminist theory (Brownmiller, 2007; MacKinnon, 1989; Rich, 1980). In this section, I want to revisit the question of how the binary positions made possible by heteronormative heterosexuality continue to structure subjectivities within, and shape the institution of, heterosexual intimacy. Thinking complicitously in this situation complicates binary notions of victimhood, while allowing us to continue to insist on structural oppression and the harm it causes.

Since we all breathe in the smog of socialization (Tatum, 1997), people gendered female are formed in specific ways, to greater or lesser degrees and by resistance as well as acceptance, by the rules connecting bodies, genders and sexualities. Active female desire, independent female agency and assertive female speech (Distiller, 2008; Distiller, 2011) remain problematic for this culture and not uncomplicated for feminized people to access (Faludi, 2006; Levy, 2006). This can be particularly acute in those moments where the rules of gender intersect with deeply individualized meanings and experiences in the realm of sexuality. If, as Mitchell (1982, p. 2) asserts in her introduction to Lacan's *Feminine Sexuality*, "a person is formed *through* their sexuality," then AFAB subjectivity cannot help but be fundamentally implicated in the misogyny of heteronormative heterosexuality.

We inhabit a rape culture (Brownmiller, 2007; Gavey, 2019; Gay, 2018; Gqola, 2015; Solnit, 2014), and all women and feminized people have to survive this. Rape culture says that girls and women exist in order to be heterosexual sexual objects, and that heterosexual men are entitled to act on their desire for these objects when and as they like. It is a norm of conduct (Young & Hegarty, 2019). Some AFAB and other females learn ways to find some profit in it, to get by or make the best of it. Some inevitably collude (see Faludi, 2006; Levy, 2006).

In *The tragedy of heterosexuality*, Ward (2020, p. 151) explores the implications for heterosexuality of the research findings, some of which are discussed below, of the fact that,

> [U]nwanted sex inside heterosexual relationships is so common and normalized that it is a core part of the scaffolding of rape culture; there's a thin line between unwanted sex (the kind that many women have with husbands and boyfriends all the time) and sexual assault.

Sexual violence has, as far as we know in this culture, always been a common experience of AFAB sexuality, and from there, all female sexuality. Ward (2020, p. 27) writes about what she calls the "misogyny paradox":

that men's heterosexual desire for women, the apparent fact that boys and men must love, need and want women, takes shape in a straight culture that also encourages them to hate, demean, hurt and control women (see Gilmore, 2001).

Consent was in the news a lot when, in 2017, the MeToo movement achieved international prominence after having been in circulation since 2006 in the work of African American feminist Tarana Burke (see Mendes et al., 2018; Rodino-Colocino, 2018). The recent public discussions about sexual harassment in the workplace, and sexual assault more broadly, mark an important cultural moment—yes, it happens! It happens a lot! No, women don't like it!—even as the predictable backlash kicked in almost as soon as the conversation began—not all men! But some women abuse their sexual power! (see Peleg-Koriat & Klar-Chalamish, 2020). The popular cultural conversation falters in its lack of focus on structural issues and its emphasis on individual intent. In a similar way to the good white/bad white binary that DiAngelo (2018) points out prevents any real discussion of the structural workings of white supremacy, the assumption is that only bad men commit only egregious acts of sexual harassment and violation. The focus is on individual intention rather than the culture that authorizes the treatment of females as objects for heteronormative male gratification. This greatly reduces the change that can come out of a mainstream conversation in American society about what it is like to navigate the public realm in a female or feminized body (see Rodino-Colocino, 2018). But the workings of rape culture do not stay only in the public realm, and its consequences are not only patently, violently egregious. In ways specific to their experiences and expectations of sexuality and sexual intimacy, heterosexual women often internalize the limiting of their agency that is part and parcel of their cultural objectification.

Ward's (2020) book dedication is, "For straight women. May you find a way to have your sexual needs met without suffering so much." She points out, by exploring straight culture, that the apparent benefits and promises of heterosexuality in a heteronormative world—that it is better to be straight, and it will make you happier than being a marginalized queer—is not at all true, especially once intersectionality is considered. "Perhaps most urgently," she (Ward, 2020, p. 3) writes,

> [A]n important indicator of the relatively negligible value of heterosexuality for many women is the fact that their sexual relationships with men have been maintained by force, both through cultural propaganda…. and more directly through sexual assault, incest, compulsory marriage, economic dependence, control of children, and domestic violence.

These forces are a direct result of the cultural objectification of women which relies on a model of gender as binary, complementary and hierarchical. This symbolic economy underlies systems, institutions and structures which oppress females and feminized people. Ward (2020) shows that in its current form, heterosexuality is misogynistic and coercive of straight women, that heterosexuality is, in fact, "a patriarchal institution" (Ward, 2020, p. 16; see Butler, 1999; Katz, 2007; Rich, 1980). Binary logic is how it works. Documenting in detail the ways that many straight men seem to disrespect and dislike women, and that many women settle for what straight men do, Ward (2020, p. 16) comments,

> Often propelled by the essentialist and heteronormative logic that male and female "energies" are incomplete without each other or that "opposites attract"…, straight culture seems to rely on blind acceptance that women and men do not need to hold the other gender in high esteem as much as they need to *need* each other and learn how to compromise and suppress their disappointment in the service of this need.

The consequences are material (women still do much more unpaid domestic labor and childcare work as well as holding down paid jobs; women still get paid less than men for the same work in America, with black women and women of color faring worse than white women, Faludi, 2006; Lockman, 2019); emotional (the sadness, disappointment, exhaustion, frustration, hopelessness and, for men, anger, insecurity and violence that come from thwarted entitlement, Ward, 2020) and, of course, sexual.

Thomas et al. (2017) track how straight women negotiate interpersonally and psychologically the "unwanted sex" that is an ordinary part of their sexual relationships and experiences. Pretending to consent becomes one way to manage sexual encounters. As this suggests, in twenty-first century consent studies, a binary view of consent is problematized: wanting is not the same as consenting; someone can be ambivalent and social scripts can conflict with bodily desires (Peterson & Muehlenhard, 2007). Straight women can and do consent without desire, disturbingly often (Thomas et al., 2017; Ward, 2020). "Unidimensional, dichotomous conceptualizations of wantedness" (Peterson & Muehlenhard, 2007, p. 72) do not capture the complexities of intrapersonal and interpersonal heterosexual dynamics (for an example of the difference that class makes, see Bay-Chen & Bruns, 2016).

This includes agreement about what constitutes sex and when sex is over, which is usually with male orgasm (see also Ward, 2020). Gattuso (2016) tells it like it is:

> Alas, friend of mine, you have had an orgasm and are falling asleep. I have not had an orgasm and am not falling asleep, which means I am awake, which means I am now going to lecture you… Who are you?… You are anyman, everyman,… You're a decent guy… No, you're not a bad guy. The sex wasn't particularly bad, either… It was normal sex. Normal, boring, vaguely dehumanizing hetero sex.
> Which is precisely the point: The normalcy…
> Here, supposedly, is what you consider sex: We make out, you play with my boobs… Penis goes in vagina, penis moves in and out of vagina… penis ejaculates.
> You roll off of me, get up, take the condom off/pee/do whatever it is people with penises do in the bathroom immediately after they've come (world's great, great mysteries), put your pants on, come back into bed, and fall asleep. Sex is now over. Sex is now over because you have decided it is over. You have decided sex is over because you are a man, and because this choreography that favors men with penises—man becomes erect, man penetrates woman, man ejaculates—is what we have been told sex is…
> [Y]ou need to know—that the way you conceptualize pleasure and its choreography is not the way sex inevitably is.

The "implicit rules of heterosex" (Thomas et al., 2017, p. 283) also include that her orgasm is a sign of his prowess, and must be clearly indicated via specific behaviors. This, suggest the authors, continues to encourage women to fake orgasm, despite "postfeminist" notions of "freedom and choice" which position women's sexual agency as equal to men's, as apolitical and as entirely personal (this is consistently understood to be a consequence of neoliberal formations, as will be seen in the next chapter; see Chowdhury & Gibson, 2019; Gill & Orgad, 2018; see also McClelland, 2010). However, "power imbalances are concealed in this repackaged construction," not least because, "female sexuality continues to be understood predominantly in relation to male sexuality and ultimately to heterosexual intercourse" (Thomas et al., 2017, p. 282).

Heterosexual women engage in a specific kind of sex work in the name of love; "In the context of gendered discourses of sexual performance that privilege male pleasure, faking orgasm can be seen as emotional labour" (Thomas et al., 2017, p. 283). At the same time, faking orgasm can also be read as a political act, to enable sex to end. Thus, "The simultaneous positioning of (fake) orgasms as emotional labour and as an agentic practice trouble the taken-for-granted understandings of female sexual desire, pleasure, and consent in heterosex" (Thomas et al., 2017, p. 283).

Consent as a construct has not been comprehensively or consistently defined (Peterson & Muehlenhard, 2007). And after conducting a literature review on the topic, Beres (2007, p. 94) comments, "Even within the literature on sexual consent there is no consensus on what it is, how it should be defined or how it is communicated." She asks how we know if sexual violence has occurred if there is no clear definition of consent. "I know it when I see it" (Beres, 2007, p. 94) does not prove to be a reliable metric, she says, and argues that the meaning of consent is produced by social discourses and cannot be assumed to have "common sense meanings … without critically reflecting on the cultural, historical, and social forces that produced those meanings" (Beres, 2007, p. 95). If we do operate on an assumption of shared meaning, she shows, gendered "miscommunications" happen, where a woman's behavior can be argued to be assumed to be consensual when she did not intend to be read as agreeing to sex. This, of course, is an example of objectification in action, justified by social assumptions as well as gendered entitlements to desire, sexual pleasure and other people's bodies. Accordingly, Beres (2007, p. 97) critiques studies that assume that consent is something given by women to men, which establishes a norm where,

[M]en are viewed as always desiring sex, and always in pursuit of sex. Through this discourse, men's consent is assumed, so to question it or develop an understanding of it would be superfluous. This places women in a position of responding to men's initiations, setting limits, and deciding if they want to participate in the sexual activity.

Thus, the active/passive gendered binary, based on a notion of sexuality as underwritten by biology, is still in play. Also evident is a false assertion of power given to women, as the ones who generate desire in men, who are less sexual than men and might not always be up for it, and who therefore control access to men's pleasure.

Beres (2007) also shows how different definitions enable consent to become "consent," when someone putatively consents because resistance seems futile, because they were drunk or for other reasons that complicate the definition of "unwanted sexual activity" under duress, which can still be read as consent under certain definitions (Beres, 2007, p. 96). Consent is not best conceptualized as something binary—where one person initiates activity and the other person then gives or refuses consent. Instead, in real time, initiation of activities can shift between partners. And of course, as Beres (2007) also acknowledges, the act of speaking, and especially speaking about something as personally and socially complicated as sex and sexual desire, is not freely done. It takes place within the context of gendered power dynamics. Even consensual sex can be "harmful" when "the consensual force is social, rather than interpersonal" (Beres, 2007, p. 99).

Social coercion, different from interpersonal coercion, cannot be dealt with legally, and is much harder to hold accountable for its harmful effects:

> Consent becomes something broader than just a "yes" to sex with a specific person, in a particular place, at a particular time. It becomes a negotiation of social expectations, a way of expressing a social identity, or of fitting in to a certain social world. It creates spaces for sex that are neither consensual nor criminal or violent, although they may be socially problematic. (Beres, 2007, p. 99)

Within a binary view of consent, there is no way to articulate the fact, or address the consequences, of what happens when women consent to sex they do not want. Thomas et al. (2017, p. 285) invented the phrase "gak sex" to try and indicate the variable experiences of violation and shifting desire that occurred under the rubric of unwanted sex that was apparently, in the heteronormative terms provided above, consented to. They eventually chose the moniker "problem sex" as more academically sound. They noticed that their study participants did not themselves have language to account for "problem sex," that is, sex that was undesired or bad or both, but which the women themselves did not identify as coerced, despite the use of hedging, disclaiming, minimizing, deflecting or qualifying when accounting for how they experienced their consenting (or not consenting). As a result, the authors tracked discursive attempts to make sense of the experiences in the face of a lack of language available to the women as they described their "unwanted sexual experiences," including experiences that the authors state can be "clearly identified" as rape, but were never described as such by the participants (Thomas et al., 2017, p. 287; see also Rutherford, 2018a). More often, the authors note, the young women in their study trailed off into silence after using negative formulations (it was bad sex, it was not good): "participants articulated what sex *was not*, however they struggled to find the language to communicate what it *was*" (Thomas et al., 2017, p. 292).

Young women (as is typical of the sampling used in much academic psychology research, the participants in Thomas et al.'s, 2017 study were undergraduates) are not always able to name sexual coercion when they experienced it. They have internalized the message that they are obliged to have sex, that consenting to sex they do not want or even, in some cases, that is consistently painful, is a normal part of heterosexual relationship management (the authors found that even while participants recounted experiences of sex without desire with other women, it was exclusively in the heterosexual encounters that they found the discursive complexities noted here). They are also not in possession of vocabulary for experiences where they felt unable to say no, or chose not to say no despite not wanting to have sex, but did not feel overtly coerced, at least not by their partners. They may well have been coerced by the rules of heteronormative binary gender in the twenty-first century, mediated as it is through thousands of years of pressure and more recently through neoliberal discourses of personal choice, postfeminism and entrepreneurial agency. It is worth noting, as we consider the WEIRD (white, educated, industrialized, rich, democratic) samples used in most of the consent studies, Young and Hegarty's (2019) calling out of the imbrication of sexual harassment as simultaneously the object of study and part of the culture of academic social psychology. They advocate, using literary metaphors, critical theory, biography and oral history, for a feminist methodology that challenges a "masculinist fantasy of unreflexive science" (Young & Hegarty, 2019, p. 453), a project of the psychological humanities if ever there was one.

Also disturbing is the implicit picture of hordes of young men who either do not know or do not care that their partners, often long-term partners, are not enjoying their sexual encounters. This implication of the research done with college women helps illuminate Ward's (2020) work on the current state of the "seduction industry," which exploits twenty-first century, feminist-derived discourses about respect and emotional intimacy to teach men how to manipulate women into the sex that these men continue to feel entitled to. Once again, these thoughts, feelings and behaviors can be understood as authorized by a binary view of gender, which makes men active subjects to the female objects they depend upon, and whose humanity, as Ward (2020) shows, they (therefore?) cannot tolerate.

Despite some cultural myths about "misunderstandings" between heterosexual partners resulting in experiences of sexual violation by women, the truth is much more complex (Beres et al., 2014), and has everything to do with binary gendered rules, the subjectivities they create and inform, and the gendered behaviors upheld by social norms and systems. The implications are relevant for all men, not just those who deliberately abuse their power. Most men need to learn to listen more honestly, to ask, to establish consent *and* desire, and also obviously to stop assuming that social, psychic and economic power entitles them to other people's bodies.

There are also implications for women, who may find it very, very difficult to speak up in the complex system of power, sexuality and gendered selfhood within which they are trying to make a living, to make a personhood. Let me be clear: Most cases of sexual violence are not ambiguous.

There are far too many "unacknowledged rape victims" (Peterson & Muehlenhard, 2007, p. 74) as a direct result of the lack of vocabulary about the interactions of social rules for gender performances, internalized gender rules, consent, wanting and the complexities and shifting nature of desire. This is not to mention the unacknowledged rape survivors who are simply disbelieved or ignored despite their clear statements of having been overpowered and violated with no ambivalence on their part or the part of their attackers. There is no onus on women to prevent their violation. In the grayer areas also, consent must be established, not assumed. And this is the point: there clearly are gray areas, because of the rules of binary gender and the kind of heteronormativity they inscribe.

So it is not the outright violence I am working so hard to establish ways to talk about here. It's the everyday, systemic, complicitous, intertwined violence that is also part and parcel of normative binary gender. Since the MeToo movement made male abuse of power in the realm of sexuality more visible and easier to insist on, since the profound cultural disbelief women and girls and other feminized people have always had to survive has been somewhat challenged by the public speaking (finally!) of sheer weight of numbers, many more female or feminized people are starting to talk about what happens to them at the hands of the men in their lives.

One of the first feminists to insist on the wide-scale scope of the problem of gender and structural violence, in the terms of modern psychology, was Herman, in *Trauma and Recovery* (Herman, 1997). She insisted that if war is the arena where men are traumatized, the family is the gendered site of female traumatization (and the traumatization of children). Her book encompasses many sites of what was then, even more than now, socially sanctioned gendered abuse, in part because her work helped bring attention to how systemic gender violence works. In constructing this argument, Herman was arguing for refusing the construction of certain spheres of life as "private" and therefore unavailable to interrogation for the relations and operations of power. She also writes in detail, and with evidence, about the gendered forms trauma can take. In so doing, she explains the behavior of women traditionally cast as hysterical, and, more recently, as borderline. She details trauma symptomology long unrecognized; she interrogates ways of understanding—or, more accurately, the ways Western societies have persisted in not understanding—women's experiences of violence and violation at the hands of those they trust.

Thus, anticipating consent studies, Herman (1997, p. 65) explained why, "Because of entrenched norms of male entitlement, many women are accustomed to accommodating their partners' desires and subordinating their own, even in consensual sex." And, not surprisingly,

> Many acts that women experience as terrorizing violations may not be regarded as such, even by those closest to them. Survivors are thus placed in the situation where they must choose between expressing their own point of view and remaining in connection with others. Under these circumstances, many women may have difficulty even naming their experience. (Herman, 1997, p. 67)

I want to make space to bring into focus the working of our inevitable complicities: not that victims are to blame, but that the rules of gender which make speaking up in intimate ways about our desires so damn difficult might be confounding of notions of female agency and of the value of female desire in heteronormative heterosexuality, and certainly in the rape culture that exists in tandem with it. Some women are not asked. Some women say no and are ignored. Some women do not say no but do not consent. Some women endure really, really bad sexual experiences, where they are used as objects, disregarded, where their desire is not honored or even expected. These are all part of rape culture, they are all damaging, and they are all unacceptable. They are not all sexual assault.

I know how easily this can be read as victim-blaming, as excusing men at best careless and at worst brutal, as missing entirely the point that not everyone has equal access to voice in systems of power. I hope the more subtle point emerges: We must find ways to resist that inhabit the complicit intersection of the personal and the systemic, that seek to clear the internal air of the social smog that teaches us we have to comply. This is in addition to, not instead of, naming criminal behavior, holding men accountable and putting the shame of violation where it belongs, on the violator.

We would be better off engaging in much more depth with rape culture as a structural formation within which binary heteronormative gender takes its shape. We would also be well-served by avoiding simplifying what are gray areas that arise in moments of intimacy because of the internalized injunctions of normative gender. Really, opening gender up beyond the binary will help everyone with this problem.

As we have seen, Thomas et al. (2017) identify that the young women in their study all fake pleasure and/or orgasm in order to end unwanted sexual encounters. They found that this strategy was used both to end unsatisfying sex and to end sex that was either unwanted or was painful. They recount an instance when the interviewer engages with this choice with one of the participants:

> [I]n another section of the interview with X, the interviewer prompted her to consider ending sex without faking orgasm:
> X: For me, like I said, the end result was just, let's get this over with and the fastest way I can get this over with is t- for him to think that I had an orgasm? So he'll have one? And we can be done. Um::
> I: Right. To play the devil's advocate for a second, a fast way- a faster way would be to say, yeah, no, let's:-
> X: Yea:::h hhh. I guess so…. I do- I don't know if I could just stop mid(hh)-w(hh)ay thro(hh)ugh, I re(hh)ally do(hh)n't.
> I: Yeah
> X: I think that would just be, almost too awkward? Like, at least if you can—if he can finish, then you can just get up and leave and kinda go do whatever you have to do, or: whatever, whereas… if ya did just sorta stop part way through and say, "you know what? This isn't working, and I'm do::ne?"
> I: Right
> X: I think that's gonna lead into a discussion that maybe necessarily I don't wanna ha::ve::? Or::. I don't know, I guess I take the easy way out? If that—pardon the pun, but, um:.
> I: ((laughing))
> X: It, uh. Yeah, to just sorta—to help him finish? Means that I could just walk away.
> As indicated by X's response, the interviewer's suggestion that she could end sex directly appears inconceivable. (Thomas et al., 2017, p. 294)

What is going on with heterosexuality when a discussion about mutual desire and pleasure is too much trouble? How is this young woman experiencing her embodiment, her intimate connections? Her selfhood? Her body becomes a tool she herself uses to maintain these gendered relations. The authors note the women's assumptions that "heterosex must and will end with male orgasm… In this way, women's ability to express the desire to end a sexual encounter outside of this prescribed 'ending' is effectively restrained both discursively as well as materially" (Thomas et al., 2017, p. 295).

Yes, this young woman is constrained, by a host of forces beyond her control, including a paucity of language for her to make different sense for herself of what is happening within and to her. Rutherford (2018b) offers a comprehensive critique of how the discourse of empowerment acts on young white women under neoliberalism to compel them to feel they can choose as individuals, while denying structural factors that may be constraining them or acting on their senses of self. And the young woman in Thomas et al.'s (2017) study is also exercising a choice, however limited. She has some agency, and she uses it complicitously. This is not a criticism. It is an acknowledgment of how we survive the systems that shape us within a culture where race, gender and other markers of difference from a mythical norm are used to keep us in our assigned places.

Here is an example of complicity in action:

> Faking orgasm can be regarded as a form of "embodied hedging" as it avoids the consequences that may come from a direct refusal to sex all the while allowing the woman to determine when the sexual encounter ends. Thus, we argue that feigning sexual pleasure is both problematic and helpful at the same time. (Thomas et al., 2017, p. 296)

The authors note that faking orgasm when there is a risk of violence is a necessary use of a normative heterosexual script, designed to mollify the man while protecting oneself from further harm. Therefore, "we are calling to puncture the established parameters of heterosex for a social reconceptualization that acknowledges, names and confronts the problems women spoke of in our interviews" (Thomas et al., 2017, p. 296). These problems cohere around the missing discourses of pleasure for the women in the study, and the apparent use of their sexual agency to make their male partners happy at the expense of their own physical and/or psychological wellbeing. The paucity of language for describing the nuances here is telling of the power dynamics at play in the system of binary gender, and the material realities they enable:

> When wanted and consensual yet disappointing/unsatisfying, sex is talked about in the same manner as experiences of unwanted and/or coercive sex and sexual assault, unwanted experiences may be at risk of being passed off as simply not pleasurable. Within dominant constructions of sexual assault, which dichotomize sex as either consensual and wanted or nonconsensual and unwanted (rape), all other experiences that do not meet either definition may be dismissed as "just (bad) sex". (Thomas et al., 2017, p. 296)

The authors conclude that the real solution is in moving beyond the "existing limiting and dichotomous conceptualizations of heterosex" (Thomas et al., 2017, 297). In other words: the binary.

Endorsing the terms of the consent studies addressed here, Ward (2020) details how one of the aspects of straight culture has always been men's sense of entitlement to women's bodies and to their emotional labor. She shows how binary-formulated heterosexuality repeatedly puts the onus on women to do the work of managing this dynamic. It also leaves men hurt and angry when it fails to deliver. Ward (2020, pp. 114–5) writes of,

> [T]he seemingly inextricable place of sexual coercion and gender injustice within straight culture… the violence and disappointments of straight culture… (the bad and coercive sex, the normalized inequalities of daily life, straight men's fragility and egomania, straight women's growing disillusionment with men's fragility and egomania, the failed marriages, the coparenting that is really solo parenting…)

One thing remains clear: The toxic rules of binary gender need to change. As much as social and political progress has been made for some women, cultural gender norms continue to structure psyches and relationships in damaging ways.

I have not spoken here about masculinities, but it is very much to the point that men are also limited and defined by, as much as they profit from, normative gender and the power relations it encodes. Beres (2007) points out that one example of a consequence of compulsory heterosexuality is to make a man who would like to be sexually involved only with other men, have sex with women. Ward (2020) shows how dependent heterosexual men are on acceptance from particular kinds of women, who carry the projections of their masculine self-worth.

Ward (2020, p. 155) looks forward to what she calls "deep heterosexuality," which is, essentially heterosexuality without heteronormativity. It is a way for people to relate intimately without their identities being structured by the complementarity of binary gender norms which, as Ward (2020) shows, means that what she calls straight culture begins with the paradox that men desire women they cannot like or respect as equals.

Transnational Lessons

The involvement of well-intentioned Western queers (as this formulation suggests, structurally in the position of well-intentioned whites discussed in Chap. 2) in matters of African sexual and gender rights can cause active harm (Epprecht, 2013; see also Hayes, 2001). For example, Epprecht (2013, p. 13) details the damage done by "homonationalism," which "means taking excessive pride in the achievements of gay rights activism in the West and showing chauvinistic regard for the Western model of outness." This overlooks that for some subjectivities, experiences of individual teleological development are not culturally appropriate or relevant. It also overlooks the complexities of social, cultural and legal strictures that many people outside of the West must navigate, as will be explored in more detail below. As a result, the use of Western LGBTQ processes and terminology for understanding African sexualities remains complicated, something "Africans and Africanists who do gender and sexuality research remain extremely reluctant to embrace… even when they make use of insights from the queer canon" (Epprecht, 2008, p. 14). At the same time, as Hawley (2001, p. 12) also acknowledges, "the 'universalizing' of gay terminology (condemned… as hegemonically Western) in fact *can* serve a local liberatory function." International human rights discourses and instruments rely on Western models of personhood and of Western legal norms, and can be helpful to some subjects in non-Western contexts even as they also interfere in local formations and overlook or inadvertently harm others. This, too, will be explored below. The construction, Western LGBTQ discourse helpful to Africa/Western LGBTQ discourse harmful to Africa, is an inaccurate binary. I hope to illustrate that on an entangled transnational level, colonial history has created its own forms of complicity, in this case in the realms of gender and sexuality. It is worth noting here, and this will be returned to below, that gender and sexuality are connected in many African places in a way they are no longer in Western LGBTQ+ discourse. This, too, creates difficulties in using Western terms to articulate some African experiences.

There is another way that Western frames are not helpful to the issue of sexuality justice in Africa. In 2016, I attended the annual conference of the American Association of Marriage and Family Therapists, the national umbrella body for my profession. One of the keynote speakers was talking about the psychological effects of homophobia on LGBTQ individuals, and to illustrate some of his points, he showed us a video he found on the internet of homophobia at work. In Nigeria. We saw a concerned white male American journalist interviewing abject black men, who spoke about their homosexual identification and the oppression they suffered accordingly. African conservatism, ignorance and dictatorial violence were set off against the West's enlightened, modern, accepting views. Because, you know, there is no homophobia in America, and Africa is by definition premodern. Epprecht (2013, p. 10) tracks some of the ways that unwitting [promotion of] stereotypes of "'Darkest Africa'—homophobic, violent, irrational… fundamentalist" only increases backlash against Western interference, as does the narratives of "those who would have us believe that nothing in Africa happens unless inspired by the West." When I challenged the speaker on his decision to pick a depiction of brutal African suppression of same sex love in order to illustrate the psychological effects of homophobia on gay-identified people, he replied that he had merely surfed the internet for illustrations of

4 Thought Bodies: Gender, Sex, Sexualities 143

homophobia to give at his talk, and that that the choice of Nigeria was random. Considering this was a plenary on the effects of culture on oppression, I found this an extraordinary response, and one that underscored an American tendency to forget that Africa is a complex collage of multiple cultures with different histories and dynamics, and a relation of power to the global system. Nigerian men articulating Western identities for American cameras as they fight for their lives is not a straightforward proposition, and certainly not an appropriate illustration of American-derived theories of the psychological consequences of homophobia for Western subjects.

Like many other Africans, although inflected differently by the country's ideological location on the continent due to South Africa's in-theory legal protections, same-sex loving South Africans and South African people who identify as genders other than the ones they were assigned at birth have to engage with the inheritances of colonialism as they live their nonnormative lives. As Desai (2001, p. 156) puts it,

> The question at this point… is not whether or not indigenous alternative sexual practices have existed or continue to exist in Africa, but rather, how one understands their historical emergence, the conditions of (im)possibility for identity formations based on these practices and in particular the relationship of these identities to racial and national identities.

The notion of "(im)possibilities for identity formation" in neocolonial, postapartheid South Africa sums it up nicely. People are expressing themselves and their sexual and gender identifications using, variously, exclusively or in combination, Western LGBTQ discourses and traditional and indigenous frames. They are using and changing what the West has brought. They are doing this in the face of African patriarchies that want to invoke versions of tradition to enforce heteronormativity, and that want to scapegoat African gender and sexual queers for the profit of national identification and politics. These constructs of authentic tradition, of modern nationhood and of heteronormativity are, of course, products of colonial history.

In order to untangle the complicities at work here, we have to see how people navigate developing personal understandings of the relationship between sex and gender, sometimes within versions of traditional culture as they are currently lived in neocolonial forms, instantiating the conditions and possibilities of late modernity, and dealing with postapartheid nationalism, which continues to be in ambivalent relation to the country's inclusive and protective Constitution (Epprecht, 2013; Munro, 2012; Sideris, 2005; Van Zyl, 2009). As Trengrove-Jones puts it in 2008, in response to yet another murder of women identified as lesbians, "To inhabit an 'alternative sexuality' in South Africa at the moment is to be a raw receptor for the clash of cultures currently underway" (p. 182).

So-called gay rights (so-called because the moniker "gay" is too narrow to accommodate all the identities and practices-without-Western-identities that are affected by this issue) is the place where postapartheid South Africa's newness and nondiscrimination commitments symbolically emerge, and it is a high-profile place where a conversation about decolonialism can be abused. It is one place where discourses of authenticity and purity become so dangerous and invested. Munro (2012, p. xiii) comments, "Homosexuality in Africa is bound up with a contradictory modernity that has been produced both within and against imperialism, and this is what makes the question of gay rights in Africa so politically fraught." As a local informant reported in a recent *Economist* article on the struggle for women's land rights in the context of postapartheid compromises with the traditional authorities used by both colonial and apartheid regimes, "If you want to resist change, it makes sense to pretend it undermines your culture" ("Trust deficit", 2020, p. 74).

These issues arose with the passage of the 2006 Civil Union Act in South Africa, which granted marriage rights to those who were intelligible to the Westernized legal system. Those same-sex-loving South Africans, often not in the metropolitan areas or not empowered to speak up in opposition to community pressure, who were to some extent or another queer-acting or queer-identified, were even more marginalized: The ship of gay rights had sailed, and they were not on board. Additionally, this situation crystallized a binary where modernity and civil protections are set up in opposition to more traditional African or Islamic cultural formations, which are then cast as by definition benighted (see Bilchitz & Judge, 2008; Bonthuys, 2008). The debates generated by this Act, about gay rights and about the new legal protections afforded women and sexual minorities in the country, were complex affairs of assertions of cultural authenticity, misogyny and homophobia, and neocolonial decolonial articulations (Reid, 2008).

Discourses that come from the West, even though—or because—they provide scope for changes to the current cultural and political systems to better accommodate some Africans whose sexuality appears "modern" (i.e., not "traditional"), also are available, by virtue of their origins, as ammunition for certain African leaders who are looking for smokescreens and decoys. Some invoke a neocolonial version of tribal law, which has passed through Christianity and also through Western political corruption to emerge abusively heteronormative and patriarchal, all in the name of an imagined authentically precolonial Africanness. Zimbabwe's Robert Mugabe, Uganda's Yoweri Museveni, Gambia's Yahya Jammeh, Nigeria's Goodluck Jonathan, to name some, have at various points over the past decade contended that homosexuality is unAfrican, a Western import, a colonial disease. Contradictorily, they sometimes invoke that other Western import, Christianity, to deny the authentic Africanness of homosexual desire. Since the identity position "homosexual" was invented in the West, to some extent they are correct. Nevertheless, those same-sex-identified Africans who identify as LGBQ or T in Western terms are surely no less African for doing so. But even without these terms, same-sex sexuality has always been part of African cultures.

Same-sex-loving Africans have always existed, and in fact, same-sex-oriented sexuality was woven into the fabric of precolonial African societies across the continent (Epprecht, 2004; Epprecht, 2008). Before colonialism, there were ways for same-sex-loving Africans to live within their societies undisturbed. In part, this was because their practices were not necessarily an identification and did not threaten the social structure.

So, for example, in Southern Africa alone, there are several social forms that facilitated same-sex intimacy in terms that utilize, and exist alongside, heteronormativity. These include the relationships among adolescent girls in Basotho, Venda and Zulu societies studied in the 1970s sometimes as "mummy-baby" friendships which involved both kinship and sexual relations (Wieringa, 2005). These relationships were seen as healthy forms of emotional connection as well as good preparation for heterosexual marriage. Part of the acceptance of same-sex female erotic interaction was, and remains, the idea that nonpenetrative sexual activity is not sex.

So-called mine marriages were a complex institution between men emerging from colonial and apartheid economic practices. Men would contract relationships with each other on highly gendered terms. The authentically homosexual emotional and sexual components of these relationships have been articulated, in opposition to the frame of purely situational homosexuality (By Zachie Achmat, Hugh McLean and Linda Ngcobo, and William Spurlin, e.g.; see Spurlin, 2010).

In addition, traditionally, marriage between women was not an uncommon practice in Southern Africa and elsewhere on the continent, before the missionaries arrived. A woman could take the structural position of a man, either in her own right or in the name of a deceased male relative. What was important was that the female husband could afford to pay for her wife, and that they used a man to help them have children, thus fulfilling their commitment as a couple to the social order (Morgan & Wieringa, 2005).

None of this is queer in the Western sense—none of it seeks to defy categories or to demand new cultural spaces for people to self-define. People engaged in these activities mostly did not intend to challenge the dominant terms or power structures. They did not, and do not, require a discourse of coming out, or self-discovery, or an oppositional placement to one's family or community. At the same time, these practices allowed people to have the space to live alternate sexual lives, in practice if not in identification.

And this history feeds into African queernesses that have emerged post colonialism and the neoliberal order it birthed, which gives some Africans access to Western modes. In South Africa today, an increasingly vocal constituency are the lesbian sangomas, whose sexual decisions are made through the proxies of the male ancestors they represent. As powerful spiritual leaders, they have a place within African traditions from which to assert their own legitimacy. Nkunzi Nkabinde was perhaps the most well-known South African lesbian sangoma, who at the time of her/his death in 2018 appeared to be exploring a gender transition; they published an autobiography (Nkabinde, 2009), as well as engaged in documentary work with others in their community.

Their writing shows that same-sex-loving female sangomas do not all identify, as Nkabinde did, at least for a time, as lesbian. Some speak a language that sounds to Western ears transgender, some hold a dual and unconflicted identity as what we might call bisexual and some identify as female men (see also Letsike, 2011; Morgan & Wieringa, 2005). This is not to suggest that the process is easy. Many of them are survivors of sexual violence and discrimination prior to and during their sangoma training processes, and some continue to be secretively sexually involved with their wives because of the stigma associated with LGBT identities in many communities. The violence they face is both on account of gender and of sexuality, as sexual violence rates are hideously high in South Africa, with same-sex-loving women being a specific targeted group (Gqola, 2015; Muholi, 2011).

Epprecht (2008) has demonstrated the ways in which traditional African social structures were disturbed by colonial rulers, missionaries and early anthropologists, who brought their Western disdain of same-sex practices to the African colonies at around the time that homosexual practices were crystallizing into homosexual identities in European discourses. As was typical of colonial processes of binary meaning-making, Western observers constructed a sense of their own superiority and rightness by relying on the putative barbarism of the cultures they encountered, and could thus be called upon to civilize. Among other things, this dynamic set up an imperative to silence on the part of Africans who were adjusting to the new order, which helped to create what Epprecht (2008, pp. 34–64) has succinctly designated an "Ethnography of African Straightness."

In addition, Western colonizers brought with them to Africa their construction of African sexuality as unbridled (Epprecht, 2008). This racist discourse relied also on a vicious misogyny, legitimized by Enlightenment science, as the case of Sara Baartman has made so clear (Crais & Scully, 2009). In life and death, Baartman's black female body was made to stand for all that was denied in nineteenth century Europe's picture of itself: exotic, hypersexual, available for consumption (see Perry, 2018). And if Africans were hypersexual, it was because they were hyper heterosexual. This Western imperative—that blackness carry the West's stigma about sexuality—intersected with another Western discourse of Otherness, to enable homosexuality to be "given" to the Orient, as its particular form of effeminized, luxurious inferiority. Africanness was by definition heterosexual, according to the West (Epprecht, 2008).

So, if homosexuality as a modern identity exists in Africa because of colonial history, so does homophobia (see Epprecht, 2004). And ironically, tragically, when those African patriarchs make use of homophobia to encode a version of the postcolonial African nation designed to funnel power to themselves, by constructing a logic for who can be in and who can be out, who can be controlled according to the old rules and who must be purged, they are profiting from a discourse that is as fundamentally racist as it is heteronormative. As we have seen, the connection between racism and heteronormative homophobia has its own history in America, too (Carter, 2007; Ward, 2020).

In contemporary Western discourse, there is a difference between transgender people and sexual queers: gay, lesbian, bisexual, asexual, same-sex loving and other people whose sexuality is nonheteronormative. Transgender identity is about gender, not sexuality. But trans people and queer people are often considered together, since all of those categories in some way disrupt the constitutive relationships between binary gender, heteronormativity, cisnormativity and the assumptions about bodies and identities they enable as complementary. All this should be familiar by now. In a South African context, the relationship between genders and sexualities is harder to articulate through a Western frame. Colonization brought political and social oppression, Christianity and bourgeois values. It set up a version of tradition which has affected postcolonial national identity politics. These histories intersect with pre-existing local expressions and enactments of alternative sexualities and gender identities. The result, in the context of decolonial imperatives to reject Western epistemologies and allow for the emergence of local ones, is, in this arena, a set of "contradictory tensions that seem to suffuse issues of gender in relation to sexuality" in Africa (Camminga, 2019, p. 18).

In South Africa, binary gender positions are sometimes invoked in service of queerness, so that same-sex relationships are expressed through male and female roles and identities, in ways which confound Western identifications, allowing, for example, straight men to be in relationships with men who identify as taking the female position because of their sexuality, but who are not trans (Reid, 2005). Some of these ladies might identify as trans, given the option, but many may not need these kinds of categories to be who they are within the terms available to them. Camminga (2019) explores the case of two people from Malawi who, from their own identifications, seem to be what Western classifications would call a heterosexual man and a transgender woman, but who were received as gay men for the purposes of drawing attention to their persecution and for the purposes of acquiring asylum, in the case of the woman (see also Epprecht, 2013). This is in part because of the lack of official recognition of Western-type transgender identities to date in the South African asylum application process.

Camminga (2019) traces how transgender as an identity travelled in specific ways to and in southern Africa. They trace the advent of what they, following Stryker (2008), call transgender phenomena in South Africa as a specific site, given its history and given its postapartheid Constitution, which uniquely in Africa protects the rights of gender and sexual minorities, as well as refugees to the country. Part of their project explores the relationship between classifications of sex and gender, imported from the West, and state mechanisms which enable national belonging; as well as the journeys toward an imagined home that are implicit in many conceptualizations of transgender, as well as in being a refugee.

Camminga's project demonstrates the ongoing conflation of transgender presentations with homosexuality, as well as the complexities of assigning a Western-developed discourse and/or the identities developed therein, to other cultural contexts, particularly given colonial histories. They conclude that because of its postapartheid legal instruments, as well as the way that transgender as a category and an identity evolved in South Africa in complex relation to both local LGB and international discourses, "South Africa represents... a space which suggests that one's orientation in terms of desire and the shape of one's body might be supported without necessarily having to use a specific discourse" (Camminga, 2019, p. 111). Transgender as a label and an identity continues to be emergent in South Africa and may always be in both dialogue and dispute with Western categorization.

And things continue to change. In 2020, a year after the publication of Camminga's book, the Professional Association for Transgender Health South Africa (PATHSA) was formed, "an interdisciplinary health professional organization working to promote the health, wellbeing and self-actualization of trans and gender diverse people" (pathsa.org.za). PATHSA presented itself to the international association of multidisciplinary transgender health healthcare workers, WPATH, in November 2020 at the online WPATH conference. It is the first South African organization of its kind, and joins Gender DynamiX, formed in 2005 (genderdynamix.org.za), as one of the very few specifically gender-focused groups in the country. Anecdotally, one of the first struggles faced by this organization is engaging with homophobic discourses authorized by a version of Christianity and the understanding it brings to the way transgender people are seen.

The Anglican Church has around 77 million members. Over 30 million of these are African (Hoad, 2007). This is, of course, thanks to colonialism. But if millions of Africans are now devout Christians of whatever denomination, including versions that blend Western modes with African ones, then Christianity surely is as African as honoring the ancestors. As Hoad (2007) details, at the third Lambeth Conference, held in 1888 when Europe was still dominating Africa in colonial terms, the bishops passed two resolutions on polygyny. The one, which applied to men, decreed that even a polygynist who converted to Christianity could not be baptized until he accepted monogamy. The other decreed that his wives could be baptized "under conditions to be decided on locally" (Hoad, 2007, p. 50). Hoad argues that if, in 1888, "[cis]gender carried the weight of cultural difference" in the Anglican Church's attempts to engage with its African constituents, then a century later, "homosexuality hands this task over to sexuality" (Hoad, 2007, p. 52). This is seen in his exploration of the complexities of Western class and sexual norms at work in twentieth-century Africa, at the World Conference of Anglican Bishops that took place in Lambeth in 1998.

In 1888, the bishops in Africa were all British missionaries. In 1998, the by-now international body of bishops had a more tolerant attitude to polygyny, and an unaccepting view of homosexual Africans. Noncelibate homosexual clergy and the officiating of same-sex unions, issues in part forced by the emergence of gay rights as a constitutional principle in postapartheid South Africa, were issues on the Lambeth agenda for the first time. The African bishops, with the exception of some from South Africa, unanimously argued that homosexuality was unchristian and unAfrican, and threatened to break ties with their European colleagues over the matter. Hoad (2007, p. 56) comments:

> Why do African bishops pledge allegiance to a literal interpretation of Scripture with the attendant… wholesale disavowal of the possibility of indigenous same-sex practices?

He goes on to suggest that attacks on homosexuality, because it is seen to be specifically Western, is one way to repudiate the construction and imbrication of African barbarity and sexual incontinence. African bishops can assert their respectability in the face of centuries of racist stereotyping of Africans, and in the terms given them by the racist West, by being the best homophobes possible. The ironies are painful, and they multiply when we remember that the tolerance of homosexuality is often constructed by developed nations as a sign of advanced civilized values, in opposition to more "traditional"—read developmentally impaired or teleologically backward—cultures.

The realm of sexuality becomes a place where the moral high ground can intersect with deep historical wounding. "Homosexuality" comes to stand for a nexus of meanings that encode contested definitions of civility. It also comes to be a frame through which to understand nonnormative genders, including transgender identification. Not surprisingly, sexual morality affects everyone's gender roles, and the version of the authentically African nation which seeks to purge its homosexuals tends to rely equally upon a version of heterosexual domesticity which needs women to stay in their proper domestic place, often revered as symbols of Mother Africa, the nurturer, the home-maker for the children. This version of bourgeois respectability is precisely the one that was used against tribalized Africans when the civilizing mission began (Epprecht, 2008). It is now being used by some Africans against African women and queers. The postcolonial African nation is, (im)possibly, formed by modernity and authorized by an invested notion of tradition. The nexus of this contradiction is the figure of the African homosexual, sometimes also transgender, and his or her repressed shadow is the "traditional" same-sex-loving African.

Violent homophobia continues to be an urgent problem in South Africa. Combined with misogyny and HIV, its expressions can be lethal. Photographer and activist Zanele Muholi has created an incredible archive which speaks to the emergence of indigenously queer communities and all they continue to endure, despite one of the most progressive Constitutions in the world. Muholi's own identity journey marks a fluidity in queer/African/nonbinary process, always centered in their race, place and nationality (Muholi, 2011; Muholi, 2018). If this is not a lesson in what binary identifications leave out, I don't know what is.

We need to problematize the ease with which African homophobia is available to underwrite the work of a Western LGBTQ politics and political identity. There is no modern/traditional binary in practice. What we are left with is the impossibility of a neat binary of us and them, of right and wrong, of good and bad. I do not mean by this to deny the effects of oppression, to suggest that the workings of power on the bodies of queers, of women, of Black people, is in any way ambiguous or excusable. Instead, I want to surface the complexities of doing something about it—the necessity of holding our locations in time and place, and of owning the messy and complicit histories that have made us all, in relation to each other.

Works Cited

Atienza-Macías, E. (2020). Some reflections on transsexuality in the New International Classification of Diseases (ICD 11): A product of the World Health Organization (WHO). *Sexuality & Culture, 24*, 2230–2235.

Aughterson, K. (Ed.). (1998). *The English renaissance: An anthology of sources and documents*. Routledge.

Azul, D. (2018). Trans-speaking voice-lessness: A fictocritical essay. *Graduate Journal of Social Science, 14*(2), 107–134.

Bay-Chen, L. Y., & Bruns, A. E. (2016). Yes, but: Young women's views of unwanted sex at the intersection of gender and class. *Psychology of Women Quarterly, 40*(4), 504–517.

Beecher, D. (2005). Concerning sex changes: The cultural significance of a renaissance medical polemic. *Sixteenth Century Journal, 36(4)*, 991–1016.

Benjamin, J. (1988). *The bonds of love: Psychoanalysis, feminism and the problem of domination*. Random House.

Beres, M. A. (2007). "Spontaneous" sexual consent: An analysis of sexual consent literature. *Feminism & Psychology, 17(1)*, 93–108.

Beres, M. A., Senn, C. Y., & McCaw, J. (2014). Navigating ambivalence: How heterosexual young adults make sense of desire differences. *Journal of Sex Research, 51(7)*, 765–776.

Berry, P. (1989). *Of chastity and power: Elizabethan literature and the unmarried queen*. Routledge.

Bettcher, T. M. (2014). Trapped in the wrong theory: Rethinking trans oppression and resistance. *Signs: Journal of Women in Culture and Society, 39(2)*, 383–406.

Bhabha, H. (1994). *The location of culture*. Routledge.

Bilchitz, D., & Judge, M. (2008). The Civil Union Act: Messy compromise or giant leap forward? In M. Judge, A. Manion, & S. de Waal (Eds.), *To have & to hold: The making of same-sex marriage in South Africa* (pp. 149–163). Fanele.

Boose, L. E. (1991). Scolding brides and bridling scolds: Taming the woman's unruly member. *Shakespeare Quarterly, 42*, 179–213.

Bonthuys, E. (2008). The Civil Union Act: more of the same. In M. Judge, A. Manions & S. de Waal (Eds.), *To have & to hold: the making of same-sex marriage in South Africa* (pp. 171–179). Cape Town: Fanele.

Bornstein, K. (1995). *Gender outlaw: On men, women, and the rest of us*. Vintage.

brown, a.m. (2020). *We will not cancel us: and other dreams of transformative justice*. AK Press.

Brownmiller, S. (2007). Against our will: Men, women and rape. In E. Freedman (Ed.), *The essential feminist reader* (pp. 311–317). Modern.

Bryant, K. (2006). Making gender identity disorder of childhood: Historical lessons for contemporary debates. *Sexuality Research and Social Policy, 3(3)*, 23–39.

Buckner, R. (2016). Whose bodies count? How experience working with transgender patients shapes conceptualizations of transgender identity. *Critical Theory and Social Justice, 6*, 52–92.

Butler, J. (1993). *Bodies that matter: On the discursive limits of "sex"*. Routledge.

Butler, J. (1999). *Gender trouble: Feminism and the subversion of identity*. Routledge.

Butler, J. (2004). *Undoing gender*. Routledge.

Califa, P. (1997). *Sex changes: The politics of transgenderism*. Cleis.
Camminga, B. (2019). *Transgender refugees and the imagined South Africa: Bodies over borders and borders over bodies*. Palgrave Macmillan.
Carter, J. (2007). *The heart of whiteness: Normal sexuality and race in America*. Duke University Press.
Chowdhury, N., & Gibson, K. (2019). This is (still) a man's world: Young professional women's identity struggles in gendered workplaces. *Feminism & Psychology, 29*(4), 475–493.
Coole, D. (1988). *Women in political theory: From ancient misogyny to contemporary feminism*. Lynne Reinner.
Cooper, B. (2018). *Eloquent rage: A black feminist discovers her superpower*. Picador.
Crais, C., & Scully, P. (2009). *Sara Baartman and the Hottentot Venus: A ghost story and a biography*. Princeton University Press.
Cruz, A. (2016). *The color of kink: Black women, BDSM, and pornography*. New York University Press.
De Bloch, A., & Adriaens, P. R. (2013). Pathologizing sexual deviance: A history. *Journal of Sex Research, 50*(3–4), 276–298.
De Lauretis, T. (1987). *Technologies of gender: Essays on theory, film, and fiction*. Indiana University Press.
Dean, T., & Lane, C. (Eds.). (2001). *Homosexuality & psychoanalysis*. University of Chicago Press.
Denny, D. (2004). Changing models of transsexualism. *Journal of Gay and Lesbian Psychotherapy, 8*(1–2), 25–40.
Desai, G. (2001). Out in Africa. In J. C. Hawley (Ed.), *Post-colonial, queer: Theoretical intersections* (pp. 139–164). SUNY Press.
DiAngelo, R. (2018). *White fragility: Why it's so hard for white people to talk about racism*. Beacon.
Distiller, N. (2008). *Desire and gender in the sonnet tradition*. Palgrave Macmillan.
Distiller, N. (2011). *Fixing gender: Lesbian mothers and the Oedipus Complex*. Fairleigh Dickinson University Press.
Distiller, N. (2012). *Shakespeare and the coconuts*. Wits University Press.
Doan, P. L. (2010). The tyranny of gendered spaces – Reflections from beyond the gender dichotomy. *Gender, Place and Culture, 17*(5), 635–654.
Dobbs, D. (1996). Family matters: Aristotle's appreciation of women and the plural structure of society. *American Political Science Review, 90*(1), 74–89.
Drescher, J. (2015a). Out of the DSM: Depathologizing homosexuality. *Behavioral Sciences, 5*(4), 565–575.
Drescher, J. (2015b). Queer diagnoses revisited: The past and future of homosexuality and gender diagnoses in DSM and ICD. *International Review of Psychiatry, 27*(5), 386–395.

Drummond, J. D., & Brotman, S. (2014). Intersecting and embodied identities: A Queer woman's experience of disability and sexuality. *Sexuality and Disability, 32,* 533–549.

Epprecht, M. (2004). *Hungochani: The history of a dissident sexuality in southern Africa.* McGill-Queen's University Press.

Epprecht, M. (2008). *Heterosexual Africa? The history of an idea from the age of exploration to the age of AIDS.* Ohio University Press.

Epprecht, M. (2013). *Sexuality and social justice in Africa: Rethinking homophobia and forging resistance.* Zed.

Erickson-Schroth, L. (2013). Update on the biology of transgender identity. *Journal of Gay & Lesbian Mental Health, 17,* 150–174.

Ettner, R., Monstrey, S., & Evan Eyler, A. (Eds). (2007). *Principles of transgender medicine and surgery.* New York: Haworth Press.

Faludi, S. (2006). *Backlash: The undeclared war on American women.* Broadway.

Fausto-Sterling, A. (1992). *Myths of gender: biological theories about women and men* (2nd ed.). Basic.

Fausto-Sterling, A. (1993). The five sexes: Why male and female are not enough. *The Sciences, 33*(2), 20–25.

Fausto-Sterling, A. (2000). *Sexing the body.* Basic.

Feinberg, L. (1993). *Stone butch blues.* Firebrand.

Fine, C. (2014). *Delusions of gender: How our minds, society, and neurosexism create difference.* Norton.

Fisher, J. A. (Ed.). (2011). *Gender and the science of difference.* Rutgers University Press.

Freud, S. (1973 [1905]). Three essays on the theory of sexuality. In S. Freud, ed., *The standard edition of the complete psychological works of Sigmund Freud, Vol. 7: A case history of hysteria, three essays on sexuality and other works* (pp. 125–245). Trans. and ed. James Strachey, in collaboration with Anna Freud, assisted by Alix Strachey and Alan Tyson. London: Hogarth Press & The Institute of Psycho-Analysis.

Garber, M. (2005). The return to biology. In I. Morland & A. Willox (Eds.), *Queer theory* (pp. 54–69). Palgrave.

Gattuso, R. (2016). What I would have said to you last night had you not cum and then fallen asleep. *Feministing,* August 4. Retrieved December 22, 2020, from http://feministing.com/2016/01/19/what-i-would-have-said-to-you-last-night-had-you-not-cum-and-then-fallen-asleep/

Gavey, N. (2019). *Just sex? The cultural scaffolding of rape culture* (2nd ed.). Routledge.

Gay, R. (Ed.). (2018). *Not that bad: Dispatches from rape culture*. HarperCollins.

Gill, R., & Orgad, S. S. (2018). The amazing bounce-backable woman: Resilience and the psychological turn in neoliberalism. *Sociological Research Online*. https://doi.org/10.1177/1360780418769673

Gilmore, D. D. (2001). *Misogyny: The male malady*. University of Pennsylvania Press.

Gqola, P. (2015). *Rape: A South African nightmare*. Jacana.

Grant, J. M., Mottet, L. A., Tanis, J., Harrison, J., Herman, J. L., & Keisling, M. (2011). *Injustice at every turn: A report of the national transgender discrimination survey report*. National Center for Transgender Equality and National Gay and Lesbian Taskforce. Retrieved May 22, 2018, from https://www.ncgs.org/research/database/injustice-at-every-turn-a-report-of-the-national-transgender-discrimination-survey/

Haraway, D. (1989). *Primate visions: Gender, race and nature in the world of modern science*. Routledge.

Harris, A. (2009). *Gender as soft assembly*. Routledge.

Hawley, J. C. (2001). Introduction. In J. C. Hawley (Ed.), *Post-colonial, queer: Theoretical intersections* (pp. 1–18). SUNY Press.

Hayes, J. (2001). Queer resistance to (neo-)colonialism in Algeria. In J. C. Hawley (Ed.), *Post-colonial, queer: Theoretical intersections* (pp. 79–98). SUNY Press.

Herman, J. (1997). *Trauma and recovery: The aftermath of violence – From domestic abuse to political terror*. Basic.

Hidalgo, M., Ehrensaft, D., Tishelman, A. C., Clark, L. F., Garofalo, R., Rosenthal, S. M., Spack, N. P., & Olson, J. (2013). The gender affirmative model: What we know and what we aim to learn. *Human Development, 56*, 285–290.

Hoad, N. (2007). *African intimacies: Race, homosexuality, and globalization*. University of Minnesota Press.

Jones, A. R. (1986). Surprising fame: Renaissance gender ideologies and women's lyric. In N. K. Miller (Ed.), *The poetics of gender* (pp. 74–95). Columbia University Press.

Katz, J. N. (2007). *The invention of heterosexuality*. University of Chicago Press.

Keo-Meier, C., & Ehrensaft, D. (Eds.). (2018). *The gender affirmative model: An interdisciplinary approach to supporting transgender and gender expansive children*. American Psychological Association.

Langer, S. J. (2019). *Theorizing transgender identity for clinical practice: A new model for understanding gender*. Jessica Kingsley.

Laqueur, T. (1992). *Making sex: Body and gender from the Greeks to Freud*. Harvard University Press.

Letsike, M. S. (2011). The "Steve" in me has a right. In A. Diesel (Ed.), *Reclaiming the L-word: Sappho's daughters out in Africa* (pp. 145–160). Modjaji.

Lev, A. (2004). *Transgender emergence*. Haworth.

Lev, A. I. (2006). Disordering gender identity: Gender Identity Disorder in the DSM-IV-TR. *Journal of Psychology and Human Sexuality, 17(3–4)*, 35–69.

Levine, L. (1994). *Men in women's clothing: Anti-theatricality and effeminization 1579–1642*. Cambridge University Press.

Levitt, H. M., & Ippolito, H. R. (2014). Being transgender: The experience of transgender identity development. *Journal of Homosexuality, 61*, 1727–1758.

Levy, A. (2006). *Female chauvinist pigs: Women and the rise of raunch culture*. Free Press.

Lockman, D. (2019). *All the rage: Mothers, fathers, and the myth of equal partnership*. Harper.

MacKinnon, C. A. (1989). *Toward a feminist theory of the state*. Harvard University Press.

Markman, E. R. (2011). Gender Identity Disorder, the gender binary, and transgender oppression: Implications for ethical social work. *Smith College Studies in Social Work, 81(4)*, 314–327.

Marotti, A. (1982). "Love is not love": Elizabethan sonnet sequences and the social order. *ELH, 49*, 396–428.

McClelland, S. (2010). Intimate justice: A critical analysis of sexual satisfaction. *Social and Personality Psychology Compass, 4(9)*, 663–680.

McKenzie, S. (2010). Genders and sexualities in individuation: Theoretical and clinical explorations. *Journal of Analytical Psychology, 55*, 91–111.

Mendes, K., Ringrose, J., & Keller, J. (2018). #MeToo and the promise and pitfalls of challenging rape culture through digital feminist activism. *European Journal of Women's Studies, 25(2)*, 236–246.

Mitchell, J. (1982). Introduction I. In J. Mitchell & J. Rose (Eds.), *Feminine Sexuality: Jacques Lacan and the école freudienne* (pp. 1–26). Norton.

Morgan, R., & Wieringa, S. (Eds.). (2005). *Tommy boys, lesbian men and ancestral wives: Female same-sex practices in Africa*. Jacana.

Muholi, Z. (2011). Thinking through lesbian rape. In A. Diesel (Ed.), *Reclaiming the L-word: Sappho's daughters out in Africa* (pp. 187–199). Modjaji.

Muholi, Z. (2018). *Somnyama Ngomyama: Hail the dark lioness*. Aperture.

Munro, B. M. (2012). *South Africa and the dream of love to come: Queer sexuality and the struggle for freedom*. University of Minnesota Press.

Namaste, V. K. (2000). *Invisible lives: The erasure of transsexual and transgendered people*. University of Chicago Press.

Nkabinde, N. (2009). *Black bull, ancestors and me: My life as a lesbian sangoma*. Fanele.

O'Shea, S. C. (2020). 'I, Robot?' Or how transgender subjects are dehumanized. *Culture and Organization, 1(26)*, 1–13.

Orgel, S. (1996). *Impersonations: The performance of gender in Shakespeare's England*. Cambridge University Press.

Peleg-Koriat, I., & Klar-Chalamish, C. (2020). The #MeToo movement and restorative justice: Exploring the views of the public. *Contemporary Justice Review, 23(3)*, 239–260.

Perry, I. (2018). *Vexy thing: On gender and liberation*. Duke University Press.

Peterson, Z. D., & Muehlenhard, C. L. (2007). Conceptualizing the "wantedness" of women's consensual and nonconsensual sexual experiences: Implications for how women label their experiences With rape. *Journal of Sex Research, 44(1)*, 72–88.

Prosser, J. (1998). *Second skins: The body narratives of transsexuality*. Columbia University Press.

Pyne, J. (2014). Gender independent kids: A paradigm shift in approaches to gender non-conforming children. *Canadian Journal of Human Sexuality, 23(1)*, 1–8.

Pyne, J. (2016). Queer and trans collisions in the classroom: A call to throw open theoretical doors in social work education. In S. Hillock & N. J. Mule (Eds.), *Queering social work education* (pp. 54–72). University of Washington Press.

Raymond, J. (1979). *The transsexual empire: The making of the she-male*. Beacon.

Reid, G. (2005). "A man is a man completely and a wife is a wife completely": Gender classification and performance amongst "ladies" and "gents" in Ermelo, Mpumalanga. In G. Reid & L. Walker (Eds.), *Men behaving differently: South African men since 1994* (pp. 205–227). Double Storey.

Reid, G. (2008). "This thing" and "that idea": Traditional responses to homosexuality and same-sex marriage. In M. Judge, A. Manion, & S. de Waal (Eds.), *To have & to hold: The making of same-sex marriage in South Africa* (pp. 73–86). Fanele.

Rich, A. (1980). Compulsory heterosexuality and the lesbian existence. *Signs, 5(4)*, 631–660.

Rippon, G. (2019). *The Gendered Brain: The new neuroscience that shatters the myth of the female brain*. Penguin.

Rodino-Colocino, M. (2018). Me too, #MeToo: countering cruelty with empathy. *Communication and Critical/ Cultural Studies, 15(1),* 96–100.
Rose, J. (1986). *Sexuality in the field of vision.* Verso.
Rose, N. (1998). *Inventing our selves: Psychology, power, and personhood.* Cambridge: Cambridge University Press.
Rutherford, A. (2018a). What the Origins of the "1 in 5" Statistic Teaches Us About Sexual Assault Policy. *Behavioral Scientist,* September 17. Retrieved April 27, 2021, from https://behavioralscientist.org/what-the-origins-of-the-1-in-5-statistic-teaches-us-about-sexual-assault-policy/#:~:text=Alexandra%20Rutherford%20is%20a%20professor,and%20its%20impact%20on%20policy
Rutherford, A. (2018b). Feminism, psychology, and the gendering of neoliberal subjectivity: From critique to disruption. *Theory & Psychology, 28(5),* 619–644.
Saini, A. (2017). *Inferior: How science got women wrong – And the new research that's rewriting the story.* Beacon.
Saketopoulou, A. (2014). Mourning the body as bedrock: Developmental considerations in treating transsexual patients analytically. *Journal of the American Psychoanalytic Association, 62(5),* 773–805.
Schiebinger, L. (1989). *The mind has no sex? Women in the origins of modern science.* Harvard University Press.
Schiebinger, L. (2004). *Nature's body: Gender in the making of modern science.* Rutgers University Press.
Serano, J. (2016). *Whipping girl* (2nd ed.). Seal Press.
Sideris, T. (2005). "You have to change and you don't know how!": Contesting what it means to be a man in a rural area of South Africa. In G. Reid & L. Walker (Eds.), *Men behaving differently: South African men since 1994* (pp. 111–138). Double Storey.
Solnit, R. (2014). *Men explain things to me.* Dispatch.
Solnit, R. (2018). *Call them by their true names: American crises (and essays).* Haymarket.
Spade, D. (2003). Resisting medicine, re/modeling gender. *Berkeley Women's Law Journal, 18,* 14–37.
Spurlin, W. (2010). Broadening postcolonial studies/decolonizing queer studies. In J. C. Hawley (Ed.), *Post-colonial, queer: Theoretical intersections* (pp. 185–205). SUNY Press.
Stryker, S. (2008). *Transgender history.* Seal.
Tatum, B. D. (1997). Why are all the black kids sitting together in the cafeteria? In *And other conversations about race.* Basic.

Thomas, E. J., Stelzl, M., & Lafrance, M. N. (2017). Faking to finish: Women's accounts of feigning sexual pleasure to end unwanted sex. *Sexualities, 20*(3), 281–301.

Tosh, J. (2016). *Psychology and gender dysphoria: Feminist and transgender perspectives*. Routledge.

Trengrove-Jones, T. (2008). Marriage and murder. In M. Judge, A. Manion, & S. de Waal (Eds.), *To have & to hold: The making of same-sex marriage in South Africa* (pp. 182–192). Fanele.

Trust Deficit. (2020). *The Economist*, December 19, pp. 72–74.

Valentine, D. (2007). *Imagining Transgender: An ethnography of a category*. Duke University Press.

Van Zyl, M. (2009). Beyond the Constitution: From sexual rights to belonging. In M. Steyn & M. van Zyl (Eds.), *The prize and the price: Shaping sexualities in South Africa* (pp. 364–387). HSRC Press.

Vickers, N. (1981). Diana described: Scattered women and scattered rhyme. *Critical Enquiry, 8*(2), 265–278.

Wall, W. (1993). *The imprint of gender: Authorship and publication in the English Renaissance*. Cornell University Press.

Ward, J. (2020). *The tragedy of heterosexuality*. New York University Press.

Wieringa, S. (2005). Chapter nine. In R. Morgan & S. Wieringa (Eds.), *Tommy Boys, Lesbian Men and Ancestral Wives: Female same-sex practices in Africa* (pp. 281–305). Jacana.

Wiggins, T. B. D. (2020). A perverse solution to misplaced distress: Trans subjects and clinical disavowal. *Transgender Studies Quarterly, 7*(1), 56–76.

Wilkinson, W. (2015). *Born on the edge of race and gender: A voice for cultural competency*. Hapa Papa.

Yeskel, F. (2015). Opening Pandora's box: Adding classism to the agenda. In S. M. Shaw & J. Lee (Eds.), *Women's voices feminist visions: Classic and contemporary readings* (6th ed., pp. 95–100). McGraw-Hill.

Young, J. L., & Hegarty, P. (2019). Reasonable men: Sexual harassment and norms of conduct in social psychology. *Feminism & Psychology, 29*(4), 435–474.

Zhou, J., Hofman, M. A., Gooren, L. J. G., & Swaab, D. F. (2007). A sex difference in the human brain and its relation to transsexuality. In G. Einstein (Ed.), *Sex and the brain* (pp. 775–779). MIT Press.

Open Access This chapter is licensed under the terms of the Creative Commons Attribution 4.0 International License (http://creativecommons.org/licenses/by/4.0/), which permits use, sharing, adaptation, distribution and reproduction in any medium or format, as long as you give appropriate credit to the original author(s) and the source, provide a link to the Creative Commons licence and indicate if changes were made.

The images or other third party material in this chapter are included in the chapter's Creative Commons licence, unless indicated otherwise in a credit line to the material. If material is not included in the chapter's Creative Commons licence and your intended use is not permitted by statutory regulation or exceeds the permitted use, you will need to obtain permission directly from the copyright holder.

5

Love and Money

We have been exploring how identities develop within the matrices available to us as humans in a world formulated by Western culture, specifically the Enlightenment and colonialism. I have been arguing that the liberal subject of this history is gendered cis male and raced white, and is dependent on binary thinking to keep his self and the systems that build and run his world intact. A theory of human complicity seeks to challenge this modus operandi, and to suggest that in practice, human being is a much more complicated and enmeshed process. Binary-structured subjectivity is an invested fiction. Oppression and suffering are caused by the processes of othering that result from the version of human being this dominant culture has evolved to experience as natural. I have been suggesting that to resist this process of othering is to think differently about what it means to be human. It is to see that we are dependent on each other to be ourselves. As such, we are made by and continue to make this world, and we can change it, but we have to move beyond the terms it wants to give us. Articulating this vision requires bringing knowledge developed in the humanities to the psy disciplines to complement some of the knowledge already in circulation in psychology, through attachment theory, object relations psychoanalysis or interpersonal neurobiology, for example. How these approaches relate to a complicit frame for therapeutic practice is taken up in the next chapter.

This chapter explores how neoliberalism, the late capitalist instantiation of the systems we have been exploring, interacts with social media, a relatively new technology at this stage of the West's game. It suggests some consequences for relational human being. The chapter comments on how by now, the logic of profit is woven into personal relationships in ways this late capitalist culture takes for granted, and the internet exploits.

I suggest that the atomization of experience and the ferocious pressure to perform a self for (emotional, social and economic) profit enabled by the direction social media has taken is a result of a specifically American understanding of what it means to be a person: liberally individualist, and invisibly gendered and raced. This is affecting young Americans in generationally specific ways, with specific consequences for how identity becomes available to the self; in short, for ways of being human today that pull away from complicitous knowing and toward an intensified, commodified individualism, with all the implications for human systems that we have been exploring. The current context, of neoliberal economic pressures and the cultural and psychological formations they create, together with the turn technology has taken in the last 20 years, creates a specific environment within which human relations and human being must form.

Although anxiety about the effects of technology on human systems is not new (Mokyr et al., 2015), there is arguably something unique about the turn that current uses of technology have taken. As my analysis will show, I am not optimistic about where things are going for young Western subjects. I will argue that the use of technology in the context of a neoliberal world order "has ushered in new organizing principles and new configurations of the self and human relationships" (Goodman, 2020, p. 333), as a lesson in how the systems I have been tracking are taking their most modern form. At the least, psychotherapists can benefit from interrogating these processes and from being aware of how the psy disciplines continue to participate in them.

Neoliberalism and Identity

Neoliberalism fractures social formations into individualized units, and focuses on competition as a force that will bring out the best in individuals, formulated in the first place as market participants. We all become entrepreneurs, responsible for our own economic survival, not entitled to rely on the state or its systems for help. In Chap. 2, we reviewed the basic definition of neoliberalism as a system that is both political and economic, and its emergence from a set of historical circumstances that went on to occlude themselves, as neoliberalism presents itself as the natural and obviously best way to do things (Rutherford, 2018). Indeed, one of the things neoliberalism does so well is to render all aspects of life depoliticized by normalizing a brutal economic status quo which replaces the state, and obviates its responsibilities to citizens by extending to us an illusion of choice. As Zuboff (2019) maps in detail, capitalism is not just an economic system. It creates social reality and culture. And neoliberalism laid the groundwork for a new kind of capitalism, which uses the technology of the twenty-first century to form its subjects.

Within neoliberal logic,

> [T]he market is construed as something that is natural to human beings. We tend to believe the mythology that markets are natural because we are now constituted as members of society according to market terms… Neoliberalism, as such, is competitive citizenship and consistently demands more competition in every area of our lives. We are on an endless hamster wheel. There is no steady ground. (Perry, 2018, p. 100)

For younger people especially, who have become subjects in the context of neoliberal systems since around 1980, life can often be fraught with anxiety; indeed, they have been called "the most anxious generation in history," an assessment linked to the impact of social media on their social-emotional development (Docu, 2018, p. 2; see APA, 2018). Schore (2012, p. 18) calls the levels of emotional distress in American youth, "this crisis at the core of our culture." They have been told that empowerment is their birthright and their responsibility (Rutherford, 2018), and that hard work will deliver success. Failure becomes a reflection of personal inadequacy, as structural limitations are rendered invisible (Sweet, 2018). Success and failure, because market terms are naturalized and reach deeply into aspects of life that used to be private, are both economic and psychological, and the two are entwined, as I will argue below.

It is within this context that the psy disciplines—whence comes the popular concept of identity in the first place (Erikson, 1968)—have helped to create an intensified version of the individual subject who is responsible for their own happiness, and for whom self-improvement is the means to manage psychological distress. Distress is conceived of as a personal issue, as the neoliberal subject does not have access to structural causes to explain their suffering. In the popular imagination and in many of the manualized approaches, psychological interventions aim at behavior changes and at helping clients find internal resources to achieve their goals, in workplace jargon which is a metric of psychic success. The focus on chemical causation for mental health symptoms helps clients achieve a sense of control over what is apparently not working correctly in their brains, without the requirement to investigate emotional processes, structural brutality or deeper pain or trauma (Davis, 2020). Such approaches help reinforce an enterprise culture where depth work is irrelevant (Sugarman, 2020).

Rose (1998, p. 153) details how enterprise culture emerged as a fundamental concept of neoliberal theorists, where,

> [T]he well-being of both political and social existence is to be ensured not by centralized planning and bureaucracy, but through the "enterprising" activities and choices of autonomous entities—businesses, organizations, persons—each striving to maximize its own advantage by inventing and promoting new projects by means of individual and local calculations of strategies and tactics, costs and benefits.

The self that is successful in such a culture is able to "maximize its own human capital,… a self that calculates about itself and that acts upon itself in order to better itself" (Rose, 1998, p. 154). This way of thinking, of course, works well with the thinking developed in the psy disciplines; Rose (1998) argues that technologies of psychology were formative for enterprise culture. Specifically, Sugarman (2020) critiques positive psychology as a technique of commodification of happiness, and as a way of thinking that renders deep wellness irrelevant. Rose (1998) explores how social psychology helped produce individuality as a technology of control under the aegis of democratic knowing. He also focuses on how the scientific stance of the psy disciplines is productive, enabling "techniques that will shape, channel, organize, and direct the personal capacities and selves of individuals under the aegis of a claim to objectivity, neutrality, and technical efficacy" (Rose, 1998, p. 155). Rutherford (2018), Sugarman (2020) and Melluish (2014) all hold the psy disciplines accountable for how they have perpetuated a model of the self-contained individual, responsible for their own choices, given how this plays into neoliberal ideologies. Gill and Orgad (2018) explore the arrival of the concept of resilience to the work of neoliberalism, part of what they term the psychological turn within neoliberalism. They trace how issues of character have become part of the discourses of neoliberalism via discourses and practices of psychology.

There is no doubt that psy approaches have helped to inform what Davies (2016) calls the Happiness Industry. Rose (1998, p. 157) links the imperative to happiness with the role of psychological experts in helping to create individuals tasked with their own improvement:

> Contemporary individuals are incited to live as if making a *project* of themselves; they are to *work* on their emotional world, their domestic and conjugal arrangements, their relations with employment and their techniques of sexual pleasure, to develop a "style" of living that will maximize the worth of their existence to themselves… Although our subjectivity might appear our most intimate sphere of experience, its contemporary intensification as a political and ethical value is intrinsically correlated with the growth of expert languages, which enable us to render our relations with ourselves and others into words and into thought, and with expert techniques, which promise to allow us to transform our selves in the direction of happiness and fulfillment.

Like Rose (1998), Melluish (2014, p. 542) also focuses on the role of the psychological expert in the intensification of psychological techniques for and on personhood:

> Increasingly, there are branded therapies, branded research methods and a connected process of marketization. Estimates suggest that there are 100–140 different schools of psychological therapy… many branded in such a way that for a psychologist to use these ideas they are required to undergo specific accredited training. This proliferation of therapeutic models is in spite of the overwhelming evidence that common factors, principally the quality of the relationship between the therapist and the client, are more important than any specific differences in models.

Melluish (2014) also points out that these scientifically endorsed methods are exported from the West to the rest of the world. As such, they participate in globalized, neocolonial relations of power with the majority world.

These, then, are some of the qualities associated with the neoliberal self, formed in relation to the psychologized individual: enterprising, responsible for themselves, energetic, ambitious, resilient, self-reliant, committed to improving as an investment in themself, flexible, mobile, calculating, active, goal-oriented, in control. Furthermore, these once-private personality traits must be displayed, in order for the neoliberal subject to ensure their marketability in this "contracting society" (Sugarman, 2020, p.76). Identity itself has been commodified:

> An individual is properly understood to be an entrepreneurial self that needs to be branded, marketed, and sold on the open market… Selves are best thought of as consumer images that can be enhanced by purchasing the proper accoutrements or experiences. (Cushman, 2019, p. 261)

Or, as Horning (2015, n.p.) put it, "if your personality can't be leveraged—then authenticity is not really available to you. You can't afford to be yourself" (qtd. Sugarman, 2020, p. 78).

The new markers of personhood, "visibility and recognition," are conferred through networks, not communities, Sugarman (2020, p. 78) points out, until "visibility and self-image become the engine of community." This new kind of community is characterized by a broadness of reach but a shallowness of connection. As we will explore in more detail below, within neoliberalism and increasingly under the surveillance capitalism to which it helped give rise, particularly for those born into this world, identity has been commodified in specific ways. What used to be of value in private, personal terms, now acquires value in twenty-first century market terms, which "presume[...] the existence of property rights over processes, things, and social relations, [presume] that a price can be put on them, and that they can be traded" (Harvey, 2007, p. 165). As we saw in Chap. 2, such an ethics of human being for trade has emerged from historical processes that are economic and political. Perry (2018, p. 104) reminds us that, "the 'free' market as a theoretical framework depends on the 'unfreedom' of those who are on the margins or outskirts of market activity and who are often dominated by those who employ them or extract their labor." She points out that while more individuals are citizens now who would, at the start of modern capitalism, have been constitutive nonpeople to the Western colonially formulated state, they are subject to inherited economic inequalities, together with the increased and intense competition of neoliberalism. Zuboff (2019) likens the new system of capitalism that has grown out of the confluence of neoliberalism, the legal and political imperatives post-9/11, and the growth of machine learning, to the process of colonialism that birthed the modern subject. Late modernity, in this formulation, bears some resemblance to early modernity.

The More Things Change

Shakespeare's historical moment, the late sixteenth century, was the time Europe started moving in newly concerted way on what was to them, "the new world." It was the time when early modernity, with its colonizing and capitalist drives, began to develop the cultural forces that continue to mutate today. Liberal, Enlightened, colonizing modernity has its roots in Shakespeare's time. As always, cultural, economic and material developments co-constituted and all participated in this long transition (for a summary of how colonial discourses were developing in England at this time and how they fed into American life, see Kendi, 2016).

English itself was changing, part of a cultural shift that impacted England's sense of itself: access to literacy was increasing, and with it, a change to who wrote, and why. This fundamentally affected the allocation of authority. Whereas previously, only priests, monks and the aristocracy produced, consumed and circulated texts, with the advent of moveable type by Johannes Gutenberg in the mid-fifteenth century, it became easier and cheaper to print and disseminate writing. This commercial development worked together with the new sense of competitive national pride that emerged with proto-colonial expansion, and helped fuel access to literacy in languages other than Latin. There was a new excitement about what English might be capable of, and a concerted effort to demonstrate that new ways of communicating could enhance the culture. New technology, new ways to create and new identities fed into each other, illustrating Rose's (1998, p. 200, n2) point that technology "produces the possibility of humans relating to themselves as subjects of certain types," an argument I continue to make below.

One of these new ways of relating is seen in how, in Shakespeare's writing and that of his peers, a particular connection was made between relationships of love, and relationships meant to enable profit, as England transitioned from a feudal economy to what would become a capitalist one. Schalkwyk (2008) has explored the intertwining of what he calls the language of love and the language of service in Shakespeare's work. Shakespeare was one of a group of newly emergent hopefuls, craving recognition of their intellectual gifts and, from there, economic and social mobility in a changing world whose rules for how to achieve success were becoming less rigid and more full of possibility, less dependent on who you were born to and more malleable to what you might accomplish for yourself. Those up-and-coming men of a newly emerging class who were smart enough to develop a network they could exploit for economic gain could change their social standing. They had to invoke and perform specific versions of themselves and in so doing, of their relationships with the aristocratic men and women who had the economic and social means to advance the careers of their apparently devoted poets (Burke, 1997; Eisaman Maus, 1995; Ferry, 1983; Greenblatt, 1984; Huntington, 2001; Warley, 2005).

The development of the technology for print was an important component in this cultural change (Febvre & Henri-Jean, 1979; Saunders, 1951). Once texts could circulate more freely, quickly and cheaply, which helped increase literacy in general, individuals could profit from the texts they produced in new ways (Marotti, 1995). Before this cultural development which quickly accrued economic imperatives, one did not think of oneself as the author of the text one produced in the sense we now take for granted after the Romantics. It was a display of one's learning, not plagiarism, to draw from and imitate the classics. Originality was not a thing. Certain forms, like drama and some kinds of elite poetry, were much more collaboratively produced than our later ideas about creative genius can accommodate (Marotti, 1986). The emergence of the personal identity of creator and author, and the profit to be gained from asserting this identity—both a psychological profit and an economic one—marked a huge shift in what it meant to write, to be addressed as a reader, to put one's work into the world (Fineman, 1986; Foucault, 1977; Greenblatt, 1984). Also to the point for the argument I want to make here, the development of print enabled the eventual constructions of modern publics, whether in the form of the nation, as Anderson (1991) has elucidated, or in the more diffuse and more modern sense of Warner's (2002) idea of the public sphere, on which more in a moment.

I have lived in four countries, and I have been struck since arriving in America by how profit is woven into personal relationships in ways this late capitalist culture takes for granted, in ways that remind me of patron–writer relationships in Shakespeare's proto-capitalist England. It is common sense that personal relationships should be pathways to economic advancement, that who you know is, and should be taken as, a valuable career resource. Part and parcel of this assumption is that how you present yourself, your personal narrative, should be carefully curated to present your best, most desirable, most valuable self to the world. Like Shakespeare's England, these cultural imperatives are facilitated by the expansion of new technologies of communication that fundamentally alter social, economic, educational, national and psychological dynamics.

In such a symbolic economy, relationships do not have value solely as themselves; they have commercial value as well, or instead. Human interactions have commodifiable potential, a fact that seems to be accepted as natural and obvious here in ways I have not experience elsewhere. If you want a job, you will likely not even be considered if you simply submit a resumé via the formal channels. Rather, you should approach someone in a position to give you that job or to introduce you to someone else who might. You approach them with strategic interest in who they are and what they have done. You approach them in the first place with your own personhood on offer, not your skills: They will help you if they like you. The purpose of the meeting or attempt to connect is not primarily to present what you can do, but who you are. If this meets with approval, you may get a step up in your career, or at least an addition to your network, which is useful because of how it may eventually yield career benefit. This is remarkably like the interweaving of the languages of love and service that Schalkwyk (2008) identified in Shakespeare's time. The personal is the commercial. The self is for sale, as is the very idea of human connection, which is assumed to exist for the purpose of profit as much as, if not more than, for its own sake. There is little intrinsic or implicit value in attachments in this universe outside of a capitalist logic. I am not suggesting intimate or family relationships are also this instrumentalized, although family connections are crucial to getting ahead in the networks that structure this country and its major institutions of power, from commerce, to elite universities, to the presidency. But certainly the ideas of friendship, and certainly the idea of what constitutes a public, are affected by this value system and this system of attributing relationship value as commodity value. If human connection is understood to be available for profit, then human selfhood is too, since the one depends upon the other.

Zuboff (2019, p. 44) tracks how neoliberalism has created an economic system which is explicitly "neofeudal" where wealth and power are consolidated in an elite, "far beyond the control of ordinary people and the mechanisms of democratic consent." In her account, the emotional malaise of the twenty-first century is a direct consequence of liberal subjects passing through neoliberal economic formations and their social and political consequence:

> This is the existential contradiction…: we want to exercise control over our own lives, but everywhere control is thwarted. Individualization has sent each one of us on the prowl for the resources we need to ensure effective life, but at each turn we are forced to do battle with an economics and politics from whose vantage point we are but ciphers. We live in the knowledge that our lives have unique value, but we are treated as invisible… Our

expectations of psychological self-determination are the grounds upon which our dreams unfold, so the losses we experience in the slow burn of rising inequality, exclusion, pervasive competition, and degrading stratification are not only economic. (Zuboff, 2019, p. 45)

This world produced what Zuboff (2019) calls surveillance capitalism, born of the way technology has been utilized to monetize our behaviors in an already neoliberal system which individualizes in order to exploit. Perhaps we are indeed returning to a version of a power hierarchy where love (friendship, connection, the meeting of curated selves for mutual profit) is money. The difference is that in Shakespeare's time, Western subjects were not yet Enlightened.

Zuboff's narrative traces the implications for subjects who have been formed in liberalism and capitalism. She (Zuboff, 2019, p. 189) invokes the internet as putatively "a mighty democratizing force that exponentially realizes Gutenberg's revolution in the lives of billions of individuals." But, she says, this potential has been colonized by the imperatives of surveillance capitalism, which uses the internet to collect information about us in order to render us the raw material of its profit-making. The small group of engineers who run this system are the new "narrow priesthood" (Zuboff, 2019, p. 189), akin to the priests of old whose preprinting press hold on literacy made them the mediators between ordinary people and their God. According to Zuboff (2019), Western culture has been quickly, oppressively and dishonestly altered by the ways the new technologies have come to be monetized. We are, she says, reverting to "a pre-Gutenberg order" (Zuboff, 2019, p. 189). The consequences for the kinds of subjects, the modes of human being, that are created accordingly are quite profound. We are left with senses of selves that expect to be autonomous and self-empowered, but are in fact radically hobbled by relations of power that we need in order to exist as subjects, but have no agency over, indeed, are controlled by.

If Shakespeare's time was emerging from feudalism and setting the stage for colonial expansion and all that came with it for the creation of modernity, then perhaps our time is indeed neofeudal, coming around in a loop to remake relationships for profit. How does one find oneself in a culture which is not only relentlessly selling one's connections, but one's identity?

Finding Oneself in the Public Eye

Warner (2002, pp. 50–1) describes how publics are created by the mode of address that assumes them into existence, what he describes as the dilemma of the chicken and the egg:

> Could anyone speak publicly without addressing a public? But how can this public exist before being addressed? What would a public be if no one were addressing it? Can a public really exist apart from the rhetoric through which it is imagined?… A public might be real and efficacious, but its reality lies in just this reflexivity by which an addressable object is conjured into being in order to enable the very discourse that gives it existence.

Publics are reliant on the words and images that call them into being, on the process of acting on the idea that they exist. A public can only exist as long as it is being addressed, and can only be invoked by its constituent members as long as they are paying attention (Warner, 2002). There is a precarity here that is also a condition of existence. There is also a clear sense of the imbrication of a public with its individual members. They make up each other. They make each other up. This dependent precarity is an excellent frame to bring to a discussion of the effects of the internet on the senses of selves of that group of younger people whose worlds are constituted by the idea of an online public.

Warner (2002) identifies several constituent factors to what makes up the idea of a modern public. These include the necessity of strangers to self-identity: in previous eras (Shakespeare's, too, Fiedler, 1973), the stranger was a threatening, external figure. The modern public relies on the idea of strangers out there who are like us, whose existence confirms our own. "In the context of a public," says Warner (2002, p. 56), "strangers can be treated as already belonging to our world. More: they *must* be. We are routinely oriented to them in common life. They are a normal feature of the social." As Warner (2002, p. 57) puts it, "stranger-relationality" is today "made normative, reshaping the most intimate dimensions of subjectivity around co-membership with indefinite persons in a context of routine action." Necessary to this process is the sheer fact of the ongoing attention of strangers, regardless of the "cognitive quality" of that attention. "Some kind of active uptake—however somnolent—is indispensable" (Warner, 2002, p. 61).

Written in 2002 (which Zuboff, 2019 times as the start of Google's consolidation of using surveillance to change the direction internet technology was taking), this certainly seems like a prescient description of how the online social media world has increasingly come to function, with quantifiable implications for those subjects formed within it (Calancie et al., 2017; Docu, 2018). Online profiles made to attract dates or sexual partners, networks of friends and their friends sought for the purposes of the upsell (personal or commercial), the use of Twitter to encourage fans who buy stuff to feel personally connected to the celebrity brand, the use of this technology to disseminate not only opinion, but now, political fiat, careers being made through blogs, the Instagramming of experience and the development of followers into both fame and, sometimes fortune, all of these depend on attracting the attention of strangers. It is the attention that matters, the attention that can be made into money and power.

Warner (2002) also explores the need for modern publics to be formulated by speech that is simultaneously both personal and impersonal. Public speech, says Warner (2002), must be understood by each of its addressees as being not exactly addressed to them, specifically, but to the stranger they were just before they were addressed, the stranger that makes possible the idea of a public to be addressed. Understanding that each addressee toggles between these two positions, strange and known, as a condition of being part of a public, is a conscious aspect of participation, he says. "The benefit of this practice is that it gives a general social relevance to private thought and life" (Warner, 2002, p. 58). Or, taken one step further, it brings private thought and life into the social as a means through which to connect with the public. This imbricates in very specific ways with the neoliberal puncturing of the sphere of the private. Private experience and personal identity become connected to the public realm through commercial imperative, which is experienced as natural, as an element of human being and relating.

To sum up: Warner (2002) offers one way to understand the pressure to be called into being as a successful self by seeing oneself in the public eye. He demonstrates the toggling between what he calls the personal and impersonal, as part of the condition of participation in this public. I suggest that what is going on with social media culture today is not a movement between, but an inseparable imbrication of, the private and the public. Warner (2002) also discusses the necessity of strangers to one's sense of self, when that self takes shape in relation to an idea of the public to which one belongs. This idea can also be articulated, using an attachment theory lesson, as the self's reliance on the mirroring back to itself by an imagined public. This public is simultaneously created by the idea, in the minds of its members, that it exists, and the work that it does in constructing its members.

Dean (2002), too, in her marvelous book on how publicity works in the internet age, writes about the ways subjectivity has been changed by the knowledge that countless others have access to (your) information, and the specific meanings made about this access by what she calls communicative capitalism. Zuboff's (2019) surveillance capitalism can be understood as the updated iteration of what was beginning in 2002, which, she (Zuboff, 2019) elucidates, was the nascent understanding that people's online activities could be translated into behavioral data that became the raw material for this new kind of capitalism. The monetization of surveillance begins with the new evaluation of online communication.

Dean (2002) argues that the secret is central to this world, where everything is connected and knowable, where the public can and should exercise their right to know. The idea that everything is knowable and shareable is given meaning only by the idea that something needs to be exposed. It is the secret which proves that "everything should be out in the open," by its very existence. If for Warner (2002), the fact of being addressed generates the public that is addressed thereby, for Dean (2002, pp. 10–11), "secrecy generates the very sense of a public that it presumes… it presupposes… that subject with a right to know." Either way, the idea of the public relies on something other than its own solidity to exist, and what it relies upon, one way or the other, is something individual, something hidden, something private. The private, the cordoned-off from the vast network of performance and visibility that constitutes the social world of the internet age, is implicated in the public eye. Under neoliberal imperatives, the private becomes an asset, and by now, under surveillance capitalism, the private's asset value is being actively tracked, mined, predicated and controlled for the purposes of generating profit (Zuboff, 2019).

Following Dean's (2002) formulation, this is a culture that is formed by the interaction between the idea of freedom as freedom of access to all information, and the idea of the secret that gives the notion of access its power. Implicit in this dynamic is both "a drive to be known, and the presumption that what matters is what is known" (Dean, 2002, pp. 12–13). People know they exist, she (Dean, 2002) argues, because they know their secrets are online. And as Zuboff (2019) has tracked, and as the many theorists cited above have argued, neoliberalism monetizes the individual who exists in this online context.

Dean (2002) says that the individual in technoculture is a cynical, ironic participant in these systems. She (2002) gives the example of participating in reward programs. We know the supermarket is doing it to make money, and that we are actually being "rewarded" very little while being interpolated into participating in making them that money. We do it anyway. Similarly, we do not have to actually believe that publicity indicates intrinsic value; we can know that it is the result of a media campaign or a reality TV show. But by participating in the structures that do this work, we participate in the valuing of publicity as a marker of worth, "materializing a belief through our actions even if we don't think we believe it" (Dean, 2002, p. 6). Drawing on the work of Zizek, Dean demonstrates how what we know is less important than what we do in the creation of ideological systems—such as the valuing of publicity as a marker of worth, even when we know that the whole thing is in the service of the generation of capital for the benefit of others. Zuboff (2019) adds an analysis of how surveillance capitalism wears us down as it profits from our behaviors, so that we become not ironic participants, but helpless puppets who do not believe we can change the power of technoculture over our lives.

Truth, Lies and Mediascape: Trump's Bullshit

As I revise this chapter, America is reeling from a coup attempt on the Capitol on January 6, 2021.

This was a direct consequence of Donald Trump's penchant for "alternative facts," a ridiculous but dangerous bit of cognitive-dissonance-inducing phrasing coined by his erstwhile senior counselor Kellyanne Conway during an interview on January 22, 2017. A lie about the size of the crowd at Trump's inauguration was countered by Conway: "You're saying it's a falsehood… And [we] gave alternative facts" (Bradner, 2017, n.p.). Thereafter, alternative facts became available to spread false information.

Alternative facts are ideas about the world informed by emotion (what someone wished had happened, or wishes to profit from), not what actually occurred in a basic historical sense. It is no coincidence that the issue of the inauguration crowd size needed to be lied about, because it arose from Trump's narcissistic need for affirmation. From early in his presidency, Trump was resisting a world in which he was unpopular, tweeting in 2017, "Any negative polls are fake news" (Kurtzleben, 2017, n.p.). But the implications for Trump's insistence on bending the world to his will are far greater than the size of his ego.

Kurtzleben (2017) tracks how Trump's repurposing of the notion of fake news undermined, as intended, the ability of news media to speak to what he was actually doing. Instead, he created a world where what he wanted the public to believe is true became the driving force behind the point of a public sphere. Subjective emotion became the touchstone for what is real, at least for Trump's supporters, of which we now know there are over 70 million, given the amount of people who voted for him in the 2020 Presidential elections. And of course, the harnessing of emotion to manipulate people's beliefs and behaviors on a new scale was possible because of the internet (d'Ancona, 2017). Zuboff (2019) argues that surveillance capitalism has an investment in keeping users online, and that it recycles the information it garners about us in order to find and target users with the most emotionally inciting information. The use of emotion to generate an online audience is an imperative of the system, which Trump exploited.

The result, as Kurtzleben (2017) shows, is a dichotomous world of real fake news and fake fake news, with different definitions of the phrase being wielded online by the far right and by the left, resulting in one more way that different groups live in "increasingly different realities" (Kurtzleben, 2017). Dean (2002) rather accurately predicted how the excess of information and its relentless accessibility would result in the advent of the idea of fake news, which cynically manipulates a suspicion of information that can be produced anywhere, anytime, by anyone saying anything. That the truth no longer actually matters in this environment is evidenced by the finding that even when presented with the actual hard facts, voters do not necessarily change their conclusions, since what has been activated is connected to what voters already think about the issue being lied about (Barrera et al., 2020; in the case of this study, immigration in France). Voters' prior schemas guide their behavior, even after factual inaccuracies have been corrected; loyalty to Trump trumps actual facts (Swire et al., 2017). We are now in a "'post-truth' era," driven by "ideological beliefs and 'common sense' assertions" (Harrison & Luckett, 2019, p. 259); in other words, what we feel to be true (it is worth noticing that it is idiomatic in America to say, "I feel like..." instead of "I think that...").

Trump's use of rhetoric, a deliberately emotion-generation use of language (Mercieca, 2020; Rowland, 2019), capitalized on the dynamics inherent in modern technologies of communication, and the communities they create. He used emotion (Rowland, 2019) instead of, or to counter, fact-based reality. This is not to endorse the idea that absolute truth exists independent of the symbolic system through which we as humans make sense of the world. But it is to argue that the amount of people who attend an event, whether or not a massacre happened at a specific place and time, or the numbers of votes counted for one politician over another, can be treated as something nonnegotiable. These things belong to the realm of the real, and are not culturally mediated.

The rise of lies in the public sphere for the purposes of political gain has been specifically linked to Trump's 2016 presidential campaign and then his ascension to power (Ball, 2017). To be more specific, Davis

(2017) differentiates between lies, which still bear some relation to the truth they distort, and bullshit, which contains no relation to external facts. Bullshit, he (Davis, 2017) says, has grown exponentially in the second decade of the twentieth century, culminating in the posttruth of Donald Trump's America.

The notion of alternative facts was not just rhetorical. It had real impact on the lives of marginalized people (Castrellón et al., 2017). It also functioned to disseminate both lies and bullshit via social media platforms and to normalize the onslaught of alternative reality, until the final lie that Trump had not lost the 2020 election to Joe Biden. Insisting repeatedly that he had won by a landslide and that the election had been stolen, Trump used emotion generated by bullshit to drive his supporters to violence in an attempt to overthrow the election results. This is typical demagoguery, but what is notable here is the use of the twenty-first century form of communication, and the kind of political public it enabled Trump to create. Trump's desire not to be a loser authorized a wholescale invention of reality, made solid through digital repetition. This is the world in which those born into the internet age must develop senses of selves.

Being Millennial

There is extensive discussion in the academic literature, the business and marketing journals, and online, about who exactly can or should be considered millennial. There are also well-placed warnings about taking the constructed notion of the "generation" as an absolute and absolutely accurate signifier. Nevertheless, generally speaking, millennials are taken to be those young adults born in the later 1970s and early 1980s, at the same time as neoliberalism began to take root. Sometimes, those born in the later 1980s and the 1990s are considered the next generation, or Gen Z (if millennials are Gen Y to Douglas Coupland's, 1991 Gen X). Now in their 20s and early 30s, millennials will soon be the largest group in the world's workforce. In addition, they, and their younger versions, are a focus of extensive corporate attention, so much so that it becomes difficult to separate out who the millennials "are" outside of the hype about them, a hype that is driven in most cases either by a gleeful focus on them as a market, or an idealized and optimistic construction of them as instantiating a new way of being thanks to the technology they live with.

Serazio (2015) warns against falling for the myth of the idea of a generation, especially now, in light of how constructed the millennial generation is by industries that want to market to them a sense of who they are or should be, and how to buy their way there, what he describes as a "project of power: summoning into being the consumer subject's sense of self so as to activate commercial activity from him or her" (Serazio, 2015, p. 601). We can see in this a version of Warner's (2002) public summoned into being by Zuboff's (2019) surveillance capitalism.

There is also the "kids these days" version of millennials and so-called Gen Zers, which bemoan their every behavior and collective value as degraded (see Bauerlein's, 2009, *The Dumbest Generation: How the Digital Age Stupefies Young Americans and Jeopardizes Our Future [Or, Don't Trust Anyone Under 30]*). The idea of the millennial generation, whatever its conceptual limits or false boundaries, has everything to do with the rise of the internet, and the accompanying new digital and social medias that have resulted in a new sense of what human being means.

The internet has brought with it new modes of subjectification, new ways of being that constitute a rupture with older ways of being individuals and of being social. Much of the writing about millennials asserts that growing up digital natives have wired millennials' brains differently. The idea of a generation shaped by access to the internet and all it entails—endless accessibility, global communities, apparent self-empowerment, the ability to influence the world on an unprecedented scale, the ability to connect across the surface of topics, images, links, and likes, automatic and effortless multitasking rather than depth thinking, cyberbullying, new forms of dopamine addiction, new forms of self-presentation and peer judgment, an expectation of interactivity in any learning experience, a psychological reliance on being instantly connected through smart phones, to name a few—is an idea whose power lies in the experiences of some members of this generation.

On May 20, 2013, *Time* Magazine ran a cover story entitled, "The Me Me Me Generation: Millennials are lazy, entitled narcissists who still live with their parents. Why they'll save us all" (Stein, 2013).

Stein (2013) offers what starts out as a rollicking, sardonic put-down of this group. He says they are influenced by their peers to an unparalleled degree, to their detriment. Their use of technology has resulted in quantifiable lower creativity and empathy. And, he says, in an about-face that hinges on the ways he is also influenced by technology, they are more tolerant and nicer than previous generations, as well as close to their parents and unconcerned by authority in general. He sums up:

> They're earnest and optimistic. They embrace the system. They are pragmatic idealists, tinkerers more than dreamers, life hackers. Their world is so flat that they have no leaders.... They want constant approval... They have massive fear of missing out... They're celebrity obsessed but don't respectfully idolize celebrities from a distance... They want new experiences... They are cool and reserved and not all that passionate. They are informed but inactive... They are probusiness... They love their phones but hate talking on them.

Many of these characteristics recur in descriptions and analyses of millennials, as we will see a little below. Many are also reductive or superficial descriptors of an inevitably more multifaceted group. Often left out is the difference material access makes—Stein (2013) says it makes no difference, but it always does. Warner (2002) makes the important point that the material form of the circulation of the texts that publics rely upon to exist, as well as the time that circulation takes, is a crucial component to bring to any understanding of a particular public. The consequences of the specific materiality upon which depends the ephemeral web, the digital cloud, are certainly relevant to any understanding of the nature of a public created by the digital media. Warner (2002) speculates briefly on this topic, in order to suggest that the internet may change the component of temporality in the constitutions of publics. A public is reliant on the channels of circulation it needs to perpetuate the discourse that creates it (Warner, 2002); access to computers and to internet literacy is a crucial, unspoken component of this process. The seamless navigation of this online public is a reality only for economically and socially enabled youth, on the global stage.

Writers responding to Stein's (2013) article also pointed out the difficulty defining the parameters of who constitutes this generation, and especially the economic constraints many young people have to manage (see Hipp, 2016; Kendzior, 2016). These are good correctives to a conversation that is often either utopian or apocalyptic. I am leaving out of the picture those components of being millennial or younger that include crushing student debt, lack of access to affordable healthcare or stable work and ongoing financial dependence on parents not through choice, but through resultant necessity. It remains to be seen what difference the coronavirus pandemic will make to these systems. These are, however, important elements of this "generation's" experience to at least acknowledge in a discussion about their emotional reliance on a public sphere that is driven by a performance of self which depends upon the commodification of the personal or private.

What millennials are consistently defined by regardless of the tone or sophistication of the argument is their access to and comfort with technology. When it is celebrated, millennial culture is usually celebrated as a discontinuity from the past, a complete break, a revolution in thinking, learning and being caused by millennials being the first generation with unique access to and comfort with computers. Perhaps one of the most well-known cheerleaders for the digital generation is Tapscott (2009):

> With their reflexes tuned to speed and freedom, these empowered young people are beginning to transform every institution of modern life. From the workplace to the marketplace, from politics to education to the basic unit of any society, the family, they are replacing a culture of control with a culture of enablement.

Their brains have been rewired in ways that make them smarter than their parents, indeed, "the smartest generation ever," and their influence on altering institutions is democratizing and fostering tolerance and diversity, he says. Tapscott's (2009) one concern was their lack of care over privacy, an attitude which may have changed in the intervening years, given how the internet has evolved (Zuboff, 2019).

He (Tapscott, 2009, p. 30) also notes they have changed "the concept of the brand" because, he says, of their insistence in participating in the process; they are not consumers, they are prosumers. Here is the line where the personal becomes not the political, but the commodifiable. Because it is clear that active participation and the insertion of agency into new media processes become a new way to market and sell both products and behavior via identity.

For Tapscott (2009), there is something intrinsic to the technology itself that causes creativity, connection, and new, better, ways of being in the world. This assumption about the technology itself as either good or bad, as seen in what it produces, is usefully called into question by Buckingham (2008; see his Growing Up Modern website). He warns of the dangers of a binary view of digital technology. He reminds us that there are, and always have been, continuities between old ways of doing things and new; that youth should not be romanticized; and that there is a material reality, or "digital divide" and not everyone who is young has equal access. He also points out that since the invention of electricity, at least, there has been a simplified debate about the benefits and risks of modern technology. This is an important set of caveats. What makes the difference, I think, what makes the current use of this technology potentially particularly pernicious, is the way the use of digital media has been so thoroughly saturated with market dynamics as imbricated with identity creation. As we have seen, Zuboff (2019) suggests that a new form of capitalism has resulted, which uses human behavior as its raw material. For generations who came of age in this universe, the implications for how they understand themselves and their relationships with others have been profoundly affected. This is not to argue that these technologies are only bad, or that they are intrinsically so.

But we are in a world where the potential of technology, whatever that means, has been thoroughly interwoven with the logic of profit, in the context of the crafting of a generation's (and future generations') psychological and social meanings, in their imaginings of themselves (Rizvi, 2006). The crafted definition of millennials as "digital natives" (the term was coined by Prensky, 2001, 2006, one of the cheerleaders of the revolutionary learning potential of computers) is dependent on not only their comfort with technology, but with the monetizing potential of this comfort. Here is an extract from a 2010 marketing report, entitled, "Millennials: Marketing to a Different Mindset":

Millennials are inherently aligned with technology. Intimacy with the digital world is one of the greatest strengths of their generation. Never having known a world without digital technology, Millennials… experience the world in a completely different way than previous generations. They recognize the power and importance of social networks and utilize the Internet as a trusted source and a platform for self-expression. In the eyes of the Millennials, personal online networks hold as much importance and authority as any conventional media channel. (Qtd. Serazio, 2015, p. 605)

Personal online networks, therefore, are marshaled for revenue in ways previously confined to what used to be conventional media channels. Again, Zuboff's (2019) recent work gives additional context to this process, asserting that the online world developed within the logic of a new kind of capitalism which relies on both capturing and controlling our online behavior to provide the information about us that creates the markets we become. This commodity-generation logic in turn creates form and meaning for personal online networks: the chicken and the egg. Corporate marketing strategies create the image of what a successful millennial is as much as they refract it, what Serazio (2015, p. 604) calls, "the industrial construction of audiences." Millennials as an idea are a public, created as much by the idea of who they each are as members and as a group as they set the terms for their group. And crucially, whereas in earlier "generations," driving forces in the construction of the public might have been the polis, or nationalism, or even counterculture, always influenced by multiple social and economic forces, today it is unapologetically and primarily capitalist—or, as Zuboff (2019) would say, surveillance capitalist, where what is for sale is human behavior, generated through the control of our thoughts, feelings and habits.

In his work, Serazio (2015, p. 601) details "how millennials are 'generationed' by commercial interests through a prism of technological bias." Serazio (2015) also confirms what my own internet search suggested: that most of the thinking and writing—the knowledge-production—about the relationship between millennials and new media (online and digital technologies) is currently being produced by marketing companies and agencies, not by academics or scholars. Even the metadiscourse is directly commodified, so that most attempts to characterize and define millennials are by their buying potential or behavior, in order to suggest ways of branding products to speak to their identities in order to capture them as consumers. And not just as consumers, but as sources of profit whose senses of themselves are tied to the product being peddled, such that the relationship is not apparently a commercial one, but deeply personal: Tapscott's (2009) prosumers. Marketers and consultants are baldly discussing how to produce the sense of agency and participation for which millennials are famous in order to profit from it (Moreno et al., 2017).

Here is the abstract from a 2017 article in the *International Journal of Marketing Studies*:

> The millennials constitute an important group of consumers. Therefore, to know how they behave has become an important issue. This paper aims to explain who the millennials are, to explain who belongs to this generational group and why they have become an attractive group for different social and economic sectors, by showing the most outstanding attitudes, tastes and buying behaviors… The findings suggest that millennials are a highly attractive market as they have grown up in an environment where technology provides a platform for personalization and immediate gratification in all aspects of life… The results contribute to the literature by providing a description of millennial consumers; showing in detailed the importance of this market segment and their buying behaviors. (Moreno et al., 2017, p. 135)

Serazio (2015) theorizes that new methods of selling to millennials increasingly commodify the cultural and the social, resulting in ways of being that make living and buying inseparable. He (Serazio, 2015, p. 600):

> [I[lluminates how millennials are "sold" in a double sense: both the online promotional tactics used to target a cohort so often decried as unreachable through traditional channels as well as the stereotypes spun about this generation's values and behaviors that, cyclically, legitimate the commercial work that is produced for them.

In his work on the constitution of modern publics, Warner (2002) also notices how more recent discourses explicitly commodify aspects of current youth and/or minority identities and cultural practices, so that the mass circulation of cultural ideas functions specifically as marketing. Marketing, display and subjectivity-creation become co-constituting. "You perform… your social placement… through [the deployment of commodified cultural memes]," says Warner (2002, p. 73).

The deployment of commodified cultural memes is otherwise known as the successful circulation of something "on brand." "Brand authenticity"; "brand community"; "brand meanings"; "brand image;" "brand trust;" "brand affinity"; "brand intimacy" and "brand advocate"; these are all terms that recur when people in business talk about attracting the millennial market. "A brand moment" means something important or meaningful has been captured, and, implicitly, rendered valuable because of its concomitant ability to get somebody to buy something, either now or upstream of the brand moment event. All of this brand energy coheres in the idea of the "personal brand"—how you present your experiences, biography, friend connections, likes and dislikes, avatars, photographs and life. Here is one of the consequences of the commodification of what was previously, in modernity at least, coded as the private, the intimate: who you are is for sale, and so the desirability of who you are is underwritten by its commodity value. It is likely quaint of me to be disturbed by this (although Zuboff, 2019 works hard to reinvigorate a sense of alarm about the turn capitalism has taken through the internet). It seems important to say, though, especially in the face of the broad characterization of internet culture as democratizing—although perhaps post-Trumpism, this will change.

Dean (2002) suggests that as the promise of decentralized information access took on the flavor of a democratic revolution thanks to the advent of personal computing, a new kind of subjectivity was generated. One of the results, as I have been arguing, was a blurring of the line between public and private as realms of experience; the new technology brought with it new "idealized norms of publicity: communication, participation, and personalization," part of a new way of being: technoculture. But it also brought with it a new "mode of subjectification." The subject in the new digital age requires publicity to know that it exists as a subject:

"People's experience of themselves as subjects is configured in terms of accessibility, visibility, *being known*. Without publicity, the subject of technoculture doesn't know if it exists at all," and, "Publicity in technoculture functions through the interpellation of a subject that makes itself into an object of public knowledge" (Dean, 2002, p. 90, p. 114).

The result of the internet age is not an enriched democratic public sphere. Instead, the result of vastly increased access to information is a new iteration of capitalism, which reaches inside the subject in new ways. The kind of communication now taken for granted on the internet produces a specific kind of public, which relies on specific ideas about its constituent members. These ideas include the assumption that the personal is and should be available for branding, and that the success of the brand is what the self depends upon to know itself. Information about all things is implicitly available, and also implicitly valuable especially insofar as it can attract marketable attention. Put another way, all attention is implicitly good because implicitly value-bearing because implicitly a revenue stream, either now or down the line, at the very least in the form of networks, whose publicity value is priceless for the self. The ultimate profiteerers from this new system are not human beings, but corporations (Zuboff, 2019), but this is obscured by a technoculture that normalizes being-for-profit.

What happens when the "nascent self is based upon mere marketed meanings" (Serazio, 2015, p. 603)? What are the consequences when the selves that are emerging in this culture are intertwined with the idea of the brand, not just as self-expression, but as self-knowledge, self-instantiation, selfhood itself? What happens when identity becomes "a product of the brand" (Serazio, 2015, p. 609)? What are the implications when branded identity becomes valuable in relation to how much publicity it can garner to itself?

Young people need self-expression, and they need community; these are appropriate developmental requirements. These have been commodified and exploited in a concerted drive that "erodes clear borders between commerce and sociocultural life."

> We ought to question the consequences of identity being channeled through digital branding schemes at such a critical developmental stage…

In some ways, this networked hypersociality and participatory exhibitionism are perhaps just the latest manifestations of more enduring phenomena of youth when it comes to needs related to community and identity. Yet the interactivity endemic to digital media use maps usefully (for brands) onto these same critical developmental needs. (Serazio, 2015, p. 600; p. 603; p. 607)

Understanding that psychological processes—the centrality of mirroring to the ability to be a self; the reliance on community for all of us, and particularly at the vulnerable developmental stage of emerging from one's family and community as Western youth do—have been publicized and commodified in ways specific to how technology has come to be utilized in technoculture, is one way to answer the question of how new processes of subjectification are taking place. And this also helps me to understand some of the patterns I see in my therapy practice.

One of the populations I serve in my work as a psychotherapist in the San Francisco Bay Area is that group of millennials who either have, or are striving to be one of the ones that have made it in the tech industry which dominates the economy and the entrepreneurial youth culture here, or did until the coronavirus started to alter life in the Bay Area (Bowles, 2021). These are young adults in their late 20s and early 30s who live in a world where personal and career success are intimately tied to self-presentation, networking, selling one's personality as much as one's ideas: to, in a word, branding.

Love and Money

The observations which follow have not been based on a comprehensive quantitative study like Tapscott's (2009), who solicited hundreds of stories via Facebook, accessed networks of thousands of millennials on the internet and interviewed over 6000 people. Or Deloitte's Millennial Survey (2019), which interviewed over 13,000 young people in 42 countries. Instead, these comments are based on in-depth therapeutic relationships developed with clients, and on conversations with colleagues who also work with this population.

I have been struck by the highly intelligent, highly resourced, highly educated, often (but not always) privileged young adults of this part of America who presented to the private therapy clinic where I first began to work with them as a group, and who I continue to see in private practice, with one of two emotional problems. Either they have made it in the tech world, working for or forming successful start-ups, weathering the pressures of self-presentation, getting good jobs with great salaries, and finding after committing all of themselves to their work that once they have achieved the prize, they are no longer sure of its meaning. These young adults are successful and miserable, feeling lonely, alienated, unsure of themselves, like they live in a world where they can never be sure which relationships are real. They feel pressured to socialize with people they do not like, and to be available for out-of-office interactions with bosses they do not respect, because the personal is the vehicle upon which they believe their commercial success rides. They do not have a sense of professional boundaries, and their interpersonal interactions at work are fraught with the need to manage office politics, grabs for power, their own ambitions, through the need to be likeable. Many of them seem to navigate the internal gap of, on the one hand, knowing they are part of an economic and social elite, and on the other, feeling unworthy—a version of imposter phenomenon. They tell me how incredibly well they have done, that they are living the start-up dream, and that they do not know who they are, exactly, or why this all should matter so much. They talk of feeling like there is a void inside them, or of feeling unaccountably depressed, or so anxious about work that they engage in maladaptive coping strategies that are making them miserable.

The other version of this I see are equally talented young people who have not yet made it, and fear they never will. Their fear of failure is woven into a fear of not being good enough, which does not mean not being smart enough, but not being likeable enough, not being lucky enough, not being connected enough. They know they are smart and talented, but they lack the networking knack, and/or they are haunted by having made the wrong choices and thereby not getting into the right elites to aid their careers. They often seem to be collapsing under the imperative to sell themselves, to measure the worth of one's life by the amount of profile and money one achieves, the sooner the more impressive and therefore the better. Those without the ego, the structural privilege, the charisma, the connections, the luck, or any necessary combination, feel like failures before they even begin, or cannot begin under the weight of the failure they feel.

Some of these psychological dynamics can be accounted for in terms of intrapersonal and family histories, to be sure. Some young people have parents for whom nothing was good enough; some have parents whose own failures haunt their children with the fear of who they might become if they do not succeed. Some come from poverty, or minority communities, and struggle with a sense of not belonging to the elite institutions and or corporate cultures they worked so hard to join. Some are immigrants, to whom American corporate individualism feels like an extremely uncomfortable costume they must wear. Some are female, which tends to bring with it a consistent struggle to embrace success while remaining feminine enough to be acceptable, and the necessity of navigating pervasive, unspoken misogyny and sometimes harassment. Taking up the right kind of space in the right kind of way is a particularly fine-tuned balancing act for some of these young women. The struggle to feel good enough in external settings has always been at least somewhat about a person's internal landscape, as well as the contexts in which that person must function. But there does seem to be a pattern here, or at least a similarity across people of the same, broadly millennial, generation.

The term "imposter phenomenon" was first coined in 1978, to describe a sense-of-self deficit experienced by high-achieving women of a particular class and race demographic, the usual WEIRD sample (Clance & Imes, 1978). Its argument seems to me a more modern version of a point made by psychoanalyst Joan Riviere, in a 1929 essay entitled, "Womanliness as a Masquerade." Riviere (1929) argued, via a case study of a woman who might have been Riviere herself, that women seeking achievements and approval in "male" environments—that is, professional life—have to compensate for the gender anxiety this causes by assuming veneers of femininity. Wanting to be seen as worthy (worth attention, worth money, worth being seen) in public has long been a cause of anxiety for those assigned female at birth and raised as such. The reasons are somewhat obvious: there are different implications for women demanding the right to be looked at and valued in the public eye, worth intellectual and commercial respect. The stigma and violence against sex workers, but not their clients, illustrates what can be at stake for women who do not conform to normative gender rules for acceptable femininity, which include highly occluded access to active sexuality/inviting public attention/ambition. That these characteristics are in fact culturally connected in Western thought Freud's discourse made clear, and any investigation into the material history of authorship in the West illustrates (Distiller, 2008; Wall, 1993; see Zambreno, 2012 for a millennial exploration of these ongoing gender issues). It is worth remembering that "imposter phenomenon" initially had a gendered meaning, and was speaking specifically about women not feeling they deserved what they had achieved at work. While these issues remain pertinent as gender issues, the emotional processes described by the fear of being a fake in the public eye clearly by now have resonance across gender.

If the number of TED Talks on the subject of what is now usually called "imposter syndrome" is anything to go by, the concept has enormous valence in this culture. Its origins in gender difference have been ameliorated. Now, it seems, the majority of high achievers in the Western world (70%, according to Solomon, 2016) suffer from not believing their achievements are based on solid ground. Many successful younger people in America struggle to believe they are worth what the public world of work says they are worth, even after hard work and sacrifice got them there. It seems they feel to some degree or another like they have faked their way to success, or like they are not as good as they appear to be.

Subsequent to the original 1978 study, which examined 150 mostly white middle and upper class professional and academic women, a literature has developed which applies the concept to other "minority" groups, and to men (McGregor et al., 2008). Recently, an exploratory 2018 study entitled, "Are all impostors created equal?" sets out to "Explor[e] gender differences in the impostor phenomenon-performance link." It found that imposter syndrome not only affects men too, but, in the study's terms, affects them worse. There are some comments that could be made about the interpretations in this exploratory study (men showed higher anxiety and less effort in response to their anxiety; women worked harder in response to the anxiety they felt, interpreted as indicating higher levels of suffering in the men). Most interesting to me here is that the cohorts recruited for the research are likely to be millennial, and were all from the United States: they were undergraduates from an American public university (Jarrett, 2018). Worth noting is that this study was framed in terms of its implications for how managers handle their personnel, once again linking the personal with the commercial.

Why are so many successful younger people convinced they have somehow fooled the world into thinking they are all that? Why do they feel that they are, in fact, charlatans and fakes? The original suggestion—that women struggle to navigate their socialized gender in the context of the public realm—needs another angle these days.

The feeling of having an internal void is a metaphor that seems to come up fairly often with my millennial clients. Why? Self-identification requires a relationship with another, ideally another that one recognizes is also another self rather than being experienced as an object, which causes problems in the process of finding oneself through the other (Benjamin, 1988; Bryson & MacIntosh, 2010), as I have argued in previous chapters. What happens to this process of self-identification when the other is an internet public, and the self knows itself through its own commodification, that is, in order to be experienced as a self, it must experience its own objectification via "[t]he act of always performing oneself with an audience's potential response in mind and the need for reciprocal exchange" (Bryson & MacIntosh, 2010, p. 115)?

The pathway to self-identification is not, in this symbolic universe, through a relationship with another self. It is through a relationship with a very specific kind of public idea of worth, of public reflection of worth. If the psychodynamic idea is that the subject reaches for the recognition of the other as a way to understand itself, perhaps the subject of technoculture suffers for reaching for the recognition of celebrity as reflected by an idea of many anonymous, networked, others, Warner's (2002) strangers. Relationship quality is not what matters here. Relationship quantity is. Alienation is the result. A sense of hollowness, an anxiety manifest in a restless, relentless superficial movement on the surface of things, across clicks and likes and happy photographs and carefully curated profiles.

Perhaps the internal feeling of the psychic void is the inevitable consequence when the self looks to find itself, not through repeated moments of neurobiologically felt presence, but through fame-based reflections in the imagined eyes of a digital public. There is no actual, embodied, there there. Instead there is a decentralized network whose psychic energy is the energy of constant, surface-based, movement. This kind of attention, by definition, is always on to the next thing. No wonder so many of my younger clients are anxious (APA, 2018).

Dean (2002) theorizes the underlying dynamics of celebrity in the technocultural symbolic economy by refiguring Lacan's ideas about desire and drive through the work of Zizek. In doing so, she accounts for the empty repetition for its own sake that characterizes much online activity: the technocultural subject is formulated by the endless, restless circularity of drive energy, not the lack at the center of the desiring subject which Lacan said propels us all into language and independent selfhood. Desire yearns for what it cannot have (in the first place, a feeling of wholeness, of return to the womb or union with the mother, according to Lacanian psychoanalysis. This loss lies at the heart of each of us, and propels us into human systems of meaning). Drive, a different kind of energy, creates restless movement in the attempt to fulfill its needs. The repetitive circle of the drive produces its own kind of empty pleasure. The circular energy of the drive becomes, in the imperative to celebrity, a "drive to make oneself seen that is crucial to publicity in technoculture." Desire impels the subject to look for the gaze of the other, but what desire cannot ever see is the point from which the other gazes; the subject cannot see the other's point of view. The energy of drive, in Dean's (2002) formulation, is the subject's work to make itself seen: "I make myself open, accessible, available, visible to that mysterious, unknown, secret thing, to the place from which I am gazed back at. In my very looking, I make myself visible to this object, the gaze" (Dean, 2002, p. 121). In my looking, I make myself visible to the gaze I need to know I exist (and which, by desire's definition, I cannot ever have). This seems to me a concise and resonant summation of the dynamics of self-constitution that millennials, those younger people who are trying to build human being in a universe structured by internet culture, have to navigate. This explains the internal void so many of them talk about.

Goodman (2020, pp. 341–2), in a discussion about how social media has altered subjectivity, recounts an experience with a student of his:

The ocean was surging against the rocks… I was enamoured with the intensity and grandness of what I was beholding. I turned to see my student pointing her phone at the water and heard her whisper "come on water, do something exciting."… She expressed that these experiences feel most real when she is able to capture them and show her friends through her social networks. She feels uneasy when she does not have this mechanism of expression… Later at dinner, she "checked in" on Facebook to allow her friends to know where she was. There was a way in which she did not feel as though she was sitting at the restaurant unless others knew her location.

Dean (2002) brings this reflexivity—I make myself seen in order to see myself being seen—into her definition of technocultural celebrity, which she says is an integral part of how publicity works in this culture. Celebrity is about being known for being known. "In celebrity, publicity is reflexivized, turned back on itself such that not only is something seen, but it *makes itself* seen—accessible to, information for—others." Because technocultural publicity is driven by the energy of celebrity, the subject produced by technoculture is itself "configured by celebrity" (Dean, 2002, p. 122, p. 13). The mediated performance of the private lives of celebrities fuels this desire and imperative to be seen publicly in order to exist. It flavors the public's idea of itself, its members and its members' ideas of themselves as members of this public.

In December 2018, *Rolling Stone* carried a cover story about Shawn Mendez, which it billed as "confessions of a neurotic pop idol." Mendez is the very young (16 when he achieved pop stardom) Canadian who became famous "not long after he picked up a guitar for the first time" by "drawing half a billion views" on Vine, a social media app which allowed him to post 6-second versions of other people's pop songs (Doyle, 2018).

The article presents us with an anxious young man who does not quite believe his own success, which Doyle gestures toward by quoting specific lyrics from the Bruno Mars song that Mendez sang the first time he sang in public: "'Easy come, easy go!'" (Doyle, 2018). These lyrics suggest the ephemerality of Mendez's position by underscoring its genesis in internet celebrity. The house of cards nature of whole enterprise is implicit in its very nature, and this, Doyle slyly suggests, accounts for Mendez's ongoing, underlying anxiety, or his "neurosis."

The story starts by recounting to us a daily encounter between Mendez and the world of social media which made him famous:

> Shawn Mendez was up late in his hotel room a few nights ago, scrolling through photos online. He kept seeing Top 40 A-listers with their partners… and he was starting to get a little jealous. "I had this thought: 'I have to get paparazzied with someone. Who am I gonna get? I'm not relevant'". (Doyle, 2018)

Doyle addresses the subtext that Mendez was made by the internet public and needs to keep courting its attention:

> It's easy to be skeptical of his success—just ask Mendez, a self-described "extremely neurotic" 20-year-old who spends much of his time second-guessing his career choices. "It's literally my biggest fear, to wake up tomorrow and nobody cares," he says. (Doyle, 2018)

Mendez's celebrity, and its vulnerabilities, exemplifies the way things now are for people seeking success online. He is one of the more successful ordinary people whose internet access brought him fame and riches. One of the rules he has to keep himself "on track… as he tries to build the long-term career of a Sheeran or a Taylor Swift" is, "*Never* say no to a selfie."

> When he walks out of the lobby of the… [h]otel…, there are already a few dozen girls waiting by the entrance. "Hold on," Mendez tells his team. "I gotta take some photos." After a minute or two of efficient chitchat—"You're amazing!" he tells one fan…—he makes his way to the van. (Doyle, 2018)

Mendez's availability to his fans is as much a part of his career profile as his music. Accessibility of his person is part of his success strategy. This is packaged as a personal exchange, where he pretends to recognize and value an individual fan's subjectivity. He is like the early modern poet, invoking his patron in language of intimacy in order to further his career, which specifically means enable the conditions of production to create something artistic (writing in the one instance, music in the other). He is also the quintessential millennial subject, caught in the endless cycle of offering himself up, through pseudo-connection, in order to ensure his commercial existence. His bankability is his likeability. How well can he make her feel connected to him? How efficiently? Because the more the better. In fact, the more connections he makes, the more he needs to keep up with the connections, because if they go away, so does "Shawn Mendez, pop idol" (Doyle, 2018).

Mendez's commitment to his fans, his willingness to always pose for selfies, suggests he is driven by technocultural celebrity. He has to have his celebrity seen by the public in order for it to exist, and he has to work constantly to tend to it in these precise terms. And *Rolling Stone*'s (2018) offer to present us with his "Confessions" contributes to the work of technocultural subject-production through the idea of accessible information, as Dean (2002) suggested. We are offered access to his secrets, which make his manufactured selfhood (seem) real and authentic. If we can access the real Shawn Mendez, the person himself, we can feel we know him, feel closer to him, know something about him and so reinscribe his celebrity by participating in the commercial exchange of personhood. We can feel connected to the pop idol who exists because we feel connected to him. Our connection to his celebrity feeds into our own awareness of our existence.

This explains his anxiety, an existential awareness of the reliance of his very existence as "Shawn Mendez... pop idol" (Doyle, 2018) on an endless reflexivity, where his work's value is not in the work, but in the extent to which the work ensures that his fans are interested in looking at him. And by "work" I mean to invoke not only his music, which he also writes, but the constant, ceaseless work of self-assertion, self-presentation, self-fashioning (Greenblatt, 1984) that was always the core of his celebrity.

Doyle describes the original publicity work Mendez did, at Meet and Greet Conventions where, along with people who were famous for vandalizing supermarkets, he participated in "a platform for teen boys with large social followings to meet the fans who felt as though they already knew them… 'We were like zoo animals,' he says. [Fans] would just stare at us and take photos with us. We would do whatever they say'" (Doyle,

2018). Somehow, this is supposed to be different from, if precursor to, what happens now:

> A wave of shrieks erupt from the parking lot. Hundreds of girls have their phones ready… Mendez takes a picture with each one, a smile pasted on his face. After he works his way through, he blows one last kiss and gets in the next van… "It's pretty dope here," he says, then goes quiet for a while. "I don't know, man," he mumbles as we approach the hotel. "I feel fucking weird". (Doyle, 2018)

I am struck, in these descriptions, by how both parties are willingly participating in an exchange which they know is not about their actual selves being seen, but about a commodified, branded interaction: Mendez pretends to care about each fan, and in return they award him celebrity. He serves up his personality, or a version of it, and in return they feel seen by him, connected to him. Some of this is, of course, typical to any dynamic of fandom. What is specific here is how it needs to be endlessly recorded and disseminated for each party to reap their full investment in the exchange. That Mendez seems to know this, and that Doyle certainly does, is encoded in the final quote above—"'I don't know, man,' he mumbles… 'I feel fucking weird'"—which ends a section of the story.

Mendez is presented as suffering from anxiety and a kind of inexplicable depression: "'You know when you're in a state of unhappiness when you have no reason to be unhappy?' he says. 'I hate that'" (Doyle, 2018). He comes across as sweet, kind, and utterly devoted to his own success, which is going well. And yet, unhappy. Mendez, of course, is barely millennial—but he is the next incarnation. His antidote to the depression, Doyle (2018) reports, is to pretend he is on stage, with "'people that love me.'"

The story ends with a tale of Mendez hooking up with a bartender for a night, and how "fans have even begun speculating about the bartender, because he followed her on Instagram that night."

> Actually, he adds, he didn't: when Mendez was in the bathroom, she grabbed his phone and followed herself from his account. He shakes his head. "Gotta give her credit for that". (Doyle, 2018)

And those are the closing words of the story. The bartender's exploitation of their intimacy, however fleeting, deserves grudging credit. Because Shawn Mendez should and does expect to have his celebrity self profited from, hall of mirrors style. This is the world he lives in.

The structural imperative to publicity demanded by the internet in the lives of all the characters is woven through this account, unremarked, but clearly telling the story of Shawn Mendez, the "neurotic pop idol." It is a story, as I have been suggesting, that illustrates Dean's (2002) theoretical model of how technoculture works to produce subjects, dependent on a kind of publicity that is constituted by twenty-first century celebrity. To this formulation I have added two characteristics of the subjects of this culture: that their love and friendship, their intimacy and connections, their personalities, are fundamentally commodities; and that they are inexplicably anxious, even when they seem to have everything they have worked for. The reasons connect through the effects of technoculture on the kind of subjectivity that can be found in this symbolic economy. It knows its own fakeness, and so does everyone else. It does not have to believe in itself. The system believes for it. But at the end of the day, it feels its own precarity. It senses the void underneath all that anxious, self-reflexive, self-fueling drive energy.

There is another component of Mendez's story that is instructive. Shawn Mendez has garnered an awful lot of online attention which speculates on his sexuality, or as he tells Doyle (2018), "This massive, massive thing for the last five years about me being gay." Doyle explains: "Examples of what he means are all over YouTube and Twitter. There are memes that pair photos of Mendez with jokes about being closeted and videos that scrutinize his gestures" (Doyle, 2018).

Mendez describes being extremely affected by this coverage. He:

> [O]ften finds himself watching his own interviews, analyzing his voice and his body language. He'll see an anonymous stranger comment on the way he crosses his legs once and try not to do it again. (Doyle, 2018)

Doyle recounts how his attempt to address the issue directly, that is, via Snapchat, backfired, and Mendez's panic after allowing Taylor Swift to post a video of her putting makeup on him:

He told her it was fine without thinking, but later that night, he woke up in a cold sweat. "I felt sick," he said. "I was like, 'Fuck, why did I let her post that?' I just fed the fire that I'm terrified of". (Doyle, 2018)

Once again, incidentally, we are reminded of how carefully celebrities have to consider and curate the information they release about themselves. But most interesting here is Mendez's horror of being considered gay when he is not. If he is not, as he insists, gay, then what is a stake, especially in his demographic, where sexual and gender fluidity is more available to public figures than ever before (see the treatment of Harry Styles in *Vanity Fair* a couple of years later, Vanderhoof, 2020)? I am not dismissing the ongoing reality of homophobia and gender-related phobias, and Mendez himself acknowledges that he is uncomfortable with the homophobia he knows his response demonstrates (Doyle, 2018). But cold sweats and sickness because of a misrepresentation of this most personal of qualities? This is the distress of misattunement, of looking into the eyes of the mirroring other and seeing something that you know is wrong reflected back at you. It is a feeling of wrongness that causes anxiety, depression, self-loathing—as queer, trans, and nonbinary folk know very well. It is further evidence that Mendez's selfhood is being formulated by this public presentation of his celebrity self, that the personal and the public, and the valuing of the inner self through commercial/celebrity success, are all dependent on each other in this world.

"Easy come, easy go": Perhaps it also lets us know that Shawn Mendez, despite how hard he has worked, also feels like he may be exposed as not all that, if he doesn't play his cards exactly right. If he cannot succeed in controlling representations of the celebrity self that create him by circulating through his fandom, will he continue to exist as a celebrity? Is imposter syndrome so much a part of this culture because its version of subjectivity depends, by definition, on the condition of celebrity? I am not presuming to diagnose Shawn Mendez, I am speculating, using this article about him as a cultural text: If the self is dependent on its public to underwrite its value, and its public is fed by the curation of the self as product, it makes sense that the person underneath all that would feel like the image had taken over.

Dean (2002) links the centrality of the promise of celebrity to the work of subjectivization it does, to "the fundamental diversity and opacity of cyberspace: we are known, but the terms of this being known are never transparent to us" (Dean, 2002, p. 122). She details the sense we all have of knowing there is information about us online that we cannot control the circulation or the content of (Zuboff, 2019 adds horrifying and extensive detail to exactly how and why this happens). She names the "insecurity" this causes—"How, exactly, are we being looked at? One never really knows who one is" (Dean, 2002, p. 123). If the internet says you are gay, does that make you so? If the internet says you are gay, does that affect your brand? In ways you cannot control? What other secrets might it make up about you? How will this affect how you are seen? It is worth noting here that we have indeed experienced technoculture as a place where reality is invented through online repetition, the key to Trump's political brand.

The subject's only option to ensure its existence is "to make itself visible over and over again. It has to understand itself as celebrity, precisely because the excess of cyberia makes it uncertain as to its place in the symbolic order" (Dean, 2002, p. 123). This is what makes Shawn Mendez like "us", and "us" like Shawn Mendez, because his celebrity was crafted by and through the internet. Mendez could easily be one of my clients: his anxiety about his own existence as "Shawn Mendez, pop idol," his ongoing commitment to keeping himself in the eye of a public that exists as an uncontrollable, fragmented gaze to which he must continually offer his self in order to make his music, and his money, these feel familiar. Technocultural celebrity doubts itself, because it is reliant not only on knowing one is known but on knowing one is not in control of how, where, when, and why one is known. Hence Shawn Mendez, terrified of being thought to be gay, anxiously monitoring his own existence insofar as it can be sustained online and through social media.

Celebrity is not a true source of identification, says Dean (2002). It is not analogous to being mirrored, because the source of the gaze in which one seeks oneself is "a point hidden in an opaque and heterogenous network. One is compelled to make oneself visible precisely because of the uncertainty as to whether one registers at all" (Dean, 2002, p. 124). Perhaps this is the central change wrought on millennial personhood by the computerized online world millennials have always traversed. What has been lost, more even than daily opportunities for human connection, is personhood based on personhood, people who are people because of other people. Instead, people are reliant on anxiously offering a commercialized version of themselves to a fragmented and unknowable network, whose attention is uncertain, capricious, and, unless constantly re-engaged by ongoing content, brief. And to reiterate, Dean's (2002) celebrity is not a simple desire for fame; it is a fundamental reliance on being known in a system where the subject cannot know or control how she is known, by whom, or why. This subject knows the public who sees her is multiple, fragmented, often hostile, often misinterpreting the information she cannot control about herself that is being shared out there. It is a self who needs to see she is seen before she can know she exists, but not in the way in which the infant is reliant on mirroring to organize her internal landscape, to learn the meaning of her experience and how to manage it. The millennial self subjectivized through celebrity is eternally anxiously caught in the circular drive to attract the right kind of attention in order to achieve its goals. And being successfully interpolated by this system, succeeding in knowing oneself because one knows, for a moment, that one has been seen, is by definition to trivialize oneself, to reduce oneself to being just another transient piece of content in an endless series of replaceable stories. Success in this system cannot but become devalued as human experience by its inevitable commodification. Every piece of content will know it is successful when it becomes the next "scoop" (Dean, 2002, p. 129). Success is successful, transient posturing.

Goodman (2020, p. 333) asks precisely the question, has the new technology, with the ways it has undoubtedly shaped human interaction, enabled "a new epoch in the shape and nature of human subjectivity, intimacy, and desire?" He answers by suggesting that psychic distance, invisibility, and invulnerability have always been elements of Western subjectivity, which during the Enlightenment came to inform the value placed on rationality and self-containment, Descartes' self-enclosed thinking subject. Not incidentally, this self, able to control what he thinks and wants, but free from being seen or controlled, unconnected to or implicated in other selves, is a subject who creates and uses others. The self-containment enables objectification of other subjects. Goodman (2020,

p. 336) thus locates the internet's mediated and avatar-based interactions not as something new, but as a radical continuation of elements in Western culture, where "we get to manage and modulate our presence."

The difference now, he suggests, is in how the subject feels compelled to make itself visible, to be seen in order to know that it exists through public declaration. Unlike attachment mirroring (In the world of social media, "Experience [becomes] owned by the recognition of a nonparticular other" Goodman, 2020, p. 342), the way this is playing out in the new public sphere dislocates, to use Goodman's (2020, p. 337) word, subjectivity from connection, and refashions it as, in my word, brand:

> I can "post" myself in the manner most conducive to my desire and to what I perceive to be the desire of others. I make myself more consumable. I become more of a commodity. What is more desirable in a capitalistic, free market economy? (Goodman, 2020, p. 337)

In other words, Goodman continues to describe the implications of neoliberalism, working together with our new technologies and the new forms of capitalism that are resulting, for human subjectivity in the twenty-first century. This will inevitably affect those born into this world more intensely than those of us initially formed in a previous iteration of this culture. As Goodman (2020, p. 344) concludes, "With the advent of personal computing devices, modern technology has become a central mediating force within human exchange, and with it, human subjectivity… The norms of connection, intimacy, and public/private experience are shifting."

To this I would reiterate that we need to bear in mind the material investments implicit in these shifts. These new developments grow out of and intensify neoliberal dynamics. Neoliberalism is itself an end-product of colonialism, which was enabled by the philosophies and economies of the Enlightenment. In Zuboff's (2019) account, we are being newly colonized by a new kind of capitalism which uses the technology of the twenty-first century to render human being itself as profit, and truncate our ability to have agency over our selves. Our behaviors are both mined and moderated. This brave new world runs the risk of collapsing our chances to think complicitously about ourselves, our world, each other.

That this is indeed happening among younger users in ever more intensive ways is evidenced by brown's (2020) recent response to the advent of cancel culture online. She (brown, 2020) issues an appeal to progressive online users to tolerate each other's mistakes, engage productively in conflict rather than shut each other down, and not to reproduce the punitive and annihilating systems that structure the state's relationship to its others, which she (brown, 2020) identifies as unconscious identification processes at work in these online communities. It is only by recognizing how we are all implicated in all of the systems at play here that we can resist its historically familiar terms. None of us is better than the other.

I write this as Joe Biden is about to be inaugurated. I write it with a sense of dread and the disempowerment Zuboff (2019) argues is a consequence of the workings of surveillance capitalism. This new force requires people to be engaged online and creates imperatives to do so. She (Zuboff, 2019) also tracks how the development of twentieth century industrial capitalism, which transmuted into neoliberalism, favored machines over people. This choice created an economically and thus socially disempowered class of Americans who previously had voice and earning potential, developed, I would add, in a society that had always conferred racialized privilege. Zuboff's (2019) economic history, together with the structuring history of white supremacy in America outlined in Chap. 3, seems to me intimately connected to the communities Trump and Trumpism have marshaled online and on the streets (Parmar, 2021). I fear that we are further than ever from a shared vision of human complicity, where hate-based othering processes are rejected as hurtful to everyone, and where human being can be experienced differently to the inheritances handed down to us by the racism and misogyny of colonialism, and the destructive, entitled individualism that found its most powerful instantiation in neoliberalism.

Works Cited

American Psychiatric Association. (2018). Americans say they are more anxious than a year ago; Baby Boomers report greatest increase in anxiety. Retrieved January 6, 2021, from https://www.psychiatry.org/newsroom/news-releases/americans-say-they-are-more-anxious-than-a-year-ago-baby-boomers-report-greatest-increase-in-anxiety

Anderson, B. (1991). *Imagined communities: Reflections on the origins and spread of nationalism*. Verso.

Ball, J. (2017). *Post-Truth: How bullshit conquered the world*. Biteback Publishing.

Barrera, O., Sergei Guriev, S., Henry, E., & Zhuravskay, E. (2020). Facts, alternative facts, and fact checking in times of post-truth politics. *Journal of Public Economics, 182*, 1–19.

Bauerlein, M. (2009). *The dumbest generation: How the digital age stupefies young Americans and jeopardizes our future (or, don't trust anyone under 30)*. Penguin.

Benjamin, J. (1988). *The bonds of love: Psychoanalysis, feminism and the problem of domination*. Random House.

Bowles, N. (2021, January 14). They can't leave the Bay Area fast enough. *New York Times*. https://www.nytimes.com/2021/01/14/technology/san-francisco-covid-work-moving.html

Bradner, E. (2017, January 23). Conway: Trump White House offered "alternative facts" on crowd size. *CNN Politics*. Retrieved January 12, 2020, from https://www.cnn.com/2017/01/22/politics/kellyanne-conway-alternative-facts/index.html

brown, a.m. (2020). *We will not cancel us: And other dreams of transformative justice*. AK Press.

Bryson, M. K., & MacIntosh, L. B. (2010). Can we play *Fun Gay*? Disjuncture and difference, and the precarious mobilities of millennial queer youth narratives. *International Journal of Qualitative Studies in Education, 23(1)*, 101–124.

Buckingham, D. (2008). Introducing identity. In D. Buckingham (Ed.), *Youth, identity and digital media* (pp. 1–19). MIT Press.

Buckingham, D. (n.d.) Growing Up Modern. Retrieved January 13, 2021, from https://davidbuckingham.net/growing-up-modern/

Burke, P. (1997). Representations of the self from Petrarch to Descartes. In R. Porter (Ed.), *Rewriting the self: Histories from the Renaissance to the present* (pp. 17–28). Routledge.

Calancie, O., Ewing, L., Narducci, L. D., Horgan, S., & Khalid-Khan, S. (2017). Exploring how social networking sites impact youth with anxiety: A qualitative study of Facebook stressors among adolescents with an anxiety disorder diagnosis. *Cyberpsychology: Journal of Psychosocial Research on Cyberspace, 11(4)*, article 2.

Castrellón, L. E., Rivarola, A. R. R., & López, G. R. (2017). We are not alternative facts: Feeling, existing, and resisting in the era of Trump. *International Journal of Qualitative Studies in Education, 30(10)*, 936–945.

Clance, P. R., & Imes, S. A. (1978). The imposter phenomenon in high achieving women: Dynamics and therapeutic intervention. *Psychotherapy: Theory, Research & Practice, 15(3)*, 241–247.

Coupland, D. (1991). *Generation X: Tales for an accelerated culture*. St Martin's Press.

Cushman, P. (2019). *Travels with the self: Interpreting psychology as cultural history*. Routledge.

d'Ancona, M. (2017). *Post-Truth: The new war on truth and how to fight back*. Random House.

Davies, W. (2016). *The happiness industry: How the government and big business sold us well-being*. Verso.

Davis, E. (2017). *Post-Truth: Why we have reached peak bullshit and what we can do about it*. Little, Brown Book Group.

Davis, J. E. (2020). Let's avoid talk of "chemical imbalance": it's people in distress. *Psyche*. July 1, 2021, from https://psyche.co/ideas/lets-avoid-talk-of-chemical-imbalance-its-people-in-distress

Dean, J. (2002). *Publicity's secret: How technoculture capitalizes on democracy*. Cornell University Press.

Deloitte Millennial Survey. (2019). Retrieved January 13, 2021, from https://www2.deloitte.com/nz/en/pages/about-deloitte/articles/millennial-survey.html

Distiller, N. (2008). *Desire and gender in the sonnet tradition*. Palgrave Macmillan.

Docu, V. (2018). Millennials and anxiety: An exploration into social networking sites as a predisposing factor. *Romanian Journal of Cognitive Behavioral Therapy and Hypnosis, 5(1–2)*, 1–11.

Doyle, P. (2018, November 26). Shawn Mendez: Confessions of a neurotic pop idol. *Rolling Stone*. Retrieved January 13, 2021, from https://www.rollingstone.com/music/music-features/shawn-mendes-cover-interview-756847/

Eisaman Maus, K. (1995). *Inwardness and theatre in the English Renaissance*. University of Chicago Press.

Erikson, E. H. (1968). *Identity, youth, and crisis*. WW Norton.

Febvre, L., & Henri-Jean, M. (1979). *The coming of the book: The impact of printing 1450–1800*. NLB.

Ferry, A. (1983). *The "inward" language: Sonnets of Wyatt, Sidney, Shakespeare, Donne*. University of Chicago Press.

Fiedler, L. (1973). *The stranger in Shakespeare*. Stein & Day.

Fineman, J. (1986). *Shakespeare's perjured eye: The invention of poetic subjectivity in the sonnets*. University of California Press.

Foucault, M. (1977). What is an author? In D. Bouchard (Ed.), *Language, counter-memory, practice* (pp. 113–138). Basil Blackwell.

Gill, R., & Orgad, S. S. (2018). The amazing bounce-backable woman: Resilience and the psychological turn in neoliberalism. *Sociological Research Online, 23*(2). https://doi.org/10.1177/1360780418769673

Goodman, D. M. (2020). The pornographic self: Technology, vulnerability, and "risk-free" desire. In D. Goodman & M. Freeman (Eds.), *Psychology and the other* (pp. 332–347). Oxford University Press.

Greenblatt, S. (1984). *Renaissance self-fashioning*. University of Chicago Press.

Harrison, N., & Luckett, K. (2019). Experts, knowledge and criticality in the age of "alternative facts": Re-examining the contribution of higher education. *Teaching in Higher Education, 24*(3), 259–271.

Harvey, D. (2007). *A brief history of Neoliberalism*. Oxford: Oxford University Press.

Hipp, P. (2016). Fuck you, I'm not a millennial. Retrieved January 13, 2021, from https://medium.com/@thehipp/fuck-you-i-m-not-a-millennial-e92e653ceb39

Horning, R. (2015, August 12). Do the robot. *The New Inquiry*. Retrieved January 7, 2021, from http://thenewinquiry.com/blog/do-the-robot

Huntington, J. (2001). *Ambition, rank, and poetry in 1590s England*. University of Illinois Press.

Jarrett, C. (2018). Research Digest. June 1. A new study claims that, under pressure, imposter syndrome hits men harder than women. Retrieved January 12, 2021, from https://digest.bps.org.uk/2018/06/01/a-new-study-claims-that-under-pressure-imposter-syndrome-hits-men-harder-than-women/

Kendi, I. X. (2016). *Stamped from the beginning: The definitive history of racist ideas in America*. Bold Type Books.

Kendzior, S. (2016, June 30). The myth of millennial entitlement was created to hide their parents mistakes. *Quartz*. Retrieved December 28, 2020, from https://qz.com/720456/the-myth-of-millennial-entitlement-was-created-to-hide-their-parents-mistakes/

Kurtzleben, D. (2017, February 17). With "fake news" Trump moves from alternative facts to alternative language. *NPR Politics*. Retrieved January 12, 2021, from https://www.npr.org/2017/02/17/515630467/with-fake-news-trump-moves-from-alternative-facts-to-alternative-language

Marotti, A. (1986). *John Donne: Coterie poet*. University of Wisconsin Press.

Marotti, A. (1995). *Manuscript, print, and the English Renaissance Lyric*. Cornell University Press.

McGregor, L. N., Gee, D. N., & Posey, K. E. (2008). I feel like a fraud and it depresses me: The relation between the imposter phenomenon and depression. *Social Behavior and Personality, 36*(1), 43–48.

Melluish, S. (2014). Globalization, culture and psychology. *International review of psychiatry, 26*(5), 538–543.

Mercieca, J. (2020, June 19). A field guide to Trump's dangerous rhetoric. *The Conversation*. Retrieved January 18, 2021, from https://theconversation.com/a-field-guide-to-trumps-dangerous-rhetoric-139531

Mokyr, J., Vickers, C., & Ziebarth, N. L. (2015). The history of technological anxiety and the future of economic growth: Is this time different? *Journal of Economic Perspectives, 29*(3), 31–50.

Moreno, F. M., Lafuente, J. G., Carreón, F. A., & Moreno, S. M. (2017). The characterization of the millennials and their buying behavior. *International Journal of Marketing Studies, 9*(5), 135–144.

Parmar, I. (2021, January 11). The Trump coup d'etat and insurrection was long in the making, and will continue. *The Wire*. Retrieved January 18, 2021, from https://thewire.in/world/the-trump-coup-detat-and-insurrection-was-long-in-the-making-and-will-continue

Perry, I. (2018). *Vexy thing: On gender and liberation*. Duke University Press.

Prensky, M. (2001). Digital natives, digital immigrants. *On The Horizon, 9*(5), 1–6.

Prensky, M. (2006). *Don't bother me, mom – I'm learning!* Paragon House.

Riviere, J. (1929). Womanliness as a masquerade. *The International Journal of Psychoanalysis, 10*, 303–313.

Rizvi, F. (2006). Imagination and the globalisation of educational policy research. *Globalisation, Societies and Education, 4*(2), 193–205.

Rose, N. (1998). *Inventing our selves: Psychology, power, and personhood*. Cambridge: Cambridge University Press.

Rowland, R. (2019). The populist and nationalist roots of Trump's rhetoric. *Rhetoric & Public Affairs, 22*(3), 343–388.

Rutherford, A. (2018). Feminism, psychology, and the gendering of neoliberal subjectivity: From critique to disruption. *Theory & Psychology, 28*(5), 619–644.

Saunders, J. W. (1951). The stigma of print: A note on the social bases of Tudor poetry. *Essays in criticism, 1*, 139–164.

Schalkwyk, D. (2008). *Shakespeare, love and service*. Cambridge University Press.

Schore, A. (2012). *The science of the art of psychotherapy*. Norton.

Serazio, M. (2015). Selling (digital) millennials: The social construction and technological bias of a consumer generation. *Television & New Media, 16*(7), 599–615.

Solomon, L. (2016). The surprising solution to the imposter syndrome. TEDXCharlotte. Published November 30.

Stein, J. (2013, May 20). The Me Me Me Generation: Millennials are lazy, entitled narcissists who still live with their parents. Why they'll save us all. *Time*.

Retrieved January 11, 2021, from http://content.time.com/time/subscriber/article/0,33009,2143001,00.html
Sugarman, J. (2020). Neoliberalism and the ethics of psychology. In D. M. Goodman, E. R. Severson, & H. Macdonald (Eds.), *Race, rage, and resistance: Philosophy, psychology, and the perils of individualism* (pp. 73–89). Routledge.
Sweet, E. (2018). "Like you failed at life": Debt, health and neoliberal subjectivity. *Social Science & Medicine, 212*, 86–93.
Swire, B., Berinsky, A. J., Lewandowsky, S., & Ecker, U. K. H. (2017). Processing political misinformation: Comprehending the trump phenomenon. *Royal Society Open Science, 4(3)*, 1–21.
Tapscott, D. (2009). *Grown up digital: How the net generation is changing your world*. McGraw Hill.
Vanderhoof, E. (2020, November 12). Harry Styles confirms that he is 2020's ideal mascot. *Vanity Fair*. Retrieved January 19, 2021, from
Wall, W. (1993). *The imprint of gender: Authorship and publication in the English Renaissance*. Cornell University Press.
Warley, C. (2005). *Sonnet sequences and social distinction in Renaissance England*. Cambridge University Press.
Warner, M. (2002). Publics and counter publics. *Public Culture, 14(1)*, 49–90.
Zambreno, K. (2012). *Heroines*. Semiotext(e).
Zuboff, S. (2019). *The age of surveillance capitalism: The fight for a human future at the new frontier of power*. Profile.

Open Access This chapter is licensed under the terms of the Creative Commons Attribution 4.0 International License (http://creativecommons.org/licenses/by/4.0/), which permits use, sharing, adaptation, distribution and reproduction in any medium or format, as long as you give appropriate credit to the original author(s) and the source, provide a link to the Creative Commons licence and indicate if changes were made.

The images or other third party material in this chapter are included in the chapter's Creative Commons licence, unless indicated otherwise in a credit line to the material. If material is not included in the chapter's Creative Commons licence and your intended use is not permitted by statutory regulation or exceeds the permitted use, you will need to obtain permission directly from the copyright holder.

6

The Complicit Therapist

Complicities offers a theory, not a therapeutic practice, but if it is taken in as a way of understanding human being, it will inevitably affect practice, as it will affect how the therapist knows what she is doing in her work, and why. And there are practices that take into account the theory of human being I have described under the rubric of complicity. In this chapter, I will detail the established ways of working that help us to apply the theory of human being I have explicated. In addition to Internal Family Systems (IFS), which understands each one of us as a system of parts carrying reactions to our experiences in the world, I will briefly explore the role of neurobiological implications for psychotherapy practice through interpersonal neurobiology (IPNB) and polyvagal theory. I will also look at how attachment theory intersects with these somatic-based ideas. *Complicities* is nothing if not a systems theory, but a systems theory that brings also the notion of the fold. We are not working with black boxes or binaries, but with complex, rhizomatic relations between self and other, constitutive relationships between inside and outside. History, both personal and community history, matters to the system's functioning. I have also referred to intersubjectivity throughout this book, and I will return to it as a useful frame for practice.

If subjects are best thought of as rhizomes or assemblages that "metamorphose or change their properties as they expand their connections" (Rose, 1998, p. 172) and not as binary structures based on self/other or subject/object, then we have a model, following Rose (1998) and Butler (1997) (who both follow Foucault), for understanding subjectification as a process embedded in regimes of power and the realities they enable. This model is responsive to the implications of attachment theory and IPNB, which demonstrate the subject's reliance on their context, including people, to be a subject. We are so far from the Cartesian lone ego. We are, in fact, imbricated on each other physiologically, vulnerable to and dependent on relationship. If there is a core to human being, that is it. Attachment theory and IPNB also illustrate the places where therapy comes in: with a physical understanding of how and why the therapist is complicit in the client's healing. This will be described in more detail below.

A complicit approach might also be seen to bring a set of values to psychotherapeutic practice. I have often been uncomfortable with the conflation of a social justice orientation with the right to judge clients, or when a client's hour is talked about as an opportunity to do advocacy work, as I have heard at some conferences for therapists with a social justice awareness. Advocacy work for a better world is important and admirable, but in my opinion, it is different to the job of a therapist, which is to hold space as nonjudgmentally as possible. IFS would say nonjudgmental acceptance is the necessary prelude to change. We all have parts that act out in rage or shame or hatred or fear. Understanding those parts and what they are trying to protect is the first step toward enabling them to transform their roles. Rage, shame, hatred and fear are burdens. Judging them is not helpful.

Of course this does not mean that we are objective. What it does mean is that if there are issues, attitudes or types of people we cannot or do not wish to tolerate, it is our responsibility not to work with those types of people or those issues or attitudes. Otherwise, in my opinion and in my practice, my job is to help clients understand themselves, in the shaping context of a relationship with me. As should be clear by now, this means also working together on understanding context—family systems; childhood experiences; what specific relationships are doing and what clients are doing in them; identity; culture and histories. The last moving piece is what happens relationally between a client and my own person-and/in-context. So a complicit mindset is a value system that brings together a theory of what human being is, as outlined in this book, and an approach to therapeutic work that takes seriously what nonjudgment means: We are none of us innocent, and we are all of us implicated in each other. I say a little more about this toward the end of this chapter.

The history of psychotherapy has marked a gradual coming together of two different approaches. One is the intrapsychic model of psychoanalysis, which at its start was concerned only with what was happening inside the client (it has since evolved, as the concept of the intersubjective third makes clear). The other is the systems approaches of community mental health and family therapy, developed partly in reaction to psychoanalysis's initial repudiation of context on the inner life of the individual psyche. A theory of complicity shows us that both models need to be taken into account, as each exists in and because of the other. In this chapter, I will account for how I think about the work I do, beginning with my idea of my role, my therapeutic stance. For me, this is feminist.

Stance

Rose (1998) details how one of the signature markers of a scientific approach is the assertion of objectivity. This value—or perhaps, more accurately, fiction—was also an informing element of classic psychoanalysis, although as mentioned above, a more sophisticated understanding of the role of the therapist's personhood is now mainstream in psychoanalysis (see Cooper, 2007). But the idea of the therapist as expert, and thereby as possessed of a scientifically endorsed objective take on a client's person, is still an informing power dynamic of the psy disciplines. This power dynamic is enforced by institutional encroachments on clients' lives and identities, especially for clients who are queer, BIPOC, indigenous, poor, trans, disabled, or at the intersections of these or other othered identities and social positions. The institutional power of the psy expert draws its authority from the history of psychology as outlined in Chap. 1, where the discipline emerged from and helped underwrite a series of related social forces, including colonialism, patriarchy, liberalism and capitalism. Psychoanalysis, a major force in the emergence of psychology as a mainstream discourse of self-understanding, also played a role, deploying a complex jargon which helped create an insiders' club, and having an original vision of the therapist as both patriarch and expert (ask Freud's client Dora, Bernheimer & Kahane, 1985).

Feminist therapy has been around since the 1970s, and started responding to and integrating with existing therapeutic approaches through the 1980s (Dankoski & Deacon, 2000; Hare-Mustin, 1978; Williams, 1995). Reviewing definitions of feminist therapy from this time period, Dankoski and Deacon (2000) summarize that feminist therapy: recognizes the historical and ongoing fact of women's oppression, which by now I would expand to include all gender oppression as I detailed in Chap. 4, as well as intersectionality; works to understand and change gender oppression; brings social context into intrapsychic models; and challenges binary gender norms. In its evolution, it has had to account for transnational and decolonial dynamics, and evolve to accommodate majority world needs and knowledges (Boonzaier & van Niekerk, 2019; Collins et al., 2019). In its Western origins, feminist therapy was more collectively formulated than many other approaches (Sang, 1995), although like white feminism in general, it needed to learn to be properly inclusive. It currently still needs to account for its relationship to hegemonic, WEIRD-driven academic psychology and to transexclusionary ideologies.

Feminist therapists are committed to "a non-hierarchical relationship… [and] empowerment" of clients (Dankoski & Deacon, 2000, p. 53). Many first-generation feminist therapists recount the experiment with informational equality in the early days of feminist therapy, where the therapist abandoned the stance of objective expert and engaged as a co-partner, including self-disclosing to address the power imbalance in the relationship. The general conclusion seems to be that respecting the relationship as an unequal one in terms of both institutional power and emotional disclosure is more advantageous (Robbins, 1995). In other words, the feminist therapist has an ongoing responsibility to acknowledge the power she has in the relationship, while also affording clients mutuality, respect and basic human, given she cannot grant institutional, equality.

Therapeutic healing is also connected to the acknowledgment that external power dynamics affect the client, and that social change is also needed to address individual suffering (see Herman, 1997). Thus, in all its complexity, it is the therapist's job to engage with power dynamics not only in the therapeutic relationship, but also in clients' lives. There is an acknowledgment that context affects and structures psyches (Dankoski & Deacon, 2000).

In other words, being a feminist therapist means acknowledging that we are not objective experts, because, being human, we all have standpoints that inform what we can see and how we understand the world and each other (Brown, 2018). It also means acknowledging that in the systems which have formed modernity, including psychotherapy, there are always power relations that need to be acknowledged and worked with. This entails recognizing injustice. As feminist therapist Greenspan (2017, p. 335) puts it, "We live in the world, and the world lives in us. It's not too far from this awareness to becoming a radical feminist activist." Brown (2018, p. 40) provides a framework for identifying power dynamics in "four realms… somatic, intrapersonal/intrapsychic, intrapersonal/social-contextual, and spiritual/existential, all in constant exchange and interaction." She (Brown, 2018) suggests that a feminist therapy understands that client distress comes from disempowerment in one or more of these realms, and not from individual pathology.

If we have an awareness of power dynamics at all levels of all systems, as well as the understanding that intersectionality and, and in, context, always matters (Zerbe Enns et al., 2020), we can acknowledge the limits of our knowledge and understanding. In this way, we also acknowledge that the client is an expert of their own experience. The feminist therapist's job is to hold the awareness of the limits of her knowing in openness, curiosity and respect, to allow the creation of a mutually enabling and respectful third space (on which more below).

In all these ways, feminist therapists are not objective scientific experts. At the same time, as therapists we bear the bulk of the responsibility for the therapeutic relationship. Holding this responsibility with awareness of our own complicit humanity I hope allows us (at least in our best moments) to be fully human in the room, and to tolerate our own limits and imperfections. Then we can better accompany our clients.

A feminist stance is against neutrality, which does not recognize power relations and does not, to my mind, work with the attachment component of the therapeutic relationship. A stance of neutrality can be withholding, even cruel. It certainly works to keep the therapist safe. But then, I am not by nature someone to sit back. Accordingly, I work to find the balance between holding space for the client's questions, concerns, feelings and experiences, and being present as myself. In psychotherapeutic practice, this process can sometimes be put in the language of directive or nondirective approaches or styles. I would suggest that a complicit therapist recognizes there is really no such thing as being nondirective. By being present with a client, we direct change, as the neurobiological theories detailed below explain. Even holding space, or unconditional positive regard, as a main intervention is engaging complicitously, because we are human. We are implicated in each other on all systems levels, and therapy is an intimate connection. It is far more of a poetry than a science. Indeed, to make the point again about the inadequacy of binaries, neuroscience proves that human being is poetic.

Trauma-Informed, Body-Based Theories

> Psychotherapists are applied neuroscientists. (Cozolino, 2010, p. 341)

Interpersonal neurobiology tracks the physiology of complicity, showing how mind, body and brain are formed in relation to the minds, bodies and brains of others (Solomon & Siegel, 2003). IPNB is interdisciplinary (Siegel, 2019). Like the psychological humanities, it recognizes that we have to get outside of silos of knowledge in order to understand the full picture of human being. Like the notion of complicity, it is all about the constitutive role of connections in the making of personhood. Somatic therapy practices like Somatic Experiencing (SE) therapy or Hakomi therapy, and body-based understandings of emotional states like Polyvagal Theory, show how emotional experiences of self and other are carried in the body, and exactly how the body's knowledge helps form the brain and mind (Kurtz, 2007; Payne et al., 2015; Porges, 2018). Together these approaches help us understand how all kinds of trauma, from single-incident PTSD to complex or developmental traumas to attachment woundings, shape an individual's internal system. More generally, they show how relationships shape us biologically. They demonstrate how individual systems co-relate, co-regulate, and co-create each other. Each individual is also a self in larger sociocultural and historical context, connected rhizomatically to other individuals, as I have been arguing. Each individual is also a self in a body, whose expressions are personal, cultural, familial and interconnected. Each autonomic nervous system and the mind it helps create is complicit in a network of others, known and inherited.

In the last few decades of the twentieth century, some academics and practitioners of psychology began to integrate neurobiological findings into their theories of human affect, exploring how we can physiologically map the ways our early years help form our subjectivities: "Both the brain and the self are built in a stepwise manner by experience" (Cozolino, 2010, p. 31). Furthermore, our minds are co-created with other minds, and are not co-terminous with our brains; we are both "mind-as-brain activity and mind-as-relational activity" (Siegel, 2019, p. 225). And the two are complicit in each other in networks of nested systems that force us to include others and the so-called outside world in each one of us, and in the therapy process.

These scientists and physicians offered theories to account for why therapy works. They married attachment theory and the awareness of processes of somatic co-regulation and the physiological, and therefore emotional and cognitive, consequences of interpersonal interactions. The constitutive role of social systems in creating a nervous system that can feel safe and work well shows us how early and ongoing reactions in the body help set the terms for the mind's sense of itself (Cozolino, 2010; Porges, 2018; Siegel, 2019; Van der Kolk, 2014).

Explicating the constitutive energies between brain, mind, relationships with others and relationships with bodies (our own and the body of the other), IPNB and other theories that explore the interweavings of self and others on a physiological level has illustrated complicity at work in the process of therapy (Afford, 2020; Badenoch, 2008; Schore, 2012). Right brain processes, body-based experiences and unconscious awareness are valued over cognitive and behavioral-based models (McGilchrist,

2009; Schore, 2003). Together with IPNB, this marks a "paradigm shift in psychotherapy practice towards the acknowledgement of the value of non-verbal, implicit processes in the clinical setting" (Peña, 2019, p. 102). Psychoanalysis accommodates this awareness and has been integrated with a neurobiologically driven theory of human being (Schore, 2012).

We know now, therefore, that nonverbal, right brain, affect-based communication is a crucial component of self (Afford, 2020; McGilchrist, 2009; Schore, 2003); that "the body keeps the score" in ways the conscious mind cannot remember (Van der Kolk, 2014); that there are "intersubjective origins of the implicit self" (Schore, 2012, p. 34); and that, "actions are automatic and adaptive, generated by the autonomic nervous system well below the level of conscious awareness… These are autonomic energies moving in patterns of protection" (Dana, 2018, p. 6). This last point, which focuses on the role of the autonomic nervous system in generating unconscious responses to implicit or perceived threat, based on previous trauma to the client's social bonding system, comes from Polyvagal Theory (Porges, 2018):

> Polyvagal Theory demonstrates that even before the brain makes meaning of an incident, the autonomic nervous system has assessed the environment and initiated an adaptive survival response. Neuroception precedes perception. (Dana, 2018, p. 6)

Neuroception describes the out-of-awareness work done by the autonomic nervous system, based on its expectations of the world. Neuroception sets the terms of possibility for a client's sense of self and other. This is one way the past lives within each of us, and helps shape the present. The process of co-regulation via the ventral vagus-linked social engagement system (Dana, 2018) is one way the therapeutic relationship can help change a client's neuroceptive responses. Polyvagal theory works well with attachment theory and its mapping of attachment styles, which, based on early relational experiences, set the terms for what we expect from the world and how we implicitly experience others. Polyvagal theory also works with trauma-informed therapies and with somatic-informed approaches (Levine, 2018; Ogden, 2018; Van der Kolk, 2018). Together, they help fill in the details of both why and how the past, including the people in past relationship with the client; the present and its stimuli and triggers; and the therapist's self (with its past and present formative markers and responses), are all complicit in and with the client.

Early childhood experiences occur before the prefrontal cortex is developed, and are experienced on a physical level. They are encoded in the brain as preverbal understandings. Before we develop the capacity for language and for explicit memory recall, we come to know things literally via our bodies and the sensations they communicate to us (Bretherton, 1992; Langer, 2019; Schore, 2003; Siegel, 2003; Stern, 1985). This knowledge is stored in implicit memory. This is one way that our early contexts are inscribed on and in our subjectivities. From a relational point of view, Harris (2009, p. 178) explores a child's dependence on their first caregivers in a way which makes clear there is no reclaimable self before attachment:

> A developmental account of identity formation must elaborate the dialectical and paradoxical idea that self, including a gendered self, emerges from an interaction in which the child is already interpreted, experienced, and understood. The experience of being mirrored becomes an inextricable element in the child's internal self-schemas in a way that forever blurs the distinction between an experience's beginning inside or outside.

So we are made by the way we are treated and how it feels in our bodies. (Langer, 2019 has pointed out the implications for transgender humans in a symbolic system that assumes cisgender human being unless explicitly told otherwise.) These early interactions with others set the terms by which we know who we are, what to expect from the world, and how and why to relate to others. These are the terms of attachment theory, of course:

> Originating in an amalgam of psychoanalysis and behavioral biology, attachment theory… posits that the real relationships of the earliest stages of life indelibly shape us in basic ways, and… attachment processes lie at the center of all human emotional and social functions. (Schore, 2012, p. 27; see Karen, 1994)

IPNB confirms this. This interdisciplinary marriage brings together a psychoanalytic awareness of the formation and consequences of the unconscious; a systems thinking understanding of the constitutive importance of context and the power of relationships to set the terms for individuals; and somatic and polyvagal understandings of how emotions are encoded in the body and implicitly in the brain, outside of prefrontal cortex awareness and control.

As therapists, we treat this by bringing our own selves to interact with the client's dysregulated, frozen or traumatically fragmented inner system (Afford, 2020; Badenoch, 2008). We have to bring our bodies and our limbic systems, as much as, or perhaps even more than, our scientific inquiring minds: "psychotherapy is not the 'talking' but the 'communicating' cure" (Schore, 2012, p. 39). The notions of the intersubjective and of the internal family system have a role to play in understanding and feeling our way through this therapeutic process, and each will be addressed in more detail below. Understanding that the therapist's sense of self is the guiding framework for the therapy process is a complicit feminist awareness. It means we cannot see ourselves as above or outside what is going on. We cannot assume the scientific, objective expert position. We are together with each client.

The therapist's right brain interacts with the client's right brain, outside of awareness and outside of and beyond language. In order to engage with and help heal a client, we literally do physical, feeling work with them (Afford, 2020; Badenoch, 2008; Geller & Porges, 2014). This is a fully complicit engagement, not only between participants but in the therapist's embodied stance too.

It follows that, in order to be as fully physiologically, implicitly available as possible for the interpersonal process, that therapist is ideally available to themself first. In IPNB terms, the therapist's own brain is integrated, allowing for a flexible mind; and in IFS terms, explored below, the therapist works best when in Self. This means knowing as much as we can about our own minds; countertransferential triggers, in psychoanalytic terms. In his explication of the neuroscience of psychotherapy, Cozolino (2010, p. 30) writes,

Each therapist-client pair creates a unique system resulting in a particular outcome... [T]he therapist's unconscious contributes to the context and outcome of therapy... [T[herapists... will be putting their imprint on the hearts, minds, and brains of their clients.

Knowing our own complicit systems is step one. Learning what we can about our client's is step two. To do this we use both our minds and our bodies, listening to information from both on their varied and connected (complicit) levels. This has been put in terms of the neurobiological role of clinical intuition, and the knowledge that gut feelings connect via the autonomic nervous system to right brain processes and implicit memory-based understandings that are embodied (Peña, 2019). Understanding that our system and our clients' interrelate—that therapy creates inter-subjective space which is biological as well as psychic—is the final step, and it is in this space that therapy happens. I hope it can be seen how this frame, which connects different approaches, makes use of both science and the art of psychotherapy (Schore, 2012); indeed, understands that they work together, or not at all.

Cozolino (2010, p. 46) suggests "a number of working hypotheses" generated from considering the neuroscientific underpinnings of a range of psychotherapeutic modalities, from depth work to systems work to cognitive behavioral approaches. These are, first, that intellectual (left brain, prefrontal cortex) understanding of a problem without (right brain) integration of feelings and sensations cannot bring about psychological change: "Whether it is called symptom relief, differentiation, ego strength, or awareness, all forms of therapy are targeting dissociated neural networks for integration" (Cozolino, 2010, p. 46). This process requires a therapist who is empathetically attuned to the client's spoken and unspoken experience, resulting in secure attachment (see also Afford, 2020; Geller & Porges, 2014). It is also reliant on the leveraging of "optimal stress" (Cozolino, 2010, p. 46), or what SE therapy calls working with the window of tolerance: emotions must have room to be safely felt and contained in the therapeutic process, and "[a]ll forms of successful therapy strive to create safe emergencies in one form or another" (Cozolino, 2010, p. 46). The resulting experience creates opportunities to change autobiographical memory, aka conscious sense of self, as well as the body's unmetabolized memories of the past (Van der Kolk, 2014): "psychotherapy involves changes not in the cognitions of the patient's… mind/brain… but in the affective embodied experiences of his or her [or their] brain/ mind/ body" (Schore, 2012, p. 12).

Schore (2012, p. 10) describes the implications of the findings that early childhood experiences shape the brain and mind, and that right brain affective processes may be more important than left brain cognition in understanding and treating mental health:

> Previously the Cartesian mind/ body split has plagued not only psychology and psychiatry but medicine in general… The current paradigm shift in research from cognition to emotion has been a major force in resolving the Cartesian problem and generating theoretical models that integrate… "nature and nurture."

Schore (2012, p. 16) also suggests that modern culture has become too invested in and reliant on left brain processes, resulting in,

> [A]n overemphasis on psychopharmacology over psychotherapy, an undue influence of the insurance industry in defining "normative" and "acceptable" forms of treatment, an overidealization of "evidence-based practice", an underappreciation of the large body of studies on the effectiveness of the therapeutic alliance, a trend towards "manualization" of therapy, a training model that focuses on the learning of techniques rather than expanding relational skill…

These critiques should be familiar to the reader by now, along with their social, historical and economic complicities. It is worth noting that these are all the same complaints made about the consequences of viewing psy work as a science, explored in Chap. 1. Schore (2012) invokes McGilchrist's (2009) warning of the development of a technocratic, neoliberal world order, also as a consequence of ignoring the importance of right brain, affective, embodied and interconnected elements of human being, as explored in Chap. 5.

From his work on the importance of the implicit, affective experience of self in the formation of later, thinking, self-awareness, and the neuroscientific evidence behind this explanation of how the unconscious works,

Schore (2012, p. 119) concludes, "The concept of a single, unitary 'self' is as misleading as the idea of a single, unitary 'brain.'" Porges (2018) suggests the brain is also in the body; and Schore's (2012, p. 119) work shows how the self begins in the preverbal right brain: "The left and right hemispheres process information in their own unique fashion" and comprise two systems, conscious and unconscious. There is no Cartesian unity here, not even on a physical level (see McGilchrist, 2009). If there is one modality that most embraces the idea of the self as a collection of parts, which takes into account systems thinking, depth work and somatic experiences, it is Internal Family Systems.

Internal Family Systems

Internal Family Systems (IFS) is both a way of understanding human being and a therapy modality. It was developed by Richard Schwartz out of family therapy approaches to clients with eating disorders (Schwartz & Sweezy, 2020). IFS has been shown to be effective with a range of clients, individual, couple and family groupings, and a range of diagnoses (Haddock et al., 2016; Lucero et al., 2018; Sweezy & Ziskind, 2017). It has been demonstrated to significantly improve the ability to mentalize and perspective-take (Böckler et al., 2017) and has been recognized by the National Registry of Evidence-based Programs and Practices as an evidence-based treatment for anxiety, depression and medical conditions (Matheson, 2015; Schwartz & Sweezy, 2020; Sowell, 2013). It has also been extensively used in therapy with survivors of childhood sexual abuse (Goulding & Schwartz, 2003).

IFS counters the mainstream Western idea of the unified self, explored in Chap. 1, by understanding subjects as made up of a collection of parts, as well as a core Self who has the innate, organic capacity to lead the system. There are two broad categories of parts, protectors and exiles, with the latter carrying the burdens of unmetabolized emotions and traumatic, horrifying or hurtful experiences.

IFS offers a sophisticated view of how systems are made up of complicit relations. It applies systems thinking, which traces relational patterns and sees a system as self-organized, complex and striving toward health:

> Systems thinking helps us examine the various systems surrounding or within a client to find and release constraints. Constraints may exist in a client's system of inner personalities, in the client's relationship with various family members, in the way the family in general is organized, in the way various institutions outside the family affect it… and in the way the client's ethnic community and the larger society affect the families values and beliefs. All of these human systems are interlocked. They affect and are affected by each other. (Schwartz & Sweezy, 2020, p. 26)

Furthermore, attest Schwartz and Sweezy (2020, p. 26), these systems mirror each other structurally at each level. There is thus "a good deal of universality" in the operating principles across systems. This framing, as we will see, allows IFS to envision its model of parts with roles that can go awry as applicable to all levels of human being and the institutions that structure our outer, and therefore help to structure our inner, lives.

IFS assumes that our parts always work for us, even if they sometimes are at odds with each other (as when one part of you wants one thing, and another part wants the opposite), or are doing counterproductive work (such as internally shaming a person to try and keep them safe from revealing a shamed part). This is a way of understanding binary positions as polarizations between two parts, which are invariably working at loggerheads for the same thing. The solution is not to take sides, but to facilitate understanding between the parts—to break the binary energy that is keeping them both stuck and escalating in relation to each other.

IFS is nonpathologizing, seeing symptoms as the behaviors caused by parts that need to be heard and understood. It is each person's unique, intrinsically healing Self that does the hearing and helping of component parts. The therapist is a guide, not an expert—how can she be expert about someone else's internal system?

The IFS process entails finding, identifying and listening to parts. Parts can be held in places in the body, and can also be frozen in a traumatic moment in time. As such, IFS offers a practice that understands and makes use of the insights of both depth and systems psychotherapies, as well as the techniques of somatic psychologies that understand how the past can be held in the body, and from there, impact the psyche.

This offers an understanding of the ecological relationship not only internally but between people and their wider systems. It is a fundamentally complicit understanding of human being, bringing an awareness of how systems both form and impact each other, as well as an optimistic, empowering view of the systemic striving for health:

> [H]uman systems—parts, individuals, families, communities, and cultures—nest, mirror, and interact. And since all systems sustain injury at times, all are at risk of developing burdens that can be passed down for generations. At the same time, all systems seek balance and make attempts to self-right. (Schwartz & Sweezy, 2020, p. 228)

Schwartz and Sweezy (2020, chapter 18) apply IFS to American society, and their findings echo the assessments made in Chaps. 2 and 3 here. They suggest that America carries legacy burdens of racism, patriarchy, individualism and materialism (what I have named as capitalism), all of which were brought by Europeans fleeing not only persecution, but a culture that brutally controlled and punished its members (Foucault graphically details these methods of control in *Discipline and Punish* Foucault, 1977). They also account for Trumpism in an interesting way, as a rigid, protective defense against economic changes of the past 40 years.

In this way, the IFS understanding of how systems work, sometimes maladaptively, to protect and maintain the status quo, layers onto historical explanations for the development and maintenance of binary systems. It also offers an alternative psychological model to the psychoanalytic self/other understanding as to why this culture has developed the processes of toxic othering that have driven value systems and the institutions that perpetuate them:

> The American legacy burdens of racism, patriarchy, individualism and materialism imbue protectors with... contempt. As a result, the United States not only exiles a greater percentage of its population than any other Western nation, it has less compassion and more contempt for its exiled populations. (Schwartz & Sweezy, 2020, p. 246)

Parts work goes well with the understanding of neural networks and the habits of being they set up and can be changed by (Badenoch, 2008). IPNB's focus on the complex system that makes up our selves—or, indeed, in IFS's term, Selves—includes the expectation that the system strives toward harmonious self-organization, which means health is achieved through flexibility and integration of systems (i.e., systems work smoothly together) (Siegel, 1999). Anderson (2013, p. 108) suggests that working with parts "can create the optimal environment for the brainstem, limbic system, cortex, and especially the prefrontal cortex to work together, promoting neural integration and creating new pathways in the brain." In other words, there may be a neurobiological explanation for how and why IFS works, which includes the interpersonal forces detailed by Siegel (1999, 2007) and the nonverbal, embodied right brain processes tracked by Schore (2003) and by somatic-based psychotherapies like Hakomi (Kurtz, 2007) and Somatic Experiencing (Levine, 1997; Payne et al., 2015). Anderson (2013) suggests that IFS helps implicit memory become explicit, integrates experience and creates new neural networks to enable new responses to situations, stimuli and people. Thus, IFS works with aspects of trauma theory which trace the ways trauma is encoded in the body (Van der Kolk, 2014). He (Anderson, 2013, p. 109) also proposes that certain reactive parts 'live' in the brainstem or amygdala, and that "over time… we will learn where all the parts are located in the brain."

In my experience, IFS's nonjudgmental, nonpathologizing approach to whatever a client is experiencing is not only appealing for a feminist therapist, it is extremely effective. As Schwartz (2017) commented in a discussion about working with racist parts as a white man, hating our parts has never worked in getting them to change. Learning to know our parts is a powerful way to understand how our internal systems work, because it allows us to see the internal connections, alliances, arguments we have going on and how these structure our responses and reactions to ourselves and others. It sees binaries as unhelpful oppositions to be mediated and resolved, so that co-operation is possible between parts. It also accounts for the impact of external systems of all kinds on the experiences and reactions of specific parts. Because IFS is collaborative in approach, it fits with a feminist stance. It does not expect the therapist to be the expert; it wants to hear from the parts. Crucially, also, IFS's main goal is to support a client's Self in taking leadership internally. IFS allows the therapist and the client to problem-solve together. While trust in the therapist is an important enabling component of this approach as all others, mutuality is a value in IFS (Schwartz, 2013).

IFS is not a system of object relations in the psychoanalytic sense. It takes parts literally, not metaphorically or symbolically, or as introjects. Intersubjectivity, as it is developed in psychoanalysis, begins by interrogating the classic psychoanalytic self/other binary, where the other is both an internalization used by the self, and, crucially, in need of recognition as an independent subject, not just material for object relations.

Beyond the Self/Other Binary: Thirdness

If IFS sees parts as literally independent entities or subpersonalities that are in relation to the Self (we are made up of others who are also ourselves), intersubjective psychoanalytic psychotherapy aims to own the self's dependence on the other. Here the other is both outside of, and then introjected into, the self. In this sense, it is a part. Crucial to the intersubjective understanding is the recognition that the other—the literal outside person upon whom the subject is dependent, in the first place the mother or first caretaker—is also a self. The object in object relations theory is thus restored to its own humanity, from whence comes its power and importance as internalized object in the subject's psyche. The self craves the other's recognition, which means the self needs the other to be also a self, and not just an object (Benjamin, 1988). This breaks the objectifying power of binary energy, and, as Benjamin (1988) points out, the constituting logic of patriarchy's rules for personhood, where the female is the first object on which the self depends.

Benjamin (1995) details how the self needs to hold the other both as its own independent self, and as an internalized other. Locating oneself between these two places of the other is necessary to respect the other's personhood as well as to inhabit one's reliance on the other, she says. This fundamentally nonbinary understanding of human being is what Benjamin (1995, p. 5) calls an "ambiphilic" approach. She explores the consequences of asking about the difference between other as another subject (a "real" object) and other as internalized part (an object relation), while acknowledging that "both are endemic to psychic experience" (p. 29). "Intersubjectivity was formulated in deliberate contrast to the logic of subject and object, which predominates in Western philosophy and science" (Benjamin, 1995, p. 30). Thus, she insists on a both-and approach.

This nonbinary approach facilitates the embrace of the intersubjective as the space where therapy occurs. The therapist's self is complicit in the process, and in the client's experience of self through the therapist as other. This third space, between and because of the dyad of two selves in the relationship, is constituted through body-based and right brain, affective, nonverbal communications (Schore, 2012). To add Benjamin's (1988, 1995) intersubjective vocabulary and perspective to this process, the client must experience the therapist as an independent subject in order to benefit from their healing presence, while at the same time taking the therapist in to facilitate a different sense of self, of what is possible inside and in relation, and therefore, to change. Once more, the complicit nature of human being—the ways our minds rely on and make each other—is core to the therapy process theoretically as well as actually, in physical reality. The focus becomes squarely relational, on attachment processes and the feelings of love, safety, recognition and pleasure that occur when selves embrace all aspects of their complicities. Gesturing toward the consequences of viewing self as self-contained, Benjamin (1995, p. 32) comments, "The idea of pleasure was lost when ego psychology put the id on the backburner, but it might be restored by recognizing the subjectivity of the other." Benjamin's (1995) definition of pleasure is pleasure in and of mutuality. It is a result of the relation between two selves, which means the rejection of the self/other binary.

The interpersonal neurobiological intersects with the idea of the creation of a third as the result of the relation between two, a model of nonbinary human complicity that describes what therapy is:

> The social synapse is the space between us... When we smile, wave, and say hello, these behaviours are sent through the space between us via sights, sounds odors, and words. These electrical and mechanical messages received by our senses are converted into electrochemical impulses within our

brains. These signals stimulate new behaviors, which, in turn, transmit messages back across the social synapse. (Cozolino, 2010, pp. 179–80)

Afford (2020) tracks in detail how this interpersonal neurobiology works in the therapy room. What does an online, mediated world, as explored in Chap. 5, do to this necessary human interaction? And what has the past year of largely online therapy conducted under the shelter-in-place rules of life during the coronavirus pandemic done to our work? What will it mean if we choose to continue virtual living once coronavirus is more contained? What will the cyborg third feel like? Certainly, Benjamin's (1995, pp. 36–7) articulation of the risk of intersubjectivity speaks to some of the relational consequences this culture is seeing in a socially mediated world:

> The need for recognition entails this fundamental paradox: at the very moment of realizing our own independent will, we are dependent upon another to recognize it. At the very moment we come to understand the meaning of *I, myself,* we are forced to see the limitations of that self. At the moment when we understand that separate minds can share similar feelings, we begin to learn that these minds can also disagree.

Ideally, we learn ultimately to tolerate the spectrum of differences between self and self, from different needs, to disagreement to conflict. We need the self not to become an objectified other, which Goulding and Schwartz (2003, p. 46) describe as the "distorted" results of polarization, where another's multiplicity is lost to the extreme reaction of a triggered part. For the other to retain their personhood in the face of conflict or disagreement, a state of "constant tension between recognizing the other and asserting the self" must be possible (Benjamin, 1995, p. 38). It is not a resting place. It is a place of ongoing doing, which requires us to manage the "sting" (ibid, p. 47) of having to engage with, manage, accommodate, speak back to, see, difference. Rather than use the other as an object to secure the borders, the stability, of the self, which is the typical use of otherness in Western colonial, patriarchal self/other psychology.

In the description above, Benjamin (1995) is tracking a developmental process in the young child: If he can learn to see his mother as a person, he can learn to tolerate her difference from him. Then he will not need to control her to feel safe. Elsewhere she (Benjamin, 1988) details how, in a patriarchal culture, the refusal of mutual recognition and the establishment of a sense of self built on the other as object set up relations of domination. The first object, in such a culture, is the mother, and the subject is the child of Freud's Oedipus complex, detailed in Chap. 2. Sexual difference becomes the lynchpin of the system. Patriarchy intersects with racism, with colonialism and with the neoliberal capitalism that resulted from the historical outspooling of all three, together with the centering of the self-contained, dependency-rejecting, left-brain-valorizing Cartesian subject as the model for Western subjectivity. Othering, cancelling, entrenched partisanship: what are these if not an inability to tolerate the subjectivity of the other? And if mutuality requires an embodied component, it is no wonder that a society increasingly built on social media is struggling to cohere as a society. As detailed in Chap. 5, my contention is that the computer age, late modernity, has exacerbated many of the dynamics of early modernity, whence began the modern systems of domination with all their consequences for human being across a globe subjected to Western norms.

The idea of the intersubjective third also includes social, political and historical dynamics, as we saw in Chap. 2. Sehrbrock (2020) calls this social thirdness, and writes about how therapists should manage the intersubjective consequences of what he calls prejudice, which creates two subjects locked in their own positionality with regard to each other. Attention to the social third—the space made of the collective and the cultural as well as the interpsychic—is crucial, according to Sehrbrock (2020), to avoid reproducing the silencing imperatives of homophobia and misogyny, and other prejudices. This is one way to understand how a social justice commitment enters clinical practice without becoming an imposition of therapist values on the client:

> Attention to the social third, to me, is thus a clinical and ethical obligation of exercising social conscience…. by silencing or ignoring the subtle and gross intersectionalities of social thirdness, psychoanalytic practice perpetuates the very injuries and pains it purports to heal. (Sehrbrock, 2020, p. 291)

His conclusion: "In order to realize psychoanalytic principles in the age of #MeToo, Time's Up, and BlackLivesMatter, we need to recognize social thirdness as an aspect of our conscience, our ethics, and our psychoanalytic politics" (Sehrbrock, 2020, p. 294). Stephens (2020) explores how the intersubjective process of knowing ourselves with and through the other can help with long-standing racialized dynamics in Western culture. An intersubjective approach, she (Stephens, 2020) suggests, can counteract the binary dynamics in self/other thinking that perpetuate dynamics of oppression and the typical affective responses of guilt and rage.

As I have been illustrating, the therapy process is an interaction between two embodied, contextualized minds. The intersubjective space, itself existing in context, is reliant on right brain, affective, intuitive, nonverbal, embodied relating between client and therapist (Peña, 2019; see Afford, 2020). In exploring the implications of intersubjectivity for a Western psychology rooted in a self-contained 'I', and intuiting IPNB, Coelho and Figueiredo (2003, p. 195) ask:

> But is it in fact possible to perceive what the other *self* feels, what it perceives? We assume that in some way it is, since psychological practices are based on elements of perception, and especially on mutual perception. Possibly most communication depends on a sophisticated interplay between the perceptions of the participants in the therapeutic process... There are pre-verbal, infra-verbal, pre-representational, corporal and perhaps even instinctual forms of communication, as well, of course, as verbal communication itself. There are conscious, pre-conscious and, who knows, perhaps even unconscious perceptions. Why not? We often transmit what we do not know we have perceived, and also recognize sensations and feelings whose origin we are unsure of. We recognize our own feelings, but are they really ours, or the other's?

IPNB answers the first question posed here ("is it in fact possible to perceive what the other *self* feels?") with a resounding "yes," and also explains how. We not only perceive the feelings of the other, through various channels of communication, as Coelho and Figueiredo (2003) detail above, but we can account for the ways the feelings of the other not only resonate within, but help to constitute, the self, physically as well as psychically.

Thus, working in the intersubjective space means working with the lessons of the somatic-informed therapy practices. It also means working within a systems focus, because culture, history and inheritances are an inevitable part of the space, within and between each participant, therapist and client. IFS therapy calls some of these inheritances, the ones that cause or carry trauma in the broad sense, burdens. It looks to see which parts of both therapist and client hold and respond to burdens, in order to help free them of their constraining roles. All of these approaches can be understood as acknowledging and responding to the fact of complicity as the fundamental marker of human being. They merely approach this fact in their own, often complementary and intersecting, ways.

A Social Justice Practice

How to engage in a discipline, psychotherapy, that stands accused, as we have seen, of co-creating the oppressive systems of modernity? How does the therapy space take full account of the social third if therapy itself is a force of Foucaultian discipline and subjectification? Despite the ongoing work of liberation psychologies, critical psychology, feminist and decolonial psychologies, psychology remains a powerful proponent and cause of binary thinking, and often reliant on the stance of scientific objectivity, with all the objectifying dynamics we have traced so far. Psychotherapy stands accused of helping to invent and perpetuate the liberal subject, today neoliberally subjected by all the institutions of the Western world.

Psychoanalysis offered the insight that the subject is a subject by virtue of its alienation from itself, and therefore cannot be the imagined masterfull, self-centered, liberal subject the West believes it to be. This has been very productive for literary theory, but less transformative of mainstream psychotherapeutic practice. In 2021, with the ongoing dominance of behavioral medicine and under the influence of the healthcare industrial complex, the psy disciplines remain "the very heartland of the self" (Rose, 1998, p. 8), helping to perpetuate the idea that, if we can afford it, we are responsible for ourselves, and for improving so as to be productive citizens of late capitalism. Rose (1998) argued that no one theory of the human subject (such as psychology) could account for the process of subjectification in which such theorizing participated. He reminds us to pay attention to the "complex of apparatuses, practices, machinations, and assemblages within which human being has been fabricated" (Rose, 1998, p. 10). Given that the humanities at least has known this for decades, what do we do now, in a Trumpified, burning, melting, drowning, contagious world? What can psychology do, given its complicity in the creation of this world?

For example, Binkley (2020) writes about the emotional postures of black rage and white listening, and how together they serve to reinforce white privilege. He details his personal experience of trying to understand his ambivalence about being invited to occupy the position of white listener, in an "unholy contract" of "raging and listening… sustaining and enriching each other, wedded in a conspiracy to keep me where and who I was, and to suppress any possibilities for an overturning of things as they were. Or imagining things as they might be" (Binkley, 2020, p. 93). He offers a genealogy of these raced emotional positions as they exist in liberal institutions. He suggests that the expressions of strong emotion as catharsis, met with an empathetic listening, are psychologized technologies: ignorant white privilege learns to know and transcend itself via an empathetic encounter with the rage of the raced other. Responsible listeners learn their own authentic personhood and how to undo racism.

The result is,

> Where once the politics of race might have been about conflicting ideas, structural analyses, and moral commitments, today it is about empathetic sensibilities, emotional states, and the capacity to sense and respond to what others around you are feeling. (Binkley, 2020, p. 93)

If Binkley is correct, this suggests that the current state of resistance to racial injustice is individualized and psychologized through the modernizing, political, processes mapped by, for example, Rose (1998) and Sugarman (2020). In being individualized, this process is rendered binary, and reduced to a self/other relation that by definition will always need someone to despise. This someone is as easily the listening white as it is the constitutive other of privilege's invisible self. It is the inadequate cis feminist or the ignorant rich kid. It allows progressive culture to fragment itself.

The feeling of being trapped Binkley describes is familiar to me, as a well-intentioned white person who is committed to interrogating the comforts of my privilege and resisting the collapses of fragility. I am not rendering structurally equivalent the oppressed subject of institutional inequality and/or structural oppression, and the well-intentioned listening white. But I am suggesting that the same binary structure, when it is the essentialized model for accounting for oppression, can undo our chance for real systemic change. Historically, oppression in Western modernity operates along a self/other binary, where the constitutive other is made to bear the self's projections so that the self can experience itself as good and whole and in control. To counter such a structure, we need a different model. We need a theory of the complicit subject, where innocence or guilt, goodness or badness, cannot be the focus. Furthermore, we need to think in more complex ways about where the language of psychology, and particularly ideas of wounding, trauma, rage, guilt, and intention have left us. To do this, we do would do better to challenge the idea of individual subjects locked in positions of privilege versus positions of victimization.

In tracking her evolution as a feminist therapist from social activist, aware of the importance of context to each human, to a more profoundly connected understanding of human being through what she calls the dark emotions, Greenspan (2017, p. 342) writes of "a new paradigm of emotional ecology in which our seemingly most personal emotions are connected to their larger social and global contexts." Goodman and Freeman (2015, p. 9) call for the need to "think *otherwise*" in psychology. To reject the bounded self of modernity, of liberal individualism, is to embrace a self open to what it does not know, which is to say, the world outside itself. For Goodman and Freeman, such a psychotherapeutic practice is "more *relational*" and, implicitly therefore, "more *ethical*." And that, finally, is what the idea of the complicit subject offers: an ethics of "*being-with*" (Goodman & Freeman, 2015, p. 9) that might help us engage with the systemic injustice that harms us all.

None of this is intended to downplay the inheritances of race, class, gender, religious, geographic, cis-privilege or ablebodied-privilege. I am not trying to excuse or ignore the abuses of power on which the neocolonial world is built. I am certainly not resisting the recent public discourse about privilege, especially white privilege, which is finally being heard by at least some white people thanks to the hard and careful work of the Black Lives Matter movement. America is built on the exploitation and suffering of Native, Black and brown people, and those foundations cannot be dug up. Western culture is built on a cisgender binary that informs all its systems of thought and meaning. It is also true that until white people and cisgender people and ablebodied people and people assigned male at birth and those with class privilege can bear to take responsibility for these foundations, outrage remains appropriate. But outrage, however painful and true its source, is easier than holding the complexity of complicit, flawed humanity. This includes learning to understand and accept all of our parts, and how they—and we—are reliant on each other.

This is one suggestion for how we truly make space for the other, what it means to hold therapeutic compassion, perhaps especially for those very different from ourselves. A theory of complicity is at odds with identity politics and the binary positionings identity politics have unfortunately sometimes come to reinscribe. Identity politics are necessary for visibility within a liberal system, as explored in Chap. 2, and also bring important self-affirming, empowering possibilities in the context of Western individualism, allowing for solidarity in the face of oppression and the concomitant negation of personhood suffered by so many. But basing a program for change on a way of thinking that defines us all according to our place in the current structure, and from there, in binary relation to each other, has its limits, in terms of ways forward out of the system. We have seen how, in political science, Brown (1995) has written about this, and from gender studies, so has Butler (1993). Gamson (1995, p. 391) also explores the paradox that in America, "fixed identity categories are both the basis for oppression and the basis for political power." In another example, this time from the discipline of history, Scott (1991) explores the importance and the implications of making visible homosexual practices and the institutions that enabled them, as a project of reclaiming a denied history:

> History is a chronology that makes experience visible, but in which categories appear as nonetheless ahistorical: desire, homosexuality, heterosexuality, femininity, masculinity, sex, and even sexual practices become so many

> fixed entities being played out over time, but not themselves historicized. (Scott, 1991, p. 778)

Thus, "The project of making experience visible precludes analysis of the workings of this system and of its historicity; instead, it reproduces its terms" (Scott, 1991, p. 779).

Scott (1991) acknowledges the importance, for someone who has experienced marginalization, of visibly experiencing oneself as part of a mass of people like oneself, of belonging to a movement, for both identity and political safety. Such movement processes allow challenges to what were previously master narratives of normality and moral goodness, which either left out or used (othered) the experiences and identities of marginalized groups. Counter-narratives, the right to make one's own meaning of one's self, life, desires and group, are powerful and important pushbacks against oppressive meanings being made of one and one's group.

At this point in history, some of us are more free of powerful institutions claiming the right to decide about who we are, who we should be and what is to be done to us to make it so. So-called conversation therapy, the attempt to change sexual orientation or gender identity, is now illegal in a number of states (Drescher et al., 2016; Newhook et al., 2018). One consequence of postmodernity, however, is that evidence becomes always partial—there can no longer be absolute proof of one absolute truth, since the postmodern reality is one of fractured, competing, different stories, narratives of and about difference. In a binary frame, difference always means power dynamics, and so meanings are contested. One result, writes Scott (1991, p. 777), is that "experience" becomes an underwriter of historical evidence, of the truth of someone's reality:

> It is precisely this kind of appeal to experience as uncontestable evidence and as an originary point of explanation—as a foundation on which analysis is based—that weakens the critical thrust of histories of difference.... these studies lose the possibility of examining those assumptions and practices that excluded considerations of difference in the first place. They take as self-evident the identities of those whose experience is being documented and thus naturalize their difference. They locate resistance outside its discursive construction and reify agency as an inherent attribute of individu-

als, thus decontextualizing it... Questions about the constructed nature of experience, about how subjects are constituted as different in the first place,... are left aside. The evidence of experience then becomes evidence for the fact of difference, rather than a way of exploring how difference is established, how it operates, how and in what ways it constitutes subjects who see and act in the world.

Scott's (1991) meta-analysis of how meanings are made in history parallels Rose's (1998) insistence that the psy disciplines cannot be taken at their word, since they have helped to construct the language in which we speak subjectivity. These lessons from the humanities have still to be taken seriously. The constructed nature of identity categories themselves, the way difference is made to do the work of meaning-making from within the terms of the dominant system, these things are elided by the reinscription of binary categories: privileged/marginalized; oppressor/oppressed. Here, we see the pull toward the construction of another binary, mentioned in Chap. 1, where material reality (suffering, exclusionary practices, actual violence) is placed against theory, the desire for meta-analysis of the meaning-making processes that underlie and enable the material suffering. My point, of course, is that they are complicit in each other, not at odds. Material reality is created by discourse, by power dynamics, by the meanings made of difference. And within, between, seeping outside of these processes, human being exceeds the binary positions imposed on it by systems of power, by history, by inheritance. If this were not true, what would be the point of therapy? Identity positions may be necessary to begin the work of resistance, but if they are also the end point, the system remains in place.

Lorde (1981) comments on being told she speaks with "the moral authority of suffering" because she is black and lesbian. Her response is, "what you hear in my voice is fury, not suffering. Anger, not moral authority. There is a difference." She details the importance of anger when there is injustice and suffering, where there is hatred of the difference represented by othered groups: "This hatred and our anger are very different. Hatred is the fury of those who do not share our goals [of liberation], and its object is death and destruction. Anger is a grief of distortions between peers, and its object is change." She asks for the creative, empowering use of anger to generate an ability to engage with difference, "to alter those distortions which history has created around our difference. For it is those distortions which separate us. And we must ask ourselves: Who profits from all this?"

The system based on binary thinking, on misogyny, racism, cisgenderism, ableism, classism, colonialism, profits. Certain groups, for whom this system was developed, profit. But even those of us who profit are intersectional, and therefore subject to the system. And since binary logic is false and artificial, as I have explored, what seems to be pure profit is always complicit, vulnerable. To use Lorde's (1981) idea, anger can be a force to break the binary, to shift us out of relations of victims and oppressors, to make us all peers in human being. Individuality, neocolonial discursive and material structures, liberal rights, neoliberal pressures and the twenty-first century imperative to profit from your personhood are forces against which rage is appropriate. And a complicit take on these dynamics allows us to start with the evidence of the experience of these systems, but not to end there, which would return us to the same terms.

Lorde's (1981) wisdom, as usual, remains relevant to our complex times. She rejects the commodification of suffering, while claiming and harnessing her righteous anger. She denies that anger has to turn into the same kind of othering hatred that generated the suffering and the anger in the first place. She refuses the charge that being angry because of racism makes her problematic or destructive to any cause, and she rightly returns the responsibility to the white women who are rendered guilty or uncomfortable by her anger. She also refuses the charge of causing hopelessness or of collapsing into victimhood: she is speaking about the productive and empowering use of anger to address injustice, and the necessity of allies being able to hear and learn from this, not collapse in the face of it, as the privileged often tend to do. She (Lorde, 1981) asks, "What woman here is so enamored of her own oppression that she cannot see her heelprint upon another woman's face? What woman's terms of oppression have become precious and necessary to her as a ticket into the fold of the righteous, away from the cold winds of self-scrutiny?"

I do not mean to minimize the real suffering caused by structural oppression. But I do mean to humbly and respectfully ask that we begin to consider our mutual entanglements in this structure. We are all complicit in each other. And if therapy nowadays can help, it can benefit enormously from getting away from reified truths.

The Complicit Therapist: How Therapy Heals

"[I]f we want to create a world in which conflict and trauma aren't the center of our collective existence, we have to practice something new, ask different questions, access again our curiosity about each other as a species" (brown 2020, p. 73). brown is talking specifically about the tendency in restorative and social justice movements to act against each other from the places of wounding caused by being the victims and survivors of histories of oppression and the systems of supremacy these histories continue to construct and fuel. This is an example of complicity, where allies are unconsciously driven by the methods they cannot help but have internalized as a result of being subject to them, subjected by them. Naming this, as brown does, is the necessary first step to finding ways to be different. We have to practice something new. But as a career in the humanities taught me via the theory I learned there, we will practice whatever the content of our common sense is. Common sense is always invested, always historically and politically produced. And it will always present itself as natural, obvious, the best and/or only way to think about things. This book has presented a way of thinking that tries to interrupt some of the common sense of Western culture: that binary thinking is inevitable, that we are not psychically and biologically co-created. If human being can be thought of as complicitous, we can open up to changes to our systems and ourselves, as the two will always influence each other.

We have looked at some psychotherapeutic approaches that, in their various ways, are systems oriented but also allow for a depth approach. I have added a focus on the necessity of a nonbinary understanding of how these dynamics work. The system is always nested in, and woven into, other systems: the individual is a system physiologically connected to their past, to their community, and to their caregivers and family, and all their systems in turn. Our parts are forged in these relationships, experiences, inheritances. The therapeutic dyad is also a system, made up of therapist and client co-creating their intersubjective third space, which itself holds all the nested systems, including the social-political inheritances and burdens at play in each unique space. The work of the therapeutic bond is neurobiological and an experience of deep human connection (Geller & Porges, 2014), poetic in its inability to be accounted for scientifically outside of affective, embodied experience. Brains, minds, bodies, hearts and souls, we are connected. Therapy heals through complicity.

Works Cited

Afford, P. (2020). *Therapy in the age of neuroscience*. Routledge.

Anderson, F. G. (2013). "Who's taking what?" Connecting neuroscience, psychopharmacology and internal family systems for trauma. In M. Sweezy & E. L. Ziskind (Eds.), *Internal family systems: New dimensions* (pp. 107–126). Routledge.

Badenoch, B. (2008). *Being a brain-wise therapist: A practical guide to interpersonal neurobiology*. Norton.

Benjamin, J. (1988). *The bonds of love: Psychoanalysis, feminism and the problem of domination*. Random House.

Benjamin, J. (1995). *Like subjects, love objects: Essays on recognition and sexual difference*. Yale University Press.

Bernheimer, C., & Kahane, C. (Eds.). (1985). *In Dora's case: Freud – hysteria – feminism* (2nd ed.). Columbia University Press.

Binkley, S. (2020). Black rage and white listening: On the psychologization of racial emotionality. In D. M. Goodman, E. R. Severson, & H. Macdonald (Eds.), *Race, rage, and resistance: Philosophy, psychology, and the perils of individualism* (pp. 90–107). Routledge.

Böckler, A., Herrmann, L., Trautwein, F., Holmes, T., & Singer, T. (2017). Know thy selves: Learning to understand oneself increases the ability to understand others. *Journal of Cognitive Enhancement, 1*(2), 197–209.

Boonzaier, F., & van Niekerk, T. (Eds.). (2019). *Decolonial feminist community psychology*. Springer.

Bretherton, I. (1992). The origins of attachment theory: John Bowlby and Mary Ainsworth. *Developmental Psychology, 28*, 759–777.

brown, a.m. (2020). *We will not cancel us: and other dreams of transformative justice*. AK Press.

Brown, L. (2018). *Feminist therapy* (2nd ed.). American Psychological Association.

Brown, W. (1995). *States of injury: Power and freedom in late modernity*. Princeton University Press.
Butler, J. (1993). Imitation and gender insubordination. In H. Abelove, M. A. Barale, & D. Halparin (Eds.), *The gay and lesbian studies reader* (pp. 307–320). Routledge.
Butler, J. (1997). *The psychic life of power: Theories in subjection*. Stanford University Press.
Coelho, N. E., & Figueiredo, L.C. (2003). Patterns of intersubjectivity in the constitution of subjectivity: Dimensions of otherness. *Culture & Psychology, 9*(3), 193–208.
Collins, L. H., Machizawa, S., & Rice, J. K. (Eds.). (2019). *Transnational psychology of women: Expanding international and intersectional approaches*. American Psychological Association.
Cooper, S. H. (2007). Begin the Beguine: Relational theory and the pluralistic third. *Psychoanalytic Dialogues, 17*(2), 247–271.
Cozolino, L. (2010). *The neuroscience of psychotherapy: Healing the social brain* (2nd ed.). Norton.
Dankoski, M. E., & Deacon, S. A. (2000). Using a feminist lens in contextual therapy. *Family Process, 39*(1), 51–66.
Drescher, J., Schwartz, A., Casoy, F., McIntosh, C. A., Hurley, B., Ashley, K., Barber, M., Goldenberg, D., Herbert, S. E., Lothwell, L. E., Mattson, M. R., McAfee, S. G., Pula, J., Rosario, V., & Tompkins, A. D. (2016). The growing regulation of conversion therapy. *Journal of Medical Regulation, 102*(2), 7–12.
Foucault, M. (1977). *Discipline and punish: The birth of the prison*. Trans. A. Sheridan. Random House.
Gamson, J. (1995). Must identity movements self-destruct? A Queer Dilemma. *Social Problems, 42*(3), 390–407.
Geller, S., & Porges, S. (2014). Therapeutic presence: Neurophysiological mechanisms mediating feeling safe in therapeutic relationships. *Journal of Psychotherapy Integration, 24*(3), 178–192.
Goodman, D., & Freeman, M. (Eds.). (2015). *Psychology and the other*. Oxford University Press.
Goulding, R. A., & Schwartz, R. C. (2003). *The mosaic mind: Empowering the tormented selves of child abuse survivors*. Trailheads Publications.
Greenspan, M. (2017). Feminism, therapy, and changing the world. *Women & Therapy, 40*(3–4), 334–345.
Haddock, S. A., Weiler, L. M., Trump, L. J., & Henry, K. L. (2016). The efficacy of internal family systems therapy in the treatment of depression among female college students: A pilot study. *Journal of Marital and Family Therapy, 43*(1), 131–144.

Hare-Mustin, R. (1978). A feminist approach to family therapy. *Family Process, 17*, 181–194.

Harris, A. (2009). *Gender as soft assembly*. Routledge.

Herman, J. (1997). *Trauma and recovery: The aftermath of violence – From domestic abuse to political terror*. Basic.

Karen, R. (1994). *Becoming attached: First relationships and how they shape our capacity to love*. Oxford University Press.

Kurtz, R. (2007). *Body-centered psychotherapy: The Hakomi method* (Rev. ed.). LifeRhythm.

Langer, S. J. (2019). *Theorizing transgender identity for clinical practice: A new model for understanding gender*. Jessica Kingsley.

Levine, P. (1997). *Waking the tiger: Healing trauma*. North Atlantic.

Levine, P. A. (2018). Polyvagal theory and trauma. In S. Porges & D. Dana (Eds.), *Clinical applications of the polyvagal theory: The emergence of polyvagal-informed therapies* (pp. 3–26). Norton.

Lorde, A. (1981). The uses of anger. *BlackPast*. Retrieved March 9, 2021, from https://www.blackpast.org/african-american-history/speeches-african-american-history/1981-audre-lorde-uses-anger-women-responding-racism/

Lucero, R., Jones, A. C., & Hunsaker, J. C. (2018). Using Internal Family Systems theory in the treatment of combat veterans with Post-Traumatic Stress Disorder and their families. *Contemporary Family Therapy, 40*, 266–275.

Matheson, J. (2015). IFS, an evidence-based practice. *Foundation for Self Leadership*. Retrieved February 22, 2021, from http://www.foundationifs.org/news-articles/79-ifs-an-evidence-based-practice

McGilchrist, I. (2009). *The master and his emissary: The divided brain and the making of the Western world*. Yale University Press.

Newhook, J. T., Pyne, J., Winters, K., Feder, S., Holmes, C., Tosh, J., Sinnott, M., Jamieson, A., & Pickett, S. (2018). A critical commentary on follow-up studies and "desistance" theories about transgender and gender-nonconforming children. *International Journal of Transgenderism, 19*(2), 212–224.

Ogden, P. (2018). Polyvagal theory and sensorimotor psychotherapy. In S. Porges & D. Dana (Eds.), *Clinical applications of the polyvagal theory: The emergence of polyvagal-informed therapies* (pp. 34–49). Norton.

Payne, P., Levine, P. A., & Crane-Godreau, M. A. (2015, February 4). Somatic experiencing: Using interoception and proprioception as core elements of trauma therapy. *Frontiers in Psychology*. Retrieved January 2, 2021, from https://www.frontiersin.org/articles/10.3389/fpsyg.2015.00093/full#h6

Peña, J. (2019). The embodied intersubjective space: The role of clinical intuition in somatic psychotherapy. *Body, Movement and Dance in Psychotherapy, 14*(2), 95–111.

Porges, S. (2018). Polyvagal theory: A primer. In S. Porges & D. Dana (Eds.), *Clinical applications of the polyvagal theory: The emergence of polyvagal-informed therapies* (pp. 50–72). Norton.
Robbins, J. H. (1995). Making changes. In E. F. Williams (Ed.), *Voices of feminist therapy* (pp. 61–70). Harwood.
Rose, N. (1998). *Inventing our selves: Psychology, power and personhood.* Cambridge University Press.
Sang, B. E. (1995). Going around in circles and coming out in the same place and different places – My development as a feminist therapist. In E. F. Williams (Ed.), *Voices of feminist therapy* (pp. 39–49). Harwood.
Schore, A. (2003). *Affect dysregulation and disorders of the self.* Norton.
Schore, A. (2012). *The science of the art of psychotherapy.* Norton.
Schwartz, R. C. (2013). The therapist-client relationship and the transformative power of Self. In M. Sweezy & E. L. Ziskind (Eds.), *Internal family systems: New dimensions* (pp. 1–23). Routledge.
Schwartz, R. C. (2017). Dealing with racism: Should we exorcise or embrace our inner bigots? In M. Sweezy & E. Ziskind (Eds.), *Innovation and elaborations in Internal Family Systems therapy* (pp. 124–132). Routledge.
Schwartz, R. C., & Sweezy, M. (2020). *Internal Family Systems therapy* (2nd ed.). Guilford.
Scott, J. W. (1991). The evidence of experience. *Critical Inquiry, 17*(4), 773–797.
Sehrbrock, J. (2020). Social thirdness: Intersubjective conceptions of the experience of gender prejudice. *Psychoanalysis, Self and Context, 15*(3), 289–295.
Siegel, D. (2003). An interpersonal neurobiology of psychotherapy. In M. F. Solomon & D. Siegel (Eds.), *Healing Trauma: attachment, mind, body and brain* (pp.1–56). New York and London: Norton.
Siegel, D. J. (1999). *The developing mind: How relationships and the brain interact to shape who we are.* Guilford.
Siegel, D. J. (2007). *The mindful brain.* Norton.
Siegel, D. J. (2019). The mind in psychotherapy: An interpersonal neurobiology framework for understanding and cultivating mental health. *Psychology and Psychotherapy: Theory, Research and Practice, 92,* 224–237.
Solomon, M. F., & Siegel, D. J. (Eds.). (2003). *Healing trauma: Attachment, mind, body, brain.* Norton.
Sowell, N. (2013). The internal family system and adult health: Changing the course of chronic illness. In M. Sweezy & E. L. Ziskind (Eds.), *Internal family systems: New dimensions* (pp. 127–142). Routledge.
Stephens, M. (2020). Getting next to ourselves: The interpersonal dimensions of double-consciousness. *Contemporary Psychoanalysis, 56*(2–3), 201–225.

Stern, D. (1985). *The interpersonal world of the infant*. Basic.
Sugarman, J. (2020). Neoliberalism and the ethics of psychology. In D. M. Goodman, E. R. Severson, & H. Macdonald (Eds.), *Race, rage, and resistance: Philosophy, psychology, and the perils of individualism* (pp. 73–89). Routledge.
Sweezy, M., & Ziskind, E. (Eds.). (2017). *Innovation and elaborations in Internal Family Systems therapy*. Routledge.
Van der Kolk, B. (2014). *The body keeps the score: Mind, brain and body in the healing of trauma*. Penguin.
Van der Kolk, B. (2018). Safety and reciprocity: Polyvagal theory as a framework for understanding and treating developmental trauma. In S. Porges & D. Dana (Eds.), *Clinical applications of the polyvagal theory: The emergence of polyvagal-informed therapies* (pp. 27–33). Norton.
Williams, E. F. (Ed.). (1995). *Voices of feminist therapy*. Harwood.
Zerbe Enns, C., Bryant-Davis, T., & Comas Díaz, L. (2020). Transnational feminist therapy: Recommendations and illustrations. *Women & Therapy*. Retrieved January 27, 2021, from https://doi.org/10.1080/02703149.2020.1776021

Open Access This chapter is licensed under the terms of the Creative Commons Attribution 4.0 International License (http://creativecommons.org/licenses/by/4.0/), which permits use, sharing, adaptation, distribution and reproduction in any medium or format, as long as you give appropriate credit to the original author(s) and the source, provide a link to the Creative Commons licence and indicate if changes were made.

The images or other third party material in this chapter are included in the chapter's Creative Commons licence, unless indicated otherwise in a credit line to the material. If material is not included in the chapter's Creative Commons licence and your intended use is not permitted by statutory regulation or exceeds the permitted use, you will need to obtain permission directly from the copyright holder.

7

Conclusion

The work of this book has been to engage with notions of human being that are mainstream in Western modernity. These common sense ideas have been forged and disseminated in the psy disciplines. I have sought to offer an alternative way of thinking about self and other that might alter how and why we think about our psychotherapeutic work. In the first chapter, I argued that the psy disciplines benefit when they learn from the humanities. In the final chapter, I outlined existing psychotherapy practices that already apply an understanding that human being is complicitous, even if those are not the terms they use. In between, I offered illustrations to bring into focus how systems of power evolve from specific historical events and from material practices, and then reinforce or underwrite these practices (see Kendi, 2016 for the example of racism in America as an illustration of how material practices can cause cultural formations as much as the other way around).

I have sought to show how the institutions, culture and material practices of the modern, currently neoliberal West assumed and perpetuated binary ways of thinking about what it means to be human. This binary thinking structured and developed common-sense notions about bodies and the identities these bodies carried, were made to carry or formed in response to the meanings placed on them. I have suggested that patriarchy, capitalism, racism, misogyny (and the homo- and trans-phobias misogyny helps to feed) and colonialism have been at play in historically specific and accountable ways (Perry, 2018 offers a detailed account of this).

This history matters because too often the mainstream psy disciplines, one of the key technologies of modern (individualized, liberal) subject formation, have operated as though human being is a series of synapses, response times, behavioral programming, chemical reactions, biological drives and other such quantifiable, individualized, scientifically explicable forces (see Tosh, 2015 for a detailed example of how psychiatry has understood sexual violence as an individual pathology, and the consequences for normative gender). As I argued in Chap. 1, drawing on the work of critical psychologists, human being is not a science.

This is one reason the psychological humanities are so important: As I hope I have illustrated here, we can only start to work our long way out of the interpersonal, environmental, structural mess we have inherited we begin to see ourselves—our humanity, and the relationships on which our individual human being depends—differently. A complicitous approach invites us to think in nonbinary ways, and to not take for granted Western cultural common sense, which, like all human meanings, is based on historical, material, relations of power, not god, nature or science—themselves cultural constructs.

I have joined the chorus which argues for the importance of understanding that culture is not a scientific enterprise, as much as some proponents of social psychology would like to offer us "scientific" studies that explain why people do the things they do (see Fine, 2014 for an incisive critique of how gendered assumptions structure the social psychological research into gendered norms and behaviors). Instead, the psychological humanities invites us to work with the complex symbolic operations of human meaning-making, always also material and embodied. If the mainstream psy disciplines can expand their frames of reference, a new way of working with the people we serve will become possible.

Of course, this requires a paradigm shift into interdisciplinarity. This in itself would necessitate massive structural change in the way medical models are taught. It also requires a greater societal valuing of the humanities as a field. These issues fill books in themselves, and I will just note them here, with the acknowledgment of their economic and institutional complexities, especially as the world starts the slow and uneven process of emerging from the coronavirus pandemic. It remains to be seen how universities and training institutes are changed by the world to come, as well as whether the citizens of the world, and our leaders, take this opportunity to consider how interconnected we all truly are.

The arguments I make here about the importance of the psychological humanities for improving the medical model of human being are by no means new. The editors (Gorski & Goodman, 2015, pp. 1–2) of *Decolonizing "Multicultural" Counseling Through Social Justice* write hopefully,

> [W]e find ourselves spending less and less energy trying to convince colleagues of the merits of approaches that acknowledge difference and challenge the imposition of Euro-, cis-male-, Christian-, or hetero-centric norms onto counseling and psychology. This is an important step forward for our professions… We do not lack frameworks and approaches for deconstructing problematic counseling and psychology paradigms and practices, nor do we lack counselors and psychologists who desire to adopt the paradigms and practices that will help them connect more effectively with the full diversity of humanity or create a more equitable and just world.

However, they detail the ways in which practices that they summarize under the title of "multicultural" approaches have tended to recapitulate the current structures of power, both symbolically and institutionally. This is what happens when underlying processes—driven by binary understandings of "cultural difference," and by liberal good intention, as detailed in Chap. 2 here—are not interrogated. I hope *Complicities* provides a rationale, and examples, of how to think differently about these matters.

I began this book with reference to one feminist dystopian vision, Naomi Alderman's (2016). I will end it with reference to another. Octavia E. Butler's *Parable* series (*Parable of the Sower* 1993 and *Parable of the Talents* 1998) tells an eerily prescient story set very close to our own time: It begins in 2024. America has been ravaged by climate change and political corruption, and has been overtaken by inequality, the breakdown of social institutions, racial division, gender violence and obscene exploitation of children and the poor. It is a brutal society, where the struggle to survive erodes human ethics, trust and connection.

Butler creates this world by magnifying existing conditions, much as Margaret Atwood does with gender in *The Handmaid's Tale* (Atwood, 1987) or biotechnology in The *MaddAddam* trilogy (Atwood, 2003; Atwood, 2009; Atwood, 2013). Butler's vision encompasses all aspects of life in modern America, to trace forward their consequences. Hers is a devastating critique of the effects of our institutions and systems of power on our planet, and on our humanity.

With one prediction, Butler's timing was late. By the second book, in 2032, despite the polls' expectations, Americans elect a populist demagogue who talks of "making America great again" (Butler, 1998, p. 21), incites his followers to violence without taking responsibility for his words and demonizes racialized others, and non-Christian Americans, "like nothing we've faced before…. I don't know that this country has ever had a leader… as bad as [he] might turn out to be" (Butler, 1998, p. 176). This leader falls from power, but not before he has done terrible damage to the lives of the marginalized.

The protagonist, Lauren in the first book and going sometimes by her last name, Olamina, in the second, is the prophet of a new religion, which she calls Earthseed. Its principle is that god is change. Lauren sees this meaning in the chaos around her:

> All that you touch
> You Change.
> All that you Change
> Changes you.
> The only lasting truth
> Is Change.
> God Is Change. (Butler 1993, p. 3)

Her message is that change is inevitable, inexorable and amoral, and that human beings have the power to anticipate and react to this universal truth whose energy drives all things. If you do not shape the change that flows all around you, you will be shaped by it, she preaches. Hers is a vision of human agency in the face of overwhelming forces. She finds the possibility for humanity's goodness precisely in the face of human brutality, because the immeasurable suffering the books present force each person to choose how they want to respond to the world that never stops assaulting them. The continuous threat presented by other people is also an opportunity to help each other. Butler explores leadership, faith, responsibility, community and family, all through what we would now call a trauma lens.

The salvation Lauren sees in embracing change, in all its uncaring, destructive dynamism, begins and ends with mutuality. One of her Earthseed verses reads:

> Partnership is giving, taking,
> learning, teaching, offering the
> greatest possible benefit while doing
> the least possible harm…
> Any entity and process that
> cannot or should not be resisted or
> avoided must somehow be
> partnered. Partner one another.
> Partner diverse communities. Partner
> life. Partner any world that is your
> home. Partner God. Only in
> partnership can we thrive, grow,
> Change. Only in partnership can we
> live. (Butler 1998, p. 132)

Lauren is unsentimental in her creed, and committed at the expense of all else to her project of building a following so she can disseminate her message, which she feels as a truth that must be spoken. She is not softhearted, but she is uncompromisingly compassionate. As this verse suggests, she sees that human being cannot succeed alone, at least not in the world America has built. Her sense of the necessity of partnership is driven by the need to survive.

Part of Butler's brilliance in these books is her ability to suggest that kindness is not softness, but strength, the key to survival. The choice to receive the humanity of others, with the mutual responsibility that follows, is how Lauren shapes her god. Again, this is not sentimental or self-sacrificing. It is difficult to maintain, and it requires the members of the community Lauren builds to pull their weight in material terms, and respect each other in their differences. The *Parable* books are simultaneously devastating social critiques and offers of hope. Butler suggests that as much as human beings made this world of inequality and suffering, and are capable of horrific exploitation of our most vulnerable, we remain agents of change within it. But only together, as we understand all the ways we are responsible for shaping the change that we cannot control.

I hope the notion of complicity is another way to say what Butler says in her novels. I hope, too, that I have illustrated the importance of learning from ways of thinking that are other than "scientific." Indeed, if we take all this to heart, it means that even the scientific, at the level at which we can understand it, is cultural, that is, human. The biological strata that interweave with the other dynamics of human being are complicit in them, and vice-versa: proverbial "nature" is not in binary relation to "nurture," but shaped by it (Gerhardt, 2004). Despite its aspirations to objectivity, psychology emerged from human history, and was shaped by relations of domination, which it went on to legitimize. It also birthed voices that resisted, insisted and enlightened. Psychology (like its related disciplines) is fundamentally human, more than the sum of its parts, and implicated in the systems that shaped it and that it went on to shape. Its institutional voices developed out of and perpetuated binary thinking, with all the implications I have detailed here. Its other voices continue to suggest otherwise. The theory of complicity aims to articulate the limits of traditional psy thinking and to suggest some of the possibilities that emerge if disciplinary boundaries change from binary either/ors. This is why *Complicities* is a project of the psychological humanities.

Works Cited

Alderman, N. (2016). *The power*. Little, Brown and Company.
Atwood, M. (1987). *The handmaid's tale*. Virago.
Atwood, M. (2003). *Oryx and Crake*. Bloomsbury.

Atwood, M. (2009). *The year of the flood*. Bloomsbury.
Atwood, M. (2013). *MaddAddam*. Doubleday.
Butler, O. (1993). *Parable of the sower*. Headline.
Butler, O. (1998). *Parable of the talents*. Grand Central.
Fine, C. (2014). *Delusions of gender: How our minds, society, and neurosexism create difference*. Norton.
Gerhardt, S. (2004). *Why love matters: How affection shapes a baby's brain*. Routledge.
Gorski, P. C., & Goodman, R. D. (Eds.). (2015). *Decolonizing "Multicultural" Counseling through Social Justice*. Springer.
Kendi, I. X. (2016). *Stamped from the beginning: The definitive history of racist ideas in America*. Bold Type Books.
Perry, I. (2018). *Vexy thing: On gender and liberation*. Duke University Press.
Tosh, J. (2015). *Perverse psychology: The pathologization of sexual violence and transgenderism*. Routledge.

Open Access This chapter is licensed under the terms of the Creative Commons Attribution 4.0 International License (http://creativecommons.org/licenses/by/4.0/), which permits use, sharing, adaptation, distribution and reproduction in any medium or format, as long as you give appropriate credit to the original author(s) and the source, provide a link to the Creative Commons licence and indicate if changes were made.

The images or other third party material in this chapter are included in the chapter's Creative Commons licence, unless indicated otherwise in a credit line to the material. If material is not included in the chapter's Creative Commons licence and your intended use is not permitted by statutory regulation or exceeds the permitted use, you will need to obtain permission directly from the copyright holder.

Correction to: Complicities

Correction to:

N. Distiller, *Complicities*, Palgrave Studies in the Theory and History of Psychology, https://doi.org/10.1007/978-3-030-79675-4

The book was inadvertently published without the acknowledgement texts of funding from the Library of the University of California, Berkeley, for this book in the front matter. This has been updated in the book.

The updated version of the book can be found at
https://doi.org/10.1007/978-3-030-79675-4

Index

A

Ableism, 16, 238
Academic psychology, 5, 17, 134, 214
Achebe, Chinua, 51
Advocacy work, 212
Africa, 88, 89, 91–93, 95–98, 142–144, 147–150
African American, 78, 81, 88, 90, 91, 93, 98, 129
Africanness, 89, 92, 94, 95, 145, 148
African patriarchies, 143
African philosophies, 90
African sexuality(ies), 141, 147
  Western constructions of, 147
Alternative facts, 58, 178, 180
Ambiphilic, 227
America, 1, 44–46, 48, 58, 68, 74–81, 85, 87, 88, 92, 93, 95, 98, 99, 111, 130, 142, 148, 171, 178–180, 190, 192, 204, 225, 235, 245, 247–249
American, xii, 4, 16, 44–46, 48, 49, 59, 68, 74–76, 78, 81, 85, 87–90, 92, 94–99, 111, 129, 142, 143, 164, 165, 169, 191, 193, 204, 225, 248
Ancient Greeks, 16, 51, 112, 114
Anger/rage, 25, 79, 80, 90, 212, 231, 233, 234, 237, 238
Anglican Church, 150
Anxiety, 19, 107, 113, 125, 164, 165, 191–193, 196–198, 200, 201, 223
Apartheid, 9, 12, 13, 15, 46, 74, 92, 94, 119, 144, 146
Aristotle, 112
Attachment theory, 9, 23, 163, 176, 211, 212, 217–219

Author, vii, 51, 82, 98, 123, 131, 134, 139, 140, 171
Autobiographical memory, 221
Autonomic nervous system, 217, 218, 221

B

Baartman, Sarah/Sara, 24, 147
Backlash, 80, 129, 142
Barbarians, 51
Benjamin, Jessica, 23, 28, 29, 52, 111, 193, 227–230
Biden, Joe, 180, 204
Biko, Stephen Bantu, 46, 47
Binary energy, 29, 224, 227
Binary gender
  logic, 111
  rules of, 136, 140
Binary systems, 7, 59, 108, 225
Binary thinking, binary logic, xi, 2–4, 6–13, 19, 23, 25, 28, 32, 43, 59, 63, 65, 66, 73, 75, 76, 80–83, 88, 99, 107, 109–111, 113, 115, 120, 123, 125, 130, 163, 232, 238, 239, 245, 250
Biology is destiny, 112
Black Lives Matter, 235
Black Panther, 75, 88–99
Black rage, 79, 80, 90, 233
Borderline, 136
Boundaries, 21, 24, 56, 181, 190, 250
Brand, 49, 59, 95, 98, 175, 183, 187–189, 201, 203
  personal, 187
Brookings Institute, 89, 96
Bullshit, 178–180
Burdens, 88, 126, 212, 223, 225, 232, 240
  legacy, 225
Burke, Tarana, 129, 170
Butler, Judith, 6, 14, 26, 50, 57, 77, 111, 115, 117, 124, 130, 212, 235

C

Cancel culture, 14, 204
Capitalism, 10, 16, 25, 43, 48, 54, 61, 75, 78, 96, 165, 169, 173, 176, 184, 185, 187, 188, 203, 204, 214, 225, 230, 232, 246
  communicative capitalism, 176
  surveillance, 48, 61, 173, 176–178, 181, 204
Castration, 53
Categorical thinking, 107
Celebrity, 175, 182, 193–202
  internet, 195
  technocultural, 195, 197, 201
Chemical causation, 166
Christianity in Africa, 150
Cisgender, 116, 117, 124, 126, 127, 150, 219, 235
Cisnormativity, 148
Citizenship, 6, 44, 45, 51, 165
  rights and race, 74, 88
Clients, vii, x, 10, 28, 31, 44, 63, 64, 66–68, 99, 110, 121, 124, 126, 166, 168, 189, 192–194, 201, 212–216, 218–221, 223, 224, 226–228, 230–232, 240
Clinton, Hillary, 113
Cognitive behavioral, 221

Colonialism, 7, 16, 25, 34, 47, 51, 52, 65, 73, 75, 76, 78, 87, 90, 92, 94–97, 143, 145, 150, 163, 169, 203, 204, 213, 230, 238, 246
Coming out, 146
Commodification of human value, 49
Commodification of identity, 59, 168, 169
Common sense, 12, 31, 132, 171, 179, 239, 245, 246
Community, 2, 5, 6, 30, 78, 98, 126, 144, 146, 147, 152, 168, 179, 181, 187–189, 191, 204, 211, 213, 224, 225, 239, 249, 250
Competition, 60, 165, 169, 173
Competitive citizenship, 165
Complementarity, 29, 115, 141
Complicit, vii, 2, 3, 8–10, 12, 14, 15, 25, 26, 33, 34, 43, 53, 55, 58, 62–68, 77, 83–85, 87, 88, 96, 111, 115, 117, 126, 137, 152, 164, 211–240, 250
Complicities, vii–xiv, 2, 3, 6–9, 11–15, 26–28, 45, 52, 62, 64–66, 68, 74, 87–99, 110, 111, 115–127, 137, 139, 142, 143, 163, 204, 211, 216, 217, 222, 228, 232, 233, 235, 239, 240, 247, 250
Complicitous thinking, 109
Compulsory heterosexuality, 141
Consent, 57, 127–141, 172
  pretending to, 130
  studies, 131, 135, 137, 140
Constitutive other, 33, 65, 76, 86, 119, 233, 234

Constraints, 18, 60, 122, 183, 224
Consumers, 61, 168, 181, 184, 186
Control of women's bodies, 113
Conway, Kellyanne, 178
Coronavirus, 44, 183, 189, 229, 247
Counter-narratives, 236
Coupland, Douglas, 180
Critical psychology, 29, 33, 232
Cultural imperialism, 92, 99
Cultural objectification, internalization of, 129
Cultural psychology, 30

D

Damaged negro stereotype, 78
Dean, Jodi, 176, 177, 179, 187, 188, 194, 195, 197, 199, 201, 202
Decolonial, 4, 74, 87, 95, 109, 145, 148, 214
  psychology, 75, 232
Decolonization, 87
Deep heterosexuality, 141
Deloitte, 189
Democracy, 10, 16, 33, 47, 48, 57, 58, 76
Democratic governance, 85
Dependence, 54, 130, 183, 219, 227
Depth work, 166, 221, 223
Desire, 13, 19, 25, 26, 49, 52, 54, 55, 61, 90, 93, 113, 121, 128, 129, 131–137, 139, 141, 145, 149, 180, 194, 195, 202, 203, 235–237, 247
  deferred, 52
  in the Oedipus complex, 52, 54
Developmental trauma, 81, 217
Deviance, 17, 32, 57, 59, 64, 76

Diagnosis, 64, 124, 126
Diagnostic and Statistical Manual (DSM), 124, 125
DiAngelo, Robin, 13, 14, 50, 66, 80, 92, 129
Difference, 5, 6, 8, 15, 17, 22, 23, 25, 31, 43, 46, 50, 52–54, 62, 63, 66, 67, 73–77, 82–86, 107, 108, 110, 112, 113, 116, 125–127, 131, 139, 148, 150, 168, 173, 182–184, 192, 203, 228–230, 236–238, 247, 250
Digital divide, 184
Digital natives, 181, 184
Directive, 216
Discipline and Punish, 225
Dominant system, 237
Domination, 29, 48, 52–54, 67, 76, 83, 93, 113, 230, 250
Dora, 214
Drive(s), drive energy, 16, 25, 115, 169, 177, 180, 188, 194, 199, 202, 246, 248

E

Early childhood experience, 219, 222
Early modern era/early modernity, 94, 112, 113, 169, 230
Ecology/ecological, 45, 225, 234
Ego, 24, 55, 178, 191, 212, 221, 228
 psychology, 228
Embodied differences, 77
Embodiment of identity, 117
England, 51, 169–171
English, 52, 87, 93, 94, 169, 170

Enlightenment, 17, 20, 43, 47, 48, 51, 73, 76, 113, 147, 163, 202, 203
Enterprise culture, 166
Entrepreneurs/entrepreneurial, 135, 165, 189
 self, 168
Epistemic violence, 68
Essentialism, 6
Essentialized, 76, 118, 234
Ethnography of African Straightness, 147
Etiology of transgender identity, 121
Eugenics, 16, 85, 111
Evidence, 86, 109, 112, 120, 136, 168, 200, 222, 236, 237
 based practice, 222
 of experience, 237, 238
Evolutionary theory, 85
Experience, 1, 3, 4, 6, 8, 9, 11, 19–24, 27–29, 32, 55, 60, 62, 74, 77, 81, 84, 89, 90, 92–95, 109, 110, 116, 119–123, 125–130, 134, 135, 137, 140–142, 163, 164, 167, 168, 171, 173, 175, 181–183, 185, 187, 188, 193–195, 202, 203, 211, 212, 215–219, 221–223, 226, 228, 233–237, 239, 240
Expertise, psychological experts, 167

F

Facebook, 189, 195
Failure, 32, 59, 80, 165, 166, 190, 191
Female
 agency, 128, 137
 desire, 128, 137

Female sexuality, 53, 128, 132
  suspicion of, 112
Femininity, 108, 191, 192, 235
Feminist/feminism, x, 1, 4–6, 8, 11, 16, 24, 25, 30, 99, 108, 109, 111, 116–119, 125, 127, 129, 135, 136, 213–215, 220, 226, 232–234, 247
  psychology, 30
Feminist therapy, 4, 214, 215
  feminist stance, 4, 214–216, 226
Fetish object, 125
Floyd, George, 44, 80
Foucault, Michele, 16, 23, 33, 48, 56–59, 65, 75, 84, 171, 212, 225
Freud, Sigmund, 25, 52–55, 78, 83, 112, 114, 125, 192, 214, 230

G

Gay gene, 33
Gender, xii, 1, 4, 10, 11, 16, 23, 25, 26, 31, 43, 49, 52, 62, 64, 67, 68, 74, 76, 82, 85, 86, 99, 107–152, 191–193, 200, 214, 234, 236, 246, 248
  affirmative model, 126
  binary, 7, 48, 76, 108, 110–116, 120, 123, 126, 127, 134, 136, 140, 141, 148, 214, 235
  clinics, 120
  as complex, 115
  as complicity, complicit content, 111, 142
  DynamiX, 150
  dysphoria, 64, 124
  incongruence, 124
  as social performance, 115
  studies, 235
  and trauma, 136
  violence as war, 136
Generation, 62, 165, 177, 180–185, 191, 214, 225
  X, 180
  Y, 180
  Z, 180
Genocide, 46, 73, 77
Google, 175
Government, 44, 45, 47, 58, 60
Governmentability, 48, 58, 59
Group differences and otherness, 82
Gutenberg, Johannes, 170, 173

H

Hakomi, 216, 226
Happiness Industry, 167
Herman, Judith, 108, 136, 137, 215
Hermeneutic perspective, 29
Heteronormative gender binary and race, 111
Heteronormativity, 91, 111, 115, 136, 141, 143, 145, 148
Heterosexual
  dynamics, 131
  intimacy, 128
  relationship management, 134
Heterosexuality, 8, 9, 25, 108, 111, 128–130, 137, 139–141, 235
Hierarchy(ies), 4, 15, 53, 85, 107, 119, 173
  of value, 107
History, xi, 2, 3, 5, 9, 10, 16, 30, 32, 34, 44, 47, 50, 51, 55, 64, 74, 78, 79, 85, 94–97, 107, 108,

115, 120–122, 124, 135, 142, 143, 146, 148, 149, 152, 163, 165, 191, 192, 204, 211–213, 232, 235–239, 246, 250
Homonationalism, 141
Homophobia, 67, 142, 143, 145, 148, 152, 200, 230
Homosexuality in Africa, 144
Human
　capital, 166
　connectedness, 52
Humanism, 6, 8, 52
Humanistic psychology, 20
Humanities, vii, xii, 3, 5, 6, 8, 15–24, 26, 27, 33, 34, 46, 49–51, 54, 61, 64, 66, 67, 83, 87, 88, 92, 95, 109, 126, 127, 135, 163, 215, 216, 227, 233, 235, 237, 239, 245–250
Hybridity, 65, 87, 122

Identity, xi, 3, 4, 7–9, 11, 13, 14, 16, 25, 30, 55, 59, 60, 66–68, 74, 77, 78, 81, 82, 84, 86, 93, 95, 96, 98, 107–110, 116–118, 120, 121, 123, 124, 127, 133, 141, 143–145, 147–149, 152, 163–171, 173, 175, 184, 186–189, 212, 213, 219, 235–237, 245
　politics, 3, 7, 8, 13, 25, 55, 93, 95, 96, 148, 235
Implicit memory, 219, 221, 226
Implicit rules of heterosex, 131
Implicit self, 218
Imposter
　phenomenon, 190–192
　syndrome, 192, 200
Indigenous African same-sex practices, 151
Indigenous psychology, 4
Individual
　pathology, 215, 246
　rights, 46–48
Individualism, 6, 17, 30, 32, 57, 59, 68, 87, 164, 191, 204, 225, 234, 235
Injustice, vii, 4, 6, 9, 10, 25, 32, 47, 140, 215, 233, 234, 237, 238
Innate essence, 112
Innocent/innocence, xi, 68, 213, 234
Institutional power, 213, 214
Intelligibility, 54, 117, 124
Intergenerational transmission of trauma, 32
Internal Family Systems (IFS), 211, 212, 220, 223–227, 232
International human rights discourses, 142
Internet, 142, 164, 173–176, 178, 180–183, 185, 187–189, 193–196, 199, 201, 203
Interpersonal neurobiology (IPNB), 11, 23, 163, 211, 212, 216–218, 220, 226, 228, 229, 231
Intersectionality, 8, 30, 67, 117, 129, 214, 215, 230
Intersubjective third, 28, 63, 90, 213, 240
Intersubjectivity, vii, 19, 27, 29, 62–68, 211, 227–229, 231
　in post-apartheid South Africa, 66
IQ testing, 16, 85

K

Kani, Atandwa, 94
Kani, John, 89, 94
   and *Black Panther*, 89
   and Othello, 94

L

Lacanian lack, 78
Lacanian Symbolic, 78
Lacan, Jacques, 54, 78, 128, 194
Lambeth Conference, 150
Language
   lack of, 134
   shaping power of, 109
   as a symbolic structure, 2
Late modernity, 144, 169, 230
Law
   of the Father, 54
Le Bon, Gustave, 114
Legal consequences of
   depathologizing transgender identity, 123
Liberal
   good intention, 49, 247
   individualism, 30, 44, 45, 48, 56, 60, 63, 234
   morality, 54
   subject, 4, 32, 43, 45, 48, 56–59, 63, 163, 172, 232
Liberalism, xii, 3, 4, 10, 43–68, 73, 77, 91, 118, 173, 213
Liberation psychology, 232
Limbic system, 220, 226
Linnaeus, Carl, 113
Literacy, 169–171, 173, 182
   theory, 232
Literature, x, 21, 51, 52, 81, 87, 94, 132, 180, 186, 192
Lorde, Audre, 8, 9, 23, 59, 81, 237, 238

M

Male entitlement, 137
Marketing, 180, 184, 185, 187
The Mark of Oppression, 79
Marriage, 5, 48, 53, 118, 130, 140, 144–146, 220
Mars, Bruno, 195
Medical model of transsexuality, 123, 124
Mendez, Shawn, 195–201
MeToo, 129, 136, 231
Millennial(s), 180–189, 191–194, 197, 198, 202
   culture, 183
   personhood, 201
Mimicry, 87, 92, 122
Misattunement, 127, 200
Misogyny paradox, 128
Modern
   liberal subject, 31, 75
   public/s, 174, 175, 187
   subject, 4, 10, 12, 24, 65, 87, 169
Modernity, 7, 10, 11, 26, 48, 61, 73–75, 78, 83, 84, 87, 96, 113, 144, 151, 169, 173, 187, 215, 230, 232, 234
Mother
   as-object, 52
Muholi, Zanele, 147, 152
Multiplicity, 229
Mutuality, vii, 66, 214, 227, 228, 230
Mythical norm, 9, 59, 139

N

Narrative therapy, 31
Nation, 4, 47, 78, 92, 148, 151, 171
Nationalism, 45, 90, 144, 185
National Registry of Evidence-based Programs and Practices, 223
The Negro Family: The case for national action, 79
Neocolonialism, 75
Neofeudal, 173
Neoliberal, 7, 24, 34, 59, 62, 65, 68, 82, 91, 97, 118, 132, 135, 146, 164–168, 172, 173, 175, 176, 203, 222, 230, 238
Neoliberalism, 10, 25, 43, 44, 48, 52, 59–62, 75, 80, 92, 118, 139, 164–169, 172, 177, 180, 203, 204
Networks, 62, 95, 115, 168, 170, 172, 175, 176, 185, 188, 189, 194, 195, 201, 202, 217
Neural networks, 221, 226
Neuroception, 218
Neuroscience, 9, 216, 220
Neutrality, 167, 216
New media, 184, 185
Nkabinde, Nkunzi, 146, 147
Non-binary gender, 108
  identity, 108
Non-binary people, 108, 122, 124
Non-binary thinking, 62
Non-directive, 216
Non-judgmental approach, 226
Nonperson(s), 48, 73, 76, 88, 118, 119
Non-verbal implicit processes, 218
Normative heterosexuality, 108
The norm/normal/normative/ normalcy/normality, 4, 6, 17, 23, 26, 32, 33, 48, 54, 56–58, 76, 80, 83, 86, 108, 109, 131, 134, 136, 138, 139, 141, 174, 192, 203, 222, 236, 246
  normative individuality, 32, 48, 131

O

Object relations, 163, 227, 228
Objective expert, therapist as, 214
Objective, therapist as, 215
Objectivity, 17, 167, 213, 232, 250
Oedipal process, 110
Oedipus complex, 52, 230
Orgasm, 131, 132, 138, 139
The other/otherness, xi, 2, 5–7, 9–12, 14, 15, 21–26, 29, 43, 51, 52, 54–57, 59, 62–64, 67, 74, 82, 87, 89, 96, 107, 113, 115, 117, 130, 133, 147, 150, 172, 176, 190, 193, 194, 197, 204, 213, 217, 227–231, 235, 245, 250
  as part of self, being other, 55
Oxford University, 94

P

Panopticon, 57
Parts, ix, x, xii, 4, 7, 8, 10, 12, 15, 18, 21, 25, 31, 32, 45–49, 59, 63, 67, 73, 76, 78, 83, 84, 87, 90, 93, 95, 99, 111, 113, 123, 124, 127–130, 134–138, 145, 147, 149, 150, 167, 169, 171,

175, 176, 187, 190, 195, 196, 200, 211, 212, 223, 224, 226–229, 232, 235, 236, 239, 250
Perry, Imani, 24, 47–50, 73, 75, 76, 78, 88, 111, 114, 118, 119, 147, 165, 169, 246
Personal narrative, 171
Perversion, 124, 125
Physiology, 216
Pleasure, 131–133, 138, 139, 167, 194, 228
  missing discourse of, 139
Poetry, 21, 171, 216
  therapy as, 216
Polarizations, 224, 229
Political science, 235
Politics
  of racial liberation in *Black Panther*, 90
  of representation, 118
Polls and polling, 58, 178, 248
Polygyny, 150
Polyvagal Theory, 211, 216, 218
Positive psychology, 166
Post-apartheid South Africa, 66, 143, 144
Postcolonial, 4, 47, 75, 87, 94, 122, 148, 151
  mourning, 92
  theory, 7, 11, 65
Postfeminism, 135
Postmodern approaches to psychology, 29
  the postmodern turn, 29
Postmodernity, 113, 236
Precarity, 174
Pre-colonial Africanness, 145

Prejudice, 14, 67, 230
Pre verbal, 219, 223, 231
Private, 48, 58, 60, 112, 136, 166, 169, 175–177, 183, 187, 190, 195, 203
Privilege, 4, 5, 7–9, 13, 30, 34, 45, 65–67, 73, 80, 82, 83, 86, 92–94, 132, 191, 204, 233–235
Problem sex, 134
Professional Association for Transgender Health South Africa (PATHSA), 150
Profit, logic of, 164, 184
Prosumers, 184, 186
Psychiatry, 3, 4, 87, 222, 246
Psychoanalysis, 3, 4, 20, 23, 28, 163, 194, 213, 214, 218, 219, 227, 232
Psychological humanities, xii, 3, 8, 15–23, 27, 43, 135, 216, 246, 247, 250
Psychology/psychoanalysis/psychiatry/and psychotherapy (the psy disciplines), vii, ix–xii, 3–5, 8–12, 15–34, 43, 44, 48, 56–59, 62–64, 67, 74, 75, 79, 81, 83–88, 99, 107–114, 124, 125, 136, 163, 164, 166, 167, 213–215, 217, 220–222, 224, 226–229, 232–234, 237, 245, 247, 250
  and democracy, 16
  as a discipline, history of, 16
  as a human science, 18, 30
  as a science, 16, 55
  as a technique of subjectification, 32

Psychopharmacology, 222
Psychotherapy practice/
   psychotherapeutic practice, xii, 3, 34, 110, 211, 212, 216, 218, 232, 234, 245
PTSD, 217
Public, xii, 14, 48, 58, 75, 76, 112, 120, 129, 136, 172, 174–176, 178, 180–182, 185, 187, 188, 191–197, 200–203, 234
   eye, 174–177, 191, 192
   speech, 113, 175
   sphere, 95, 171, 178, 179, 183, 188, 203
   modern, 171, 174, 175, 187
   online, 174, 182
Publicity, 176, 177, 187, 188, 194, 195, 197, 199

Q

Queen Elizabeth I, 113
Queer, 5, 6, 8, 25, 108, 109, 116, 125, 141, 143, 146, 148, 151, 152, 200, 213
Queer theory, 6, 8, 11, 24, 99, 108, 115–117, 121, 125

R

Race
   as a construct, 73, 76
   as a cultural problem, 79
   and racism in psychology, 84–88
Racialization, processes of, 84, 85
Racialized type, 79
Racism, 10, 16, 47, 48, 56, 66, 73–75, 77–88, 90, 111, 113, 148, 204, 225, 230, 233, 238, 245, 246
Racist structures, 82, 87
Rape, 112, 114, 134, 136, 140
   culture, 128, 129, 137, 138
Recognizability, 50
Relations of power, 1, 5, 8, 30, 44, 74, 83, 84, 168, 173, 246
Resilience, 81, 167
Reward programs, 177
Rhizome, 15, 212
Right brain, right brain processes, 217, 218, 220–223, 226, 228
Riviere, Joan, 191
Rolling Stone, 195, 197
Rose, Nikolas, 10–12, 16, 23, 29, 31–34, 48, 56–58, 77, 84, 107, 111, 166, 167, 170, 212, 213, 232, 233, 237

S

Safe emergencies, 221
Same-sex intimacy, traditional African forms
   female husbands, 146
   lesbian sangomas, 146
   mine marriages, 146
   mummy-baby friendships, 145
Same-sex practices and nationalism in Africa, 147, 151
Sanders, Mark, 12–15
San Francisco Bay Area, 189
Schwartz, Richard, 223–227, 229
Science as a system of classification, 76
Scientific language *vs.* poetry, 22

Scientific method, 18, 20, 21, 23, 84, 87, 107
Scientific objectivity, 232
Scientific racism, 16, 24, 74, 84, 85
Scientific stance of the psy disciplines, 167
Secret, 176, 177, 194, 197, 201
Seduction industry, 135
Self, vii, 1, 3, 5, 7, 9–12, 14, 15, 17, 20–26, 29, 30, 33, 34, 43, 45, 50, 52, 54, 55, 58, 62, 64, 65, 76, 78, 80, 110, 118, 120, 139, 163, 164, 166, 168, 171, 172, 175, 176, 181, 183, 188, 189, 193, 199–202, 211, 216–224, 227–234, 236, 245
The self as fold, 9
Self-contained individual, 167
Self-identification, 193
Self/other, xi, 3, 7, 11, 23–26, 52, 54, 65, 77, 87, 115, 212, 225, 229, 231, 233
Self-other binary, 2, 10, 11, 14, 24, 84, 227–232, 234
Sex, xii, 86, 107–152, 235
  bad sex, 134, 140
  gak sex, 134
  unwanted sex, 128, 130, 134
  workers, 192
Sexism/misogyny, 2, 16, 51, 54, 56, 67, 111, 113, 128, 145, 147, 152, 191, 204, 230, 238, 246
Sexology, 16, 111, 118
Sexual agency, 108, 132, 140
Sexual difference, 2, 46, 85, 111, 116, 125, 230
Sexual harassment, 129, 135

Sexuality, xii, 8, 10, 23, 60, 64, 67, 76, 107–152, 192, 199
Sexual normativity, 109
Sexual orientation, 108, 236
Sexual violence, 128, 132, 135, 147, 246
  in South Africa, 147
Shakespeare, William, 50, 51, 88, 94, 169–174
  and colonialism, 94
  and cultural politics, 94
  sonnets, 51
  and universal humanity, 50, 88
Sin of Eve, 112
Slavery, 46, 47, 49, 73, 75, 76, 78, 81, 95
Snapchat, 199
Social
  bonding system, 218
  justice, x, 3, 4, 30, 32, 33, 74, 212, 230, 232–239, 247
  media, xii, 59, 68, 113, 164, 165, 175, 176, 180, 181, 194–196, 201, 203, 230
  psychology, 31, 57, 135, 167, 246
  thirdness, 28–29, 67, 230, 231
Somatic Experiencing (SE), 216, 221, 226
South Africa
  Civil Union Act, 144
  gender fluidity/transgender, 149
  post-colonial national identity politics, 148
  same-sex love, 143–145
  traditional culture, 144
  transgender phenomena, 149
South African Constitution, 144
Speech pathology, 122

Spivak, Giyatri, 7, 65, 66, 68
Split subject, 54
Standpoints, 4, 5, 76, 215
Start-ups, 190
Straight culture, 129, 130, 140, 141
Stranger-relationality, 174
Strangers, 174–176, 193, 199
Structural definition of racism, 75
Structural racism, 80, 85, 87
Styles, Harry, 200
Subaltern, 7, 65, 66, 87
Subjectivity, ix, xi, 3, 6, 9, 11, 12, 15, 17, 26–29, 32, 48, 53–56, 60, 63, 66, 68, 77, 79, 84, 89, 107, 110, 112–114, 119, 120, 126, 128, 135, 141, 163, 167, 174, 176, 187, 194, 196, 199, 200, 202, 203, 217, 219, 228, 230, 237
Subject-object binary, 7, 11, 212
Subject of psychology, 5, 20, 24, 27–33, 43, 44, 56–59, 62, 63
Success, 95, 98, 165, 166, 170, 188–192, 195, 196, 198, 200, 202
Surveillance capitalism, 48, 61, 168, 173, 176–178, 181, 204
Swift, Taylor, 196, 199
System
 complex, 135, 226
 of oppression, x, 45, 75, 96, 115, 123
 of power, 1, 2, 5, 6, 11, 13, 15, 32, 34, 52, 64, 83, 87, 96, 107, 109, 137, 237, 245, 248
Systemic inequality, 52, 75
Systems work, systems thinking, 220, 221, 223–226

Tech industry, 189
Techne, 31
Technoculture, 177, 187–189, 193–195, 199, 201
Technology, xi, 4, 11, 12, 18, 26, 48, 56–59, 61, 62, 96, 97, 109, 118, 164–167, 170, 171, 173, 175, 179, 181–187, 189, 202, 203, 233, 246
Thatcher, Margaret, 60
Therapeutic healing, 215
Thinking complicitously/complicit thinking, 13, 44, 67, 107, 120, 122, 128
Third, x, xii, 20, 28, 63, 109, 228, 229
 cultural third, 28
 intersubjective third, 28, 63, 90, 213, 230, 240
 social third/thirdness, 28, 29, 67, 230–232
 space, vii, 28, 67, 90, 91, 96, 215, 228, 240
Time Magazine, 181
Traditional African social structures, effects of colonialism on, 147
The tragedy of heterosexuality, 128
Trans exclusionary feminism, 214
Transgender, 108, 109, 115–127, 147–149, 151, 152, 219
 authenticity, 120
 emergence, 117
 identities in South Africa and asylum, 149
 people, 7, 108, 116–120, 122, 124–127, 148, 150
 rights, 99
 transsexual self-narratives, 116

Transnational, 4, 91, 109,
    141–152, 214
    psychology, 30
Transphobia, 28, 126
Trauma, 9, 32, 81, 90, 136, 166,
    216–218, 226, 232, 234,
    239, 249
    single incident, 217
Trauma and Recovery, 136
Trumpism, 44
Trump/Trumpism/Trumpocalypse,
    44, 204, 225
Truth and Reconciliation
    Commission (TRC), 13
Twenty-first century market
    terms, 169
Twitter, 175, 199

U

Uncomplicit thinking, 14
Unconditional positive regard, 216
Unified self, 5, 57, 223
Universal humanity/the universally
    human, 27, 50–56, 67, 88

V

Ventral vagus, 218
Vine, 195
Voice-lessness, 122, 123

W

Warner, M., 171, 174–176, 181,
    182, 187, 193

Western
    epistemologies, xi, 90, 95, 148
    LGBTQ processes and
        terminology, 141
    models of outness, 141
    queerness, 146, 148
    subject of psychology/modern
        subject of
        psychotherapy, 3, 10
White
    listening, 80, 233
    supremacy, 77, 79, 80, 96, 119,
        129, 204
    violence, 77
    women's tears, 92
Whiteness, xi, xii, 23, 46, 66, 67, 77,
    78, 80, 81, 85, 86, 91, 92,
    94, 95, 111
Window of tolerance, 221
Women as sexual objects, 128
World Conferences of Anglican
    Bishops, 150

Y

Young Western subjects, 164
Young woman and
    heterosexuality, 139

Z

Zizek, Slavoj, 91, 177, 194
Zuboff, Shoshana, 60–62, 165,
    169, 172, 173, 175–178,
    181, 183–185, 187, 188,
    203, 204

GPSR Compliance

The European Union's (EU) General Product Safety Regulation (GPSR) is a set of rules that requires consumer products to be safe and our obligations to ensure this.

If you have any concerns about our products, you can contact us on

ProductSafety@springernature.com

In case Publisher is established outside the EU, the EU authorized representative is:

Springer Nature Customer Service Center GmbH
Europaplatz 3
69115 Heidelberg, Germany

www.ingramcontent.com/pod-product-compliance
Lightning Source LLC
LaVergne TN
LVHW012248070526
838201LV00092B/160